Education and Democracy

Education and Democracy

Paulo Freire, Social Movements, and Educational Reform in São Paulo

Maria del Pilar O'Cadiz
Pia Lindquist Wong
Carlos Alberto Torres

WestviewPress

A Division of HarperCollins*Publishers*

Copyright © 1998 by Westview Press, A Division of HarperCollins Publishers, Inc.

Published in 1998 in the United States of America by Westview Press, 5500 Central Avenue, Boulder, Colorado 80301-2877, and in the United Kingdom by Westview Press, 12 Hid's Copse Road, Cumnor Hill, Oxford OX2 9JJ

A CIP catalog record for this book is available from the Library of Congress.
ISBN 0-8133-8962-3

The paper used in this publication meets the requirements of the American National Standard for Permanence of Paper for Printed Library Materials Z39.48-1984.

10   9   8   7   6   5   4   3   2   1

In Memoriam

Paulo Reglus Neves Freire (1921-1997)

This book has been almost seven years in the making. Though the work has certainly not been continuous for all those years, it was a major focus of the three of us for most of them. It is a tribute to Paulo Freire, his courage, his humanity, and the timelessness and relevancy of his ideas that our work on this manuscript was never tedious, never dull, and never a burden, but rather a constant source of joy, inspiration, and discovery. Although the book was always intended to be a critical but friendly description and analysis of Freire's efforts as Secretary of Education, the need to disseminate information about this radical educational reform became even more urgent after the sad news of Paulo Freire's death in May 1997. Thus, while this text is the result of the scholarly efforts of three researchers, it is also a celebration of a revolutionary thinker who had the unique opportunity to make his ideas concrete and therefore affect the lives of countless young children in his native country. We dedicate our efforts on this volume to Paulo Freire and to the hundreds of educators in São Paulo whom he inspired to work tirelessly in creating a happy, democratic school dedicated to serving poor and working class children and their communities. It has been our pleasure and privilege to have worked with Paulo Freire and the many educators involved in educational reform in São Paulo. Their commitment, courage, political clarity and struggle for social justice and equality are a constant source of motivation and inspiration for us to renew and reinvigorate our own efforts in the fight for equal rights, decency and justice.

Contents

Tables and Figures

Acknowledgments

Pia Lindquist Wong

Almost 10 years ago, I made a "career change" from working in community development to working in education. Paulo Freire and the educational framework put forth in *Pedagogy of the Oppressed* were instrumental in helping me to blend together a commitment to social transformation and a budding interest in education. *Pedagogy of the Oppressed* changed the way I thought about the educational process; the Inter Project changed the vision I had about the potential beauty and liberatory qualities of that same process. I feel forever indebted to Paulo Freire and to the many Brazilian educators who showed me that formal learning can indeed by a joyful and transformative act.

I would also like to acknowledge several people without whose unswaying support this book would not have come to fruition. It has been a wonderful experience to have worked with Pilar O'Cadiz and Carlos Alberto Torres. I have learned a tremendous amount from each of them, as they willingly shared their expertise and brilliant insights while we worked together writing this book. Their patience, grace, and good humor have made these seven years pass quickly. I can only hope that all my future collaborations are as pleasant and fruitful as this one has been. In a way, this whole book came to fruition because of a certain Stanford University connection—with the important link being Martin Carnoy, who was my mentor and who served as Carlos Alberto Torres' advisor years earlier. I would like to thank him for introducing me to Paulo Freire when I was just beginning the doctoral program there, and for the subsequent intellectual guidance that he provided in the ensuing years. One Brazilian educator in particular deserves mention in this opening—Antonio Fernando Gouvêa, the *grande Gouvêa*. For some reason he had special patience for this *norteamericana* who appeared at his school with countless questions and a need to sit in on every meeting, visit every classroom and interview all the staff and students. His understanding of the Inter Project and his insights into the implementation of this reform are present in all aspects of my analysis; his guidance was as illuminating as his friendship was invaluable.

In addition, heartfelt thanks to my dear friends, Lexie and Daltro Morandini, to whom I feel indebted forever for their unflagging good humor, generosity and hospitality in hosting me in their home for eight months.

Finally, I would also like to thank my family who have always given willingly and generously of their time and love. My husband, Bruce Griesenbeck, has remained interested, curious, supportive, and patient throughout all of the work on this book, which included an eight month period of separation. His limitless capacity for backrubs, late night discussions, dishes, laundry, and international phone bills cannot be overappreciated. My parents, Yen Lu Wong and Herbert Shore, have been a constant source of intellectual guidance. I have always felt privileged to have had their support, both emotionally and intellectually. But most of all, I want to thank our young son, Riley Hui Griesenbeck, whose entry into this world made me full of wonder and gratitude. More than anything else, his young life, curious mind, and innocent smile make me more determined than ever to do what I can to make this world (in the words of Paulo Freire) "less ugly, less cruel, and less inhumane." I hope this book and the understandings derived from it will be one step in that direction.

Pilar O'Cadiz

In carrying out the research for this book, I had the fortune of meeting many committed educators in São Paulo whose creativity, diligence and perseverance in the face of seemingly insurmountable obstacles never ceased to astound me. I owe my deepest gratitude to them for allowing me into their classrooms and homes, for maintaining interest in my work and offering me their insights and much-esteemed friendship. Although I appreciate the input of all the Brazilian teachers who contributed to this research, I would like to give a special thanks to Gouvêa, Maria do Carmo, Francisca, Flavio, Sonia, Rosa, Carolina, Marlene, Nanci, and Elza. *Obrigada!*

I could not have spent so many months in the field without the generosity of my dear Brazilian friends, Doni and Miriam Atunes, Rogerio and Liana Belda, Adima Aith and family, Luciana Chaui, Claudio Coutinho and Marcio Aith, Maria do Carmo Mendonça and family, Vera and Marcos Madeiro, Evanete Caldas, José and Zuleide Bezerra, whom I would like to thank for providing me with a place to stay and all the rest.

In addition, I recognize the gracious opportunities offered to me by various Brazilian scholars—who played leading roles in the PT administration of the Secretariat of Education—to discuss my research: Moacir Gadotti, Mario Sergio Cortella, Mario D'Olne Campos, Ana Maria Saúl, and Marta Pernambuco. I also acknowledge the ongoing guidance of professors Jose Carlos Sebe Bom Meihy, Oswaldo Humberto Cheschio of the University of São Paulo and Nelly Stromquist of the University of Southern California at various stages of my research.

The valuable orientation and encouragement provided to my research by professors Concepción Valadez and Peter McLaren of the Graduate School of Education & Information Studies and Edward Telles of the Department of Sociology at UCLA is greatly appreciated. Moreover, the wise, caring and constant guidance of Professor Carlos Alberto Torres deserves special recognition. I am especially grateful to Pia Lindquist Wong for her untiring collaborative spirit and genuine friendship over the years as we worked on this project together.

I would also like to thank my colleagues Gustavo Fischman, Rachel Chapman, and Carmen Nava for their ongoing support in this endeavor, as well as the much-appreciated editing assistance of my dear friend Diana Sancetta.

Of course, there are two individuals without whom I could never have carried out the work that such a book entails, Covadonga O'Cadiz and Javier Gómez Serrano: they lovingly cared for my children Román, Mayáhuel, and Cala while I was away doing field work and spending long hours at the computer writing. I am forever grateful for their unconditional love and support. I am also indebted to my father, Sergio O'Cadiz, who has endowed me with the discerning vision of the artist and a passion for the cultural and historical richness of my Latin American heritage.

I also salute the children, parents, and "teacher-leaders" and tutors of the Boyle Heights Elementary Institute (BHEI). They constantly reminded me, while carrying out the intellectual work of research and writing, of the challenges and joys of practicing a dynamic, culturally based and dialogical educational exchange. Their enthusiasm, despite the risks, to build community through critical learning provided more than sufficient inspiration for this book. Thanks to Kenny Rogers and the BHEI Board of Directors for allowing me the opportunity to work at the Institute while completing my dissertation: their patience and understanding is much appreciated.

The UCLA Latin American Center, International Studies and Overseas Programs (ISOP), and the Graduate School of Education and Information Studies must be recognized for providing crucial financial support for my research.

Finally, I would like to express my eternal indebtedness to Paulo Freire for providing me—since I first read *Pedagogy of the Oppressed* 17 years ago— with the philosophical foundation of a critical-utopian outlook on living, learning, and knowing. Having finished this book one year after my youngest daughter, Cala, was diagnosed with autism, I believe that my Freirian foundation provides an enhanced perspective on how to seek at all times new ways in which to teach and learn with my daughter.

Under these circumstances, Freire would point to the obvious: to the eternal conflict between our being and our acting in the world. Knowledge—he would say—is not something to be encapsulated, frozen in time, possessed by some and not by others, to be denied or uncritically embraced. Knowledge is co-created among men and women in the world. Knowledge is power and knowledge can liberate. This is because we know not only with our minds—the neurological makeup of our organic brains— but with our bodies, our senses, our soul, with the history of those who came before us and with a vision of what we imagine the future to be.

Carlos Alberto Torres

This book grew out of friendship and mutual intellectual stimulus. Yet it could not have been accomplished without Pia Linquist Wong's and Pilar O'Cadiz' successful doctoral dissertations from which I learned so much. Nor this book could have been accomplished without their hard work in reconciling a manuscript written "*a tres voces*." The life of any intellectual is always a complicated design of ceaseless travel, interminable field work, long hours of reading, thinking and dialogue, trying to decipher exactly what are the most pressing questions of the time; and finally, many hours of writing, which as Freire so persistently argued, involve a great deal of agony and pain, but also joy and liberation. It is also very taxing on the family, and I wish to remember Maria Cristina Pons, the person who, with her sensibility, inquisitive mind, literary suggestions, smile, love, and patience, has always supported my work, teaching me many things that I cannot describe here. My gratitude to her and to my children Carlos, Pablo, and Laura.

We all are indebted to Paulo Freire, "*maestro*," friend, mentor, incomparable "*compañero*" of dialogue and praxis for two decades. He is within us. With you, "*maestro*," has died a living myth, he who struggled with his contradictions, who educated with his parables, who captivated with his smile framed by a white beard and straight hair whisping in the breeze, in that incomparably beautiful head. We will miss you Paulo.

I cannot conclude this acknowledgment without thanking Moacir Gadotti for his friendship and inspiration. With him and with Paulo we lived imaginary dreams and we searched together for possible utopias. In 1991, at Paulo's request, we created, with Moacir and few other friends, the Paulo Freire Institute in São Paulo. It is because of Moacir's inspiration, leadership, hard work and tremendous sense of responsibility that the Institute is now a reality, with its own offices, and with activities already impacting upon the cultural and educational life of São Paulo and Brazil. In my many dialogues with Moacir, I have learned philosophy and pedagogy but he has also taught me that, as the book of Proverbs said, "When there is no vision, the people perish." I acknowledge here Moacir Gadotti, a man of vision who as Freire's Chief of Staff at the Secretariat of Public Education in São Paulo, was responsible for many of the wonderful experiences that we critically analyze here. To him my friendship, gratitude and respect.

This research could not have been accomplished without financial resources and the assistance of many graduate students, including Julie Thompson. I benefited from a generous fellowship from the National Academy of Education Spencer Fellowship (1990-1992), the support of the Department of Educational Foundations at the University of Alberta, and later the support of the Graduate School of Education & Information Studies, the Senate Research Committee, the Latin American Center and the International Studies and Overseas Program at UCLA to carry out this research between 1988 and 1995. An important motivation was my appointment by Paulo Freire in 1989 as one of his advisers in the educational administration of the City of São Paulo. Chapter III is based on an article entitled "Paulo Freire as Secretary of Education in the Municipality of São Paulo." published in *Comparative Education Review*, Vol. 38, No. 2 (May 1994), pp. 181-214. Segments of this article are reprinted here with CER permission, which I acknowledge with gratitude.

I

From a Pedagogy of the Oppressed to a Pedagogy of Hope

Introduction

This book is a critical examination and analysis of the ideas and per-formance of the educational administration headed by Paulo Freire, Secre-tary of Education of the municipality of São Paulo, Brazil between 1989-1991. Under Freire's leadership, the Municipal Secretariat of Education (MSE) implemented a process of educational reform that reflected the demo-cratic-socialist ideology and objectives of the Workers' Party (*Partido dos Trabalhadores*, PT), which won municipal elections in 1989.

With a focus on theory and praxis, we discuss, on one hand, the rela-tionship between the state and social movements and, on the other, the relationships between teachers and curriculum reform. In so doing, the book thoroughly examines the intersection of politics and education in a fascinating and ambitious project of educational reform in a major Latin American urban center.

A central focus of the book is the Interdisciplinary Project or "Inter Project." The Inter Project, along with other reforms implemented by the PT-MSE, had far-reaching effects on curriculum, instruction and teacher training, and as such, represents the primary effort of the Secretariat to create one of its fundamental policy objectives: the initiation of the Move-ment for the Reorientation of the Curriculum (MRC). The central concepts of interdisciplinarity, generative themes, critical consciousness and democ-ratization of education formed the foundation of this Freirean program for curriculum reform.

Although this study centers on a particularly Brazilian educational reform experience, its political rationale, planning techniques and curriculum organizing, and teaching methods could be modified and applied in different local, national, and international contexts. Moreover, the personal involvement of Paulo Freire makes the total reform experience all the more intriguing because of the fact that Freire was an internationally renowned intellectual icon of education for liberation and critical pedagogy. But, despite his fame and the global dissemination of his revolutionary philosophy of education, until 1989, Freire had not yet had the opportunity to extensively implement his ideas in a formal elementary public school setting in his own country.

More than indulging in the exaltation of politics and mystification of personalities, the analysis tries to understand how students and teachers were engaged in the process of curriculum change and democratization of school governance. We additionally expose the kind of political awareness emerging in the São Paulo schools and communities that participated in Freire's radical educational reform.

Justification of the Study

Why study educational reform in São Paulo, and why focus on teachers and curriculum? There are few successful models of educational reform undertaken by a socialist political party in Latin America in the last part of this century, a period when Latin America has been undergoing sweeping models of neoliberal reform of state governance and social institutions alike. The theoretical richness of the Freirean educational reform experience—one built not on mere improvisation or crude pragmatism, but on the implementation of many different yet overlapping political and educational philosophies—as well as the new knowledge created because of it, offer a story needing to be told. Many of the activists who participated in reshaping São Paulo's educational system and the pedagogic vision of its schools, including teachers and members of social movements, still carry out major tenets of the Freirean program today in São Paulo and elsewhere in the country. This book, then, also constitutes a report on the social history of a contemporary educational reform movement in Brazil which continues to play an essential role in developing alternative models of education policy and planning in the country and possibly worldwide.

The Reform Challenge

The challenge to change public education in the city of São Paulo is not idiosyncratic. Large and sprawling urban environments like Los Angeles,

Boston, Chicago, or New York share many of the same issues that, by and large, the Freirean administration confronted in São Paulo (e.g., overcrowded classrooms, dilapidated facilities, dwindling public resources, overworked and underpaid teachers, communities plagued by economic despair and social violence). Moreover, the nature of educational decentralization in the United States, with its tradition of local control is comparable to the nature of educational decentralization in Brazil. Brazil's historical legacy of municipal and state control in elementary and secondary education makes the São Paulo experience even more relevant for debates in the United States.

What the government can do to improve public education is a question that resonates throughout the corridors of schools and colleges of education, a query heard in the boardrooms of the many bureaucracies concerned with educational policy making, and an issue discussed in government policy making committees. But, more importantly, government's role in public education is a central topic in the homes of common citizens striving for better education, and by implication, a more promising future for their children. Thus, trying to improve the purpose and efficiency of public schooling demands tireless effort and creative imagination. The São Paulo experience, inclusive of the Inter Project, is a refreshing perspective. In offering a set of innovative suggestions and concrete avenues for positive change, it advances the theoretical discussion on educational policy making, and at the same time proposes a set of experiments to promote learning in schools that are full of imagination and hope.

Freire always argued, and with him the practitioners of critical pedagogy—that educators are not merely technicians, they are artists and intellectuals and, above all, human beings. Teachers are caring, loving, human beings whose prime impetus in life is their commitment to educate children, youths and adults. Freire acknowledged this to be the utopian origin of the educator's efforts before they become suffocated by the contradictory realities of schooling and the pressing straight jacket of educational bureaucracy, state authoritarianism, and limited political economy endowments.

Teachers, more often that not, are energetic and willing to experiment. Encountering the right leadership and vision, they want and are able to create new horizons of pedagogic imagination and social realities in schools. In some cases, educators are able to transgress the self-imposed limits of the particular school systems in which they are or feel embedded. From the basis of a fundamental trust and faith in teachers, Paulo Freire has insisted in his many writings, lectures, and dialogical books, that ideology plays a central role in the social reproduction of schooling. Specifically, teachers are agents continuously negotiating their place among structures, rationales, norms, symbols, and routines. The notion of *the teacher*, like the notion of democracy or the concept of the "good life," is also a social construction.

With this foundational perspective, the educational policies of the PT mobilized teachers to achieve important changes in the process of policy making; changes that the Freirean administration identified as inextricably linked to the process of human liberation, and not as just a matter of making technical, legal, ethical, or piecemeal political improvements in schools. To carry out its reform objectives, the PT-MSE projected an entirely new vision of the public school; a vision that some pedagogues within the PT called the *Escola Pública Popular,* or the Popular Public School. This book, therefore, also dissects the operationalization of a utopian educational project, and evaluates how influential and effective it was. As expected, not everything goes according to plan in an extensive social experiment like this one, but the accomplishments that Freire, his colleagues at the Secretariat and the teachers in the schools managed to bring about, despite immense political and logistical obstacles, deserve to be highlighted.

Another salient aim of the book is to study the ways in which the Freirean administration linked a historical tradition of social struggle in Brazil and Latin America—based on notions of liberation, dialogue, collective organization, and social movements that necessarily implicate political risk—with the traditions of socialism and critical theory in educational research. Thus, a second goal of this book is to discuss a particular aspect of the reform experience, which is not merely context-dependent but, we propose, has global appeal.

Perhaps what makes the Freire-led PT-MSE project so intriguing is that it reflects some of the contradictions of public policy built into the relationships between state and social movements. The PT administration boldly took on the challenge of collaborating with social movements through its policy-making efforts in literacy training, as well as made the proposal to create a social movement within the schools. It did this by initiating the "Movement for the Reorientation of the Curriculum" (MRC, the general rubric uniting all the reforms designed to improve the quality of schooling in São Paulo). Most notably, this curriculum reform project sought to politically mobilize teachers for pedagogic reflection and action, along the lines of Freire's own idea of education as liberatory praxis.

Yet regardless of its idealistic notions and courageous aims, like any reform, it can only prove worthy if it works. There have been few studies of the PT educational reform plan in São Paulo, and as with a host of other proposals for educational improvement in the region and internationally— we must stress—few researchers have been able to prove, conclusively, that changes have enhanced the quality of education provided.

For seven years we studied this singular experience in educational reform with avid curiosity and, admittedly, a sense of amazement at its audacity and solidarity with its purpose, yet striving always to maintain a critical gaze. As a result of our scholarly labor of love, this book, we believe, offers richly textured evidence of what seems to work and what could be improved in radical educational reforms, pinpointing some of the more significant successes and failures of the reform project.

Throughout this book, we assist the reader in understanding fully both the theoretical tenets and the practical application of the PT-MSE educational reform in the city of São Paulo, and the various degrees to which the modifications have been effective on several levels. First, at the level of classroom practice and change, we asked if the reforms were creating critical and active citizens. Then, we considered the issue of content; that is, what kind of knowledge is being produced and distributed in the process of reform?

Second, a focus on teachers must be present when analyzing actual reform processes. Did the new policy orientation increase their theoretical knowledge of the profession? Did teachers experience an increase in dialogue and exchanges with their colleagues, thus overcoming the feeling of isolation caused by their immersion in bureaucratic dynamics and authoritarian administrations? Did teachers come to see their students and colleagues in a different (more favorable) light?

Third, our inquiry prompted us to learn more about school governance in São Paulo. In so doing, we examined whether the PT administration's innovative approaches for collaboration between state and social movements have been productive enough. There was the intention that the Freirean-led policies would change the way the capitalist state would relate to educational and social movements. There was a consciousness on the part of some Secretariat personnel that policy formulation must occur hand-in-hand with efforts to eliminate the legacy of an authoritarian past. Effective decision making, increased parent, teacher, and student participation in public policy-making, better relationships with teacher unions, new alternatives for governance such as the "School Councils," and the overall internal democratization of the system were all goals which the new socialist administration set its high hopes for achieving. This book gives some clues as to whether these stated goals where clearly proposed and eventually achieved.

Fourth, a serious concern is whether teaching and learning actually improved in the São Paulo municipal schools, during the Freirean experiment. The authors choose a qualitative approach to assess the efficiency, success, and failures of the PT-MSE school system reforms. This was achieved primarily through field research, direct observation of classrooms and administrative settings, ethnographic interviewing, administration of teacher surveys, in addition to literature review and the collection and analysis of Secretariat documents and teacher produced materials pertinent to the reform. We thought that information about the efficiency of the system in promoting actual learning was a central consideration for an investigation assessing successes and failures of a far reaching public school reform.

Fifth, we were concerned with the question of legitimation. It is important to assess whether increased awareness about the nature of public education and its role in society (e.g., that schools serve as a battleground for social and class interests), will offer more legitimation to the process of political change if propelled by a particular leadership. Likewise, we were curious to know whether these distinctively Freirean and socialist policy changes—which persistently stressed the importance of addressing those issues relevant to the concerns and interests of the popular sectors and to fomenting popular participation in the public institution of the school—and any accompanying improvement efforts were noticed and, more importantly, appreciated by the population of São Paulo at large. Thus, an important fifth question is: Did the new policies result in an improved image of education in São Paulo?

We also take into account the particularities of schooling experiences discriminating by social class in São Paulo. All parents care about their children's welfare. However, parents will relate differently to state initiatives in Brazil (as they do elsewhere) depending on their economic, political and cultural endowments. For this reason we studied schools which reflect, by and large, the life experiences of the popular classes in Brazil; that is, working or lower and lower-middle class parents and children, and by implication the teachers who work with them. Research indicates that in a country as segmented culturally and economically as Brazil, the middle and upper classes send their children to private schools, and therefore they have little, if any involvement with public schooling. By all accounts, public schooling in Brazil is for the poor, as such, it is a system suffering from the nightmares of the iron cage of an unchecked bureaucracy, diversion of resources, and the predominance of private interest over the public good.[1]

The Brazilian Context

We have a cultural and political history of almost 500 years of submission. We have a "race" of politicians that have, in fact, refused to concern themselves with education. We have the sad inheritance of the dictatorship with the resulting deterioration of cultural and economic possibilities. We have spaces, almost always very unsightly, which we call schools, which more often that not are permeated by an overwhelming sense of hopelessness. We have a dominant class that throughout our history has privileged foreign interests, or interests that were simply foreign to the majority of working people. In summary, from this apocalyptic vision there remains the certainty that we have but two paths to take: a hurried rush to give up, and the tenacity to begin again; nihilistic self defeatism or a small hint of that strange and elucidating hopefulness that they say overtakes the hearts of those, throughout the world, who survive earthquakes.[2]

Scholars of Brazilian contemporary society are quick to point out the dire conditions of the country's public educational system. They invariably signal the inequities that exist between the private and public sectors and the skewed distribution of limited public resources, with primary schooling—attending the educational needs of the country's poorest—being short changed in favor of federally funded higher education that mostly benefits the wealthiest. In addition to numerous factors of a political and economic nature, the Brazilian state has lagged in its efforts to build a public education system as compared with other countries of early industrialization in Latin America (e.g., Argentina and Mexico).[3]

The root of the problem is found in two decisive historical factors: 1) Brazil's imperial legacy and resulting lack of any far-reaching educational policies on the part of the Colonial and Imperial regimes or the first Republic (with the limited though honorable exception of the educational efforts carried by the Jesuits); 2) the prolongation of a slavocratic regime which ended formally in Brazil with the proclamation of emancipation as late as 1883 [though illiterates were not allowed to vote until 1988, for the most part keeping the descendants of slaves disenfranchised]. This slavocratic system and the plantation structure associated with its historical roots kept the demand for an educated work force at a minimum. Given the aristocratic social order of the Lusobrazilian Empire, and the limited rights relinquished to a large portion of the work force (i.e., slaves), it is not surprising then that despite the fact that Brazil's first constitution of 1824 declared basic education to be free for all citizens, it would not be until a century later that any serious political effort to organize universal primary schooling for the country's citizenry even took place.[4]

As a consequence, even as we approach the end of the Twentieth Century, nearly four million children between the ages of 7 and 14 receive no formal schooling. And when children in Brazil do enter the first grade 23 percent repeat their initial year of schooling and eventually drop out due to the precarious material conditions of public schooling, limited teacher preparation, and the poor quality of education provided. School evasion, therefore, offers the most glaring evidence of Brazil's educational failure with 15 percent of first graders and 19 percent of fifth graders leaving school, and only 32 percent of children who begin their eight years of elementary schooling finishing in that time period.[5] Indeed, as Plank argues: "[e]nrollment rates nevertheless remain low. In 1990, according to the MEC [Ministry of Education and Culture], only about 16 percent of children between the ages of fifteen and nineteen were enrolled in secondary schools. Only 5 percent of those who complete eight grades of primary schooling enter post-secondary institutions."[6]

From Pedagogy of the Oppressed to a Pedagogy of Hope

One of the basic tenets of an emancipatory educational paradigm, which takes seriously the presuppositions of critical and emancipatory pedagogy, is the adoption of a "language of possibility" as Henry Giroux has expressed in countless writings,[7] and a language that emerges quietly in the final moments of Regis de Morais' scathing indictment of Brazilian society presented above. This utopian outlook forms the core of Brazilian progressive pedagogic thought and is the philosophical premise of Paulo Freire's own vision, as expressed in his book *Pedagogy of Hope,* a book revisiting his own history in writing his seminal book *Pedagogy of the Oppressed.*[8]

Moving from the "Pedagogy of the Oppressed" to a "Pedagogy of Hope" is the guiding principle of De Morais' claim: "In this tumultuous and misunderstood century, to believe in ourselves can begin to be painful, but it is necessary. We must lunch and dine utopias, for, as the philosopher reminds us, it may very well be that the greatest of utopias is to believe that we can live without utopias."[9]

In the final decade of the century, the authenticity and idealism that kept Freire's educational philosophy alive in his country during his 16 years of exile (1964-1980) and gave it its universal appeal, inspiring myriad of educational projects aiming for the conscientization of learners, was to meet its greatest challenge yet: utopia meets the realities of bureaucratization, institutionalization, and the concrete conditions of educating children in the context of São Paulo's urban schools in the 1990s. Therefore, individuals who participated in the development of a critical approach to educational thinking in Brazil in the 1980s, in particular, progressive academics at the University of São Paulo, the Pontifical Catholic University of São Paulo, and the University of Campinas, found themselves in the face of a golden opportunity to actually put their ideas into practice with the appointment of Paulo Freire as Secretary of Education for the city. In this regard, by applying Freirean pedagogic principles to the schooling of children, the São Paulo experience offers a extraordinary opportunity for reflective analysis on critical educational theory and the practice of an emancipatory educational program being carried out in a social milieu marked by stark economic and political contradictions and various social and cultural complexities.

The research problem was clear. The research questions, as outlined above, helped us to begin to understand the pedagogic and political problems of school reform that the Freirean administration addressed during its four year tenure. Yet, while we were designing the overall research project, we were confronted with the challenge of identifying the kind of theoretical framework that would help us to understand a radical educational reform process, undertaken by a democratic socialist party, in São Paulo, the heart of capitalist Brazil.

Theoretical Framework

A neo-Marxist, post-structuralist and post-liberal theoretical framework which seriously takes into account the political economy as well as the politics of culture has guided this research.[10] This analysis places emphasis on the role of critical theory and critical pedagogy in Freire's administration of the PT-MSE, framing the process of social transformation in the context of theories of social and cultural reproduction.

Despite seemingly contradictory standpoints, insights from critical postmodern theory are also part of our theoretical construct. Postmodernism plays a serious role in the analysis of Brazilian society and in considering the role of schooling in the definition of identities of students, educators, and communities. Rather than an attempt to validate some of the key theses of postmodernism, paradoxically, the emphasis of our study is to understand the creation of political actors. Hence, a central theoretical dilemma is to discuss the intersection between politics and education—Brazilian style—in São Paulo, while at the same time keeping in mind that democratic socialism operates within the confines—but also tries to go beyond—liberal democracy. Hence the title of this book, *Education and Democracy*, reversing the famous title of Dewey's seminal work, *Democracy and Education*. But there is more.

A political sociology of education, offering concrete analysis of specific situations, informs our work as well. We have resorted to methodological pluralism to carry out this research, which took place over an extended period of time. As previously mentioned, our methodology included narrative analysis, ethnographies, systematic interviewing with elites, government officials, teachers, students and people in the *bairros* of the schools studied. But we also conducted archival review, documentary review, classroom and non-participatory observation in our inquiry.

Despite a fairly elaborated methodological paraphernalia, our enthusiasm for the events happening in front of our eyes made us think about the notion of objectivity. We could not and even refused to feel at the margins of the process, as traditional—and we are afraid obsolete—research strategies advised us. In fact, there were many occasions in which we felt totally consumed by the political passion and imagination of Brazilians, and we found ourselves engaged in all sorts of dialogues which went well beyond the detachment of a positivistic ethnographer or scientist. It is clear that we have no apologies for that, quite the contrary. Not only did this engagement make our research more enjoyable, and perhaps even more useful for our Brazilian colleagues, but it also made our own processes of learning more experiential, down to earth, indeed multifaceted.

Finally, we have situated our own theoretical perspective in our commentaries above for those who always want to label origins and development in a particular text. Yet, we would like to emphasize that our perception of the process of teaching and learning is based on a position which is close to the philosophy of constructivism. Hence our work considers very favorably the critical pragmatism of John Dewey's progressive democratic educational ideals and Paulo Freire's revolutionary and utopian pedagogy of the oppressed, but we also relate to the contributions of Jürgen Habermas from a post-liberal perspective.[11]

Constructivism is understood here in the context of multiculturalism and post-colonial analysis, especially with a focus on the discursive practices in education. Therefore, we make ours a central claim of feminist knowledge production theory: that is, its concern for an epistemology that recognizes the difficulty of establishing a fact-value distinction, or upholds a notion of value neutrality in education. A similarly important standpoint is the notion that science constructs identities by legitimizing principles of rational organization of society, and legitimating as well the rationales which underline the evolving constitution of institutions. We agree with Sandra Harding when she questions the assumption that there is no scientific contestation of these identities and challenges the dominant notion that societies which are multi-ethnic, multi-lingual, and multi-cultural are virtual melting pots.[12] Nothing could be further from the truth.

Constructivism, when incorporating post-colonial discourses, offers a unique perspective for the democratic analysis of scientific findings in several domains, including education. Constructivism, as an epistemological approach, is in agreement with a basic principle of the Inter Project, that is, the distinctively Freirean notion of the generative theme—central to the Project's methodological approach to the validation of popular knowledge in the school and the interdisciplinary organization of universal knowledge in the curriculum—making it even more suitable for our research. Since this is a central theoretical claim of this book, we need to explain it in more detail.

Although the Inter Project is informed by various pedagogical, psychosocial, and constructivist theories of learning and cognitive development, including the work of Emilia Ferreiro and Lev Vygotsky, as analyzed in Chapter V, at its foundation is the Freirean methodology of thematic investigation.[13] It is a methodology which calls for the collective investigation of the school community's socio-cultural reality in order to discover the generative themes or situations most significant to that particular population. The generative themes, based on the real life situations, problems and concerns of the learners, are used as the building blocks in the construction of a locally relevant curriculum which at the same time relates that local reality to a broad range of individual, community and societal problems, e.g., peer group relations in the school, public transportation, violence and public safety, and air and water contamination in an industrial city like São Paulo.

Hence, the Inter Project fully adopted the Freirean methodological strategy of "problematization," dialogue and reflective praxis throughout its planning, implementation, and evaluation processes. This bold marriage between the critical theoretical tenets of a popular education tradition, mostly carried out in nonformal educational settings, to the large bureaucratic body and setting of São Paulo's municipal school system, inevitably led to slippery situations between the theoretical and philosophical universe of its actors and the practical day to day, administrative, pedagogical, and political work of the new administration. This slippage could become even more severe if and when the task at hand called for establishing a movement for the reorientation of the curriculum, pursuing the democratization of the administration of the municipal schools, and the improvement of the quality of education offered in the schools, while promoting literacy training for adults in collaboration with existing social movements.

Therefore, our constructivist approach seemed not only appropriate for the research design but almost appeared as an epistemological demand to carry out a study which followed, step by step, and as it was unveiling itself in front of our eyes, a fascinating attempt of radical democratic educational reform. While the richness of the whole process cannot be captured in its integrity, texture and dynamics by a single research project, the organization of this book accounts for key dimensions of this experience.

Organization of the Book

We hope that this introduction has set the right tone for the inquiry and has offered some insights into the complexity of the research problem. Chapters II and III offer an historical and political analysis of Brazilian and Latin American education, within a context of the dual conditions of structural adjustment and neoliberalism. In this sense, this book discusses one of the most important experiences of this decade, and offers a preliminary assessment of its conflicts and contradictions as well as its successes. Particularly, Chapter II discusses, as a necessary preface, the historical and contemporary relationships among education, the state, and social change in Latin America. Chapter III discusses how the administration led by Paulo Freire tried to create a popular public schooling model, offering a generic set of arguments developed in more detail in Chapter IV which outlines the major administrative and structural reforms and policy initiatives in reorienting the curriculum that supported teachers' work in the Interdisciplinary Project. Chapter V focuses on the Inter Project in greater detail, analyzing its goals, methods, curriculum design, and outcomes, while chapter VI offers an ethnographic account of the reform experience through an in-depth set of case studies of four São Paulo schools. The chapter focuses on teachers' lives, opinions, aspirations and expectations regarding educational reform and curriculum change in São Paulo in light of the PT-MSE's utopian political-pedagogic project. Finally, chapter VII provides a set of conclusions for an ongoing dialogue on a pedagogy of hope, social movements and educational reform. Through a painstakingly detailed empirical analysis and pluralistic theoretical perspective, this book provides an assessment of an original, far-reaching, and radical process of educational reform and does so from the vantage point of the teachers, classrooms and schools that were affected.

Notes

1. David N. Plank, *The Means of Our Salvation: Public Education in Brazil, 1930-1995* (Boulder, CO: Westview Press, 1996).

2. Regis de Morais, *Educação em tempos obscuros* (São Paulo: Autores Associados-Cortez Editores, 1991), p. 58.

3. David Plank, "Public Purpose and Private Interest in Brazilian Education," *New Education* 2 (1990), pp. 83-89. For an expanded argument, see David Plank, *The Means of Our Salvation*, Op. Cit., chapters 1 and 4.

4. Raymundo Moniz de Aragão, *A Instrucão Pública no Brasil* (Rio de Janeiro: Instituto de Documentação, Editora da Fundação Getulio Vargas, 1985), pp. 1-30.

5. 1988 Inep statistics cited in *Almanaque Abril* (São Paulo, Brazil, 1994), p. 79. For a more detailed statistical treatment, see Plank, Op. Cit., pp. 29-62.

6. David Plank, Op. cit. p. 87.

7. Henry Giroux, *Schooling and the Struggle for Public Life: Critical Pedagogy in the Modern Age* (Minneapolis: University of Minnesota Press, 1988).

8. Paulo Freire, *Pedagogia da Esperança. Um reencontro com a Pedagogia do Oprimido* (Rio de Janeiro: Paz e Terra, 1992).

9. Regis de Morais, *Educação em tempos obscuros* (São Paulo: Autores Associados and Cortez Editores, 1991), p. 58.

10. One such theoretical perspective can be found in Raymond A. Morrow and Carlos A. Torres, *Social Theory and Education. A Critique of Theories of Social and Cultural Reproduction* (New York: State University of New York Press), 1995.

11. For a theoretical conceptualization, see Raymond Morrow and Carlos Alberto Torres *Critical Theory and Education: Freire, Habermas and the Dialogical Subject* (Alberta and Los Angeles), manuscript.

12. Harding, Sandra, *The Science Question in Feminism*. Ithaca: Cornell University Press, 1986.

13. For a detailed analysis of this methodology see Moacir Gadotti and Carlos Alberto Torres, eds., *Educação popular: Utopia latinoamericana (ensaios)* (São Paulo, Cortez Editora-Editora da Universidade de São Paulo, 1994); Moacir Gadotti and Carlos Alberto Torres, eds., *Educación popular: Crisis y perspectivas*. (Buenos Aires, Miño y Davila editor, 1993); Carlos Alberto Torres and Guillermo González Rivera, eds., *Sociología de la educación: Corrientes contemporáneas*. Third edition, with a new introduction (Buenos Aires, Miño y Davila, 1994); Carlos Alberto Torres, ed., *Paulo Freire: Educación y concientización* (Salamanca, Spain: Sígueme Publishers, 1980); Carlos Alberto Torres, ed., *Paulo Freire en América Latina* (Mexico: Editorial Gernika, 1980); Carlos Alberto Torres, ed., *La praxis educativa de Paulo Freire* (Mexico: Editorial Gernika, 1978, 5th edition, 1987); Carlos Alberto Torres, ed., *Entrevistas con Paulo Freire* (Mexico: Editorial Gernika, 1978, 4th edition, 1986).

II

Setting the Stage:
Politics, Policy, and Education
in Brazil

The State as a Political Actor in Public Education

Latin America has been marked by patterns of conflict and coordination between the state and organized labor. Collier and Collier point to the introduction of corporatism as the distinctive characteristic of Latin American capitalism and politics in the 20th century.[1] Corporatism involves a set of structures which integrate society in a vertical manner, thus leading to the legalization and institutionalization of a workers' movement which is formed and largely controlled by the state.

In Latin America, the state itself is redefining its role in economic development and educational expansion. Historically, the state in Latin America has actively intervened in the development of national economies by means of redistributionist policies. During the second half of the 19th century and the first three decades of the 20th century, the predominant state model in Latin America was a liberal one controlled by rural landowners or oligarchy.[2] In this form, the state consolidated the nation and generated relative political stability and the oligarchy maintained tight control over the political process, at times by means of direct control over the state, and at other times through control of the parliament and important political parties. In order to implement this control, occasional electoral fraud or open repression were employed.[3]

Public education played a major role in the legitimation of the political systems and the integration and modernization of the countries of Latin America.[4] Public education systems in the region were all developed as part of the project of liberal states seeking to establish the foundations of the nation and citizenship. The role and function of public education in the creation of a disciplined citizen; the role, mission, ideology, and training of teachers; and the prevailing notions of curriculum and school knowledge were all deeply marked by the prevailing philosophy of the liberal state.[5]

Furthermore, as part of its development project, the state extended social benefits to vast sectors of the population, as is evident, for example, in Argentina, Brazil, Costa Rica, and Mexico. Education played a key role in these social programs because mass schooling was viewed as a means of building a national citizenry, training a productive labor base, and increasing social mobility. Ultimately, mass schooling was seen as a prerequisite for liberal democracy. This contributed to educational expansion and increased investment in public education.

Educational expansion in Latin America during the early phase of industrialization in the 1960s represents the highest rates of educational growth in the world.[6] Between 1960 and 1970, the indices of growth for higher education and secondary education were 247.9 percent and 258.3 percent, respectively. However, the enrollment in primary basic education grew only 167.6 percent, while the illiteracy rate remained more or less constant in most countries of the region.[7] One study of the late 1970s shows a fundamental continuity in this pattern of educational development.[8] Ernesto Schiefelbein argued that in the last four decades Latin America made significant progress toward democracy by "(i) expanding access to education for most children reaching school age; (ii) extending the years of schooling; (iii) improving timely entrance to school; (iv) providing early care to an increasing number of deprived children; and (v) increasing the provision of minimum inputs and eliminating tracks for social levels."[9]

In contrast to previous achievements in the expansion of public education, the past two decades have witnessed a decline in quantity and quality of schooling in the region.[10] Reimers argues that ministries of education in the region have been forced to sacrifice equity and efficiency in order to reduce educational expenditures under the constraints imposed by internationally-mandated structural adjustment policies. These cuts have disproportionately affected primary education and are reflected in the limited resources available for teaching materials, school facilities and in falling school enrollment rates.[11]

Economic and Socio-political Background: Crisis, Austerity, and Structural Adjustment in Contemporary Latin America

The 1980s have been labeled as the "lost decade" in Latin America.[12] It was during this decade that the region witnessed a cycle of high inflation, even hyper-inflation, and recession never before experienced. The oil crises of 1973 and 1982, coupled with the debt crisis of the 1980s, left the region in a state of economic disarray. Faced with rising international interest rates, Latin American countries found it increasingly difficult to meet their debt repayment schedules. International financial organizations (for instance, the International Monetary Fund and the World Bank) required governments in the region to adopt structural adjustment policies to address balance of payment difficulties and fiscal deficits.

This model of stabilization and adjustment involves a number of policy recommendations, including the reduction of government expenditures, currency devaluations to promote exports, reduction in import tariffs, and an increase in public and private savings. Key aims of this model are a drastic reduction in the state sector, the liberalization of salaries and prices, and the reorientation of industrial and agricultural production toward exports. The overall purpose of this policy package is, in the short-run, to reduce the size of fiscal deficits and of public expenditures, to drastically reduce inflation, and to reduce exchange rates and tariffs. In the medium-term, structural adjustment relies on exports as the engine of growth. To that extent, structural adjustment and subsequent policies of economic stabilization seek to liberalize trade, to reduce distortions in the price structures, to end "protectionist" policies, and therefore to facilitate the rule of the market in the Latin American economies.[13]

These economic changes are taking place in the context of re-democratization of political structures. Latin American societies have a long tradition of political authoritarianism which has, to some extent, permeated many different policy arenas, including education. The historical irony is that the return to democracy in the eighties and the overall project of redemocratization was marked by unusual economic constraints.

Trends toward economic globalization, deteriorating political economic conditions, particularly hyper-inflation in countries like Argentina and Brazil, the upsurging of neoliberal governments, the political debacle of the region's left, the failure of socialist revolution in Central America in the 1980s (i.e., Nicaragua, El Salvador, Guatemala), and the collapse of the socialist economies, created the "right conditions" for structural adjustment policies to be fully implemented region wide, despite past populist experiences of governance and the strength of unions.

Economic stabilization came about in Latin America as a response to debt crisis, fiscal crisis, industrial recession, and inflation (in some contexts hyper-inflation). This happened however, only after key social actors in the distributional conflict (the working class, campesinos, and even sectors of the middle classes) relinquished, consciously or by default, their ability to challenge cuts in public expenditures. There was a deadlock between the programs of the lower class sectors (particularly trade unions) and the economic and political preferences of elites which was finally broken with the onset of this period of adjustment.[13]

While the extent of the social consequences of the crisis and stabilization policies are still a matter of debate, it is evident from a number of international studies that the overall welfare of the people in the region is worse, in many respects, than it was 20 years ago.[15] For instance, according to the Economic Commission of Latin America (ECLA), approximately 44 percent of the continent's population (183 million people) in 1990 were living below the poverty line—an increase of 112 million over 1970. ECLA attributed this growing impoverishment to "the dramatic fall in average income, which marked a tremendous step backwards in the material standard of living of the Latin American and Caribbean population."[16] Similar analyses are presented in a report by the Inter-American Dialogue.[17]

To address the economic and fiscal crisis and its social and political consequences, stabilization and structural adjustment programs have been carried out under different names—by regimes with diverse ideological orientations—within the context of a general and deep crisis. The state's reform reduced its interventionist role in society and facilitated, through privatization and diminishing welfare policies, the rule of market forces in Latin American societies. This, of course, has implications for state legitimacy and for the role of public education in the region.

Democratizing Education in Brazil: Early Movements

Efforts to democratize access to education have appeared at different moments throughout the history of Brazilian public schooling. Yet, it is not until after the First World War that initial steps toward building a public educational system are taken. During this period Brazil underwent a period of profound structural change. The import-substitution industrialization that took place during World War I spurred the rapid urbanization of the country's population resulting in the development of a strong urban middle class and expanding working class sector which in turn created an increased demand for schooling. This changing social fabric also called for the crafting of a new pedagogic vision commensurate with the evolving edifice of modern Brazilian society.

The single most significant move in that direction is exemplified by the *Escola Nova* Movement of the 1920s and 1930s which grew out of the economic and social trends of industrialization and urbanization of the time. The emergent urbane liberal elite—inspired by the North American educational progressivism and pragmatism (i.e., Dewey)—created the *Escola*

Nova movement to champion the modernization of Brazilian society through the realization of universal, free and laic schooling as an obligation of the State. In their 1932 "Manifesto dos Pioneiros da Educação Nova," the *Escola Novistas* not only promoted the expansion of public schooling but insisted on numerous pedagogic innovations that would move Brazilian education away from the archaic practices and content inherited from its ecumenical and oligarchic past, towards a more relevant and active educational program (e.g., "ensino ativo") that worked to link the teachings in school to the economic and social reality of the community.[18] Moreover, the *Escola Novistas* framed their vision of public schooling within the overriding goal of achieving modernization and democracy for Brazil, which translated into the inclusion of vocational training and citizenship building in the public school curriculum.[19]

Named the country's first Minister of Education in 1930, Francisco Campos, spearheaded an extensive educational reform effort that culminated in the 1934 Constitution which guaranteed universal schooling. Furthermore, the Constitution of 1934 was the first to directly address the problem of educational expansion in terms of specific governmental policies and financing: "representing an advance in relation to the previous constitutions, [it] designed the outline of an organized educational system based on guidelines drawn up by the Union, it sought to democratize schooling and created the means by which to implement these measures." It did so by guaranteeing financial resources for education obligating the Federal government and municipalities to allocate 10 percent of their tax revenues and the state and federal districts never less than 20 percent.[20]

With the onset of the political regime of the *Estado Novo* (1937-1945) under the populist leader, Getulio Vargas, many advances made by the *Escola Novistas* were lost. The Constitution of 1937—albeit largely drafted by Francisco Campos, who had previously, as secretary of the Interior for Minas Gerais, strongly advocated the principles of the *Escola Novistas*— declared as foremost the freedom of private initiative in the area of education.[21] It further reserved secondary schooling for elites and determined prevocational or professional education as sufficient for lower socio-economic groups. As Helenir points out, "with such measures, the Constitution of 1937 [. . .] only worked to reinforce the antidemocratic [spirit] and dualism characteristic of Brazilian education."[22]

As a consequence, even with the legal foundation for a public educational system having been established with the 1934 and 1937 Brazilian Constitutions, a divide was created between the public and private, relegating the majority of the population to limited access to education in the public sphere at the elementary level and reserving the right to a quality and extended education for a small elite who could afford private schooling and then gain access to the prestigious public institutions of higher learning. Therefore, in addition to its late start, advocates of Brazilian public education have had to consistently battle the powerful interests behind private education, namely the church and the middle class and upper classes that benefit from the continual subsidy of private and higher education by the State. This conservative opposition has held firmly to two principles: (a) that a course on religion be taught in public schools and (b) that the inherent rights of parents to choose the kind of education their children receive translates into the obligation of the state to subsidize private and religious schooling. In opposition to this conservative position, Liberal and Leftist advocates of public education have fought a long hard battle against entrenched elite views of the purpose of public schooling and the obligations of the State to fulfill the educational demands of the majority of the population. In recent years the Workers' Party has been at the forefront of this struggle to provide a quality education for the popular classes.

Politics and Education in Latin America: Paulo Freire and Popular Education

> Truly, only the oppressed are able to conceive of a future totally distinct from their present, insofar as they arrive at a consciousness of a dominated class. The oppressors, as the dominating class, cannot conceive of the future unless it is the preservation of their present as oppressors. In this way, whereas the future of the oppressed consists in the revolutionary transformation of society, without which their liberation will not be verified, the oppressor's future consists in the simple modernization of society, which permits the continuation of its class supremacy.[23]

In Latin America, models of popular education spring from the original Freirean pedagogy of the oppressed developed in the early 1960s, and they are connected to the tradition of working class education initiated in Spain in the 19th century which further evolved until the Spanish Civil War (1936-1939), and was later continued in Latin America as characterized by the liberal project of public education. Popular education and public education (free, compulsory, secular education) were at some point synonymous, and the Freirean experiences of the sixties served to deconstruct and recreate the meaning of the experience of public education or education for all.

During this same period, the imagination of Brazilian educators was awakened amidst a general tide of revolutionary fervor that swept the continent. Central to this radical time were the Second Vatican Council (Vatican

II) which formally opened the Catholic Church to a progressive social agenda as embodied by Liberation Theology, and its secular counterpart, Popular Education. In Brazil, the Movement for Popular Culture (MCP)— of which Paulo Freire stands as a foremost visionary—gained momentum. Like other counter-hegemonic popular educational experiences that emerged throughout Latin America at the time, the MCP sought to shake loose from its centuries-old shackles of oppression the critical conscious- ness of the Brazilian masses—descendants of Indigenous peoples, African slaves and the European dispossessed—by means of a transformative edu- cational praxis. Hence, the popular education movement of the early 1960s emerged as part of a political-pedagogic imperative to not only make liter- ate those who had been kept out of the school house and forced into the slums of the country's burgeoning urban centers or the isolation of a desti- tute rural life, but also to arm them with the knowledge of how to trans- form that repressive reality.

Popular education à la Freire arose from a political and social analysis of the living conditions of the poor and their outstanding problems (such as unemployment, malnourishment, poor health), and attempted to en- gage the poor in individual and collective awareness of those conditions. There are key features in this theoretical and practical educational model. The pedagogical practices drew from prior collective and individual expe- riences (understood as previous knowledge) and stressed work in groups rather than individualistic approaches. The notion of education provided by these projects is related to the concrete skills or abilities that they try to instill in the poor (i.e., literacy or numeracy), and these projects strive to arouse pride, a sense of dignity, personal confidence, and self-reliance among the participants. Finally, these projects can be originated by gov- ernments, as in Colombia and Dominican Republic, with projects related to integrated rural development, or, as in Nicaragua, with the collective of popular education; and they may be directed toward adults as well as chil- dren.[24]

Therefore, conscientization is a goal, and knowledge appears as an instrument of struggle. Local community empowerment is a central con- cern of popular education, and a key strategy is to expand the connections between social movements and new forms of state governance. Given the experience of public education systems in the eighties and nineties, popu- lar education models have struggled vehemently to defend and expand public education while preserving quality of educational provision in neoliberal times.

The experience of the municipality of São Paulo with Paulo Freire as Secretary of Education is an illustration of how popular education can develop with a socialist orientation.[25]

Freire, the PT, and Educational Reform in São Paulo

In October of 1992, in the official organ of the municipal government, *Diário Oficial do Município de São Paulo*, the PT mayor Luiza Erundina de Sousa, former Secretary of Education Paulo Freire (1989-1991) and Freire's successor Mario Sergio Cortella (1991-1992) signed a letter addressed to "those who together with us construct a public education of quality for São Paulo." In this letter the educators of the city are reminded of one of the initial statements made to them in February of 1989, on the part of Secretary Freire, when the PT first took hold of the Municipal Secretariat of Education:

> We should not call the people to the school to receive instructions, postulations, recipes, threats, reprimands and punishments, but to collectively participate in the construction of a knowledge, that goes beyond purely empirical knowledge, and that takes into account their necessities and turns it into an instrument of struggle, allowing for their transformation into protagonists of their own history. Popular participation in the creation of culture and education breaks with the tradition that only the elite is competent and knows what the needs and interests of the society are. The school should also be a center for the irradiation of popular culture, at the service of the community, not to consume it but to create it.[26]

The same letter goes on to recount the frustrations and successes of the PT's project for educational reform in the city during its four year tenure, citing the construction of 65 new schools and the renovation of 178 of the total of 691 municipal schools and the extension of preschool education to 145,000 more children as well as literacy training to 312,000 adults and youths. In the letter Erundina, Freire and Cortella also point to one of the PT administration's major accomplishments: the passing of a new municipal legislation, *Estatuto do Magistério*, which protects teachers' salaries and promotes the value of teachers as professionals. The authors of the letter finally point to efforts made to facilitate school autonomy through participatory planning and administration. They affirm that it is through such a process of increased autonomy for local schools that the planning of education in the city will "stop being the sole domain of technicians and specialists, making progressively more explicit the priorities and necessities, the difficulties and the interests of various social groups and the limitations of the municipal government as a sphere of power, [hence making the autonomy of the schools] an excellent instrument for the construction and affirmation of citizenship."[27]

But the Mayor, the former Secretary of Education and his successor concluded by asserting that although they are "certain that this process was not free of errors, [they believe that such mistakes] can not be taken in isolation for they are situated within the framework of a politics which seeks to value public education."

Freire's role as a protagonist in the trajectory of a critical approach to popular education has significant implications for the educational reform carried out by the Workers Party under his leadership as Secretary of Education in the Municipality of São Paulo. The ideal of a Popular Public School erected three decades after the emergence of the popular education movement in Brazil is linked both historically and theoretically to Freire's initial arrival onto the educational scene in his country in the late 1950s [this relationship will be explored in more detail in Chapter III]. In this sense, the analysis in this book maps out the development of contemporary progressive pedagogic thought and the leftist politics of schooling in Brazil, in which both Paulo Freire as an individual and the PT as a political party have taken part, each contributing in different ways to the particular characteristics of the educational reform project carried out in the municipal schools of São Paulo over the course of the PT's four-year administration.

The two primary initiatives that evolved from this reform experience, the Interdisciplinary Project and MOVA (the Literacy Movement for Adults and Youths), represent in some respects a unique combination of elements borne of the popular educational movements that flourished decades previous and matured through a decade of the social democratic politics of the Worker's Party. Thus, they are a marriage between collective critical pedagogy and political work oriented toward constructing a collective consciousness for a new democratic society. In this way, many of the educators encountered at all levels of this reform, from its planners at the Secretariat to the teachers in the schools, seemed motivated by forces greater than simply a bureaucratic mandate to carry out a plan of educational action. These were individuals who had participated in the realization of an historical moment of transition from dictatorship to democracy. In many respects their proposal of radical reforms seemed that much more part of a continual and integrated process of pedagogic practice and political struggle with roots extending backwards into several decades of contemporary efforts to defeat the oppressive oligarchic forces of Brazilian society, and branches stretching forward in a fight for the future of democratic life in the country.

The PT itself is composed of a broad spectrum of the political left in Brazil. An understanding of the party's historical formation, its popular base and intellectual leadership and the socialist ideals that it has promoted since its arrival on the Brazilian political scene is necessary in order to fully grasp both the intention and the outcome of the São Paulo experience in educational reform under the helm of the Workers Party.

The Workers Party (*Partido dos Trabalhadores* or "PT") first arrived on the Brazilian political scene at the end of the decade of the seventies, signaling the organization of significant opposition forces to the Brazilian military regime that had seized power in the 1964 coup d'etat. The bureaucratic authoritarian regime would eventually succumb to this democratization movement, in which the PT played a pivotal role, leading to the first (indirect) presidential elections in 1985. A diverse coalition of labor union leaders and workers, intellectuals and leftist community activists came together to debate the formation of the party in January of 1979 and by May First of that year published an unofficial *"Carta de Princípios do PT"* which included in its initial political platform the "democratization of schooling, with free public education for all, and a guarantee of access to school at all levels for the entire population." [28] The Party was officially founded on February 10, 1980 with the launching of its *Manifesto*, which reiterates the Party's commitment to universal public schooling at all levels and under the Manifesto's *Plano de Ação* (Action Plan) adds that such an education should be "oriented to the necessities of the workers." [29] According to Gadotti and Pereira: "In this way, the first "mass" political party in Brazil was born from "the base up," by virtue of the very will of the workers. [It was] the first party of our political history which emerged from the base." [30]

More than a decade and a half after its inception, the PT boasts of 700,000 members; 120,000 militants; 2,304 municipal directorships; 53 municipal governments (four representing state capitals: Belo Horizonte, Porto Alegre, Goiânia and Rio Branco); 77 state representatives, one senator (Eduardo Suplicy, who presented himself as mayoral candidate in the 1992 municipal election which the PT lost to the current mayor of São Paulo, Paulo Maluf of the conservative right wing *Partido Democratico Social*, PDS); 36 federal deputies, and 1,400 local representatives in municipal governments (i.e., *vereadores*).[31] Today the PT is made up of five major tendencies: *Opção Esquerda* (the democratic socialists wing of the party making up 32 percent of its membership including its president, Rui Falção); *Unidade e Luta* (30 percent of the membership representing Lula's socialist positions); *Na Luta PT* (the more radical Trotskist wing of the party, making up 22 percent of its active membership); *Democracia Radical* (representing 10 percent of the Party and a moderate position); *Independentes* (5 percent of members who remain unaligned with a particular tendency, e.g., Senator Eduardo Suplicy).[32]

> The distinctiveness of the PT among the many political parties that have sprouted during the past two decades of the post military years has been its strength: The PT is a unique organization in Brazilian politics. It has militants, regular meetings and a permanently functioning structure that operates at the local regional and national level. It has about 600,000 militants distributed between 2,304 regional directorates, as its local groups are known. Most other parties do not have any significant structure, few militants and function only at election time. For its militants, the PT is more that just a party; it is a lifestyle, a meeting point, a culture, the PT is the "let's party party," as many activists acknowledge.[33]

In terms of the party's ideological orientation, its intellectual leadership emphatically rejects the idea that socialism has been defeated arguing for the reconstruction of a new socialist vision, moving away from the "scientific socialism" that buttressed the recently fallen communist bureaucratic authoritarian regimes of Eastern Europe and the Soviet Union. It is a party that allows for a great deal of philosophical and ideological pluralism among its diverse membership made up of workers of all categories (industrial, agricultural, urban, rural and independent workers, as well as "white-collar" professionals like bank workers and teachers), along with small property owners and other middle class groups joined by a variety of Marxist intellectuals (ranging from the seasoned university professor to the student activist), labor organizations, and diverse social movements. Consequently, its principal political project is not to immediately dismantle the bourgeois capitalist state but to construct a "Popular Democratic Government" that can begin to seek viable alternatives to the existing capitalist social formation and defunct models of anti-democratic socialism.[34] Reflecting the nondogmatic spirit prevalent in the party, one member asserts:

> The PT should be a laic party, open to all perspectives of the world, *that they may verify and reciprocally produce each other,* in a broad process of the reconstruction of the socialist utopia. I am a Marxist but I want to have non-Marxists at my side. Perhaps because, as Norberto Bobbio would say, *in order to be a good Marxist it is necessary to not only be a Marxist.*[35]

In effect, the party not only encompasses individuals and groups of various Marxist tendencies, it also has made room for militants and grassroots movements that subscribe to other ideologies, or that do not necessarily identify themselves with a particular political philosophy but more so with a proactive position with respect to a specific problem of contemporary Brazilian reality (e.g., literacy movements, neighborhood rights groups, public health, ecological, feminist and race issues). In this manner the PT claims to "fight for the right of workers and the poor to speak with their own voices and in their own names." Such a broadened conception of the Marxist notion of class struggle necessarily has led to the party's advancement of a revised notion of citizenship and democracy in Brazil.

Margaret E. Keck, author of *The Workers' Party and Democratization in Brazil* (1992), points to the PT's crucial role in redefining the parameters of political participation and in contributing to the revitalization of democracy in Brazil:

> [S]ince 1980 the Workers Party has brought hundreds of new actors into politics. It has created new constituencies that expect political leaders to be responsible and accountable. And it has insisted that the capacity to participate politically comes not from status or specialized learning, but from the experience of everyday life. The PT has had a marked impact on the new generation. Its strongest support is among the young, and the party may be playing a crucial role in socializing youth into a radically revised vision of what politics is about.[36]

Education, therefore, is seen as a powerful and necessary tool in the development of a critically conscious citizenry active in the construction of a democratic socialist society. Consequently, the struggle for a quality public education represents one of the fronts around which popular groups affiliated with the PT have galvanized and constitutes a major area of policy effort among the municipalities that the PT has held in recent years.

As an indication of the Party's evolution from its origins in the labor movement of São Paulo to an increasingly institutionalized, comprehensive and broad based national party, it is important to note the significant role the PT has played in Brazil's first two presidential elections since the demise of the military dictatorship. Indeed the PT expanded its national base of support as a consequence of its leadership during the Direitas Já (Direct Elections Now) campaign of 1983 which called for direct presidential elections. The PT's charismatic leader of working class origin, Luís Inácio "Lula" da Silva, rose to a leadership position in the early days of the Party's efforts to organize the steel workers of São Paulo's industrial belt. The politically seasoned labor leader ran in both the 1989 and 1994 presidential elections. He lost by a very slim margin in the first instance, to Fernando Collor de Mello, the prodigal—and as it turned out later, the distinctly dishonorable—son of an oligarchic family of the Northeastern state of Alagoas. Brazil's conservative elite panicked at the prospect of a socialist president and lavishly financed Collors' electoral campaign. Rede Globo, Brazil's powerful television network, launched a fierce campaign to discredit Lula's person, ultimately resulting in Collor's triumph with 49 percent of the vote over Lula's 43 percent. Four years later, despite the fact that six months prior to the October 1994 elections he enjoyed a 22-point lead over Fernando Henrique Cardoso, the eminent sociologist of the Brazilian Social Democratic Party (Partido Social Democratica Brasileiro, PSDB) in the polls, Lula ultimately gained only 27 percent of the vote, losing to Cardoso by a margin of 27 percentage points.[37]

Despite these two national losses, the PT achieved multiple victories in local and state elections. In 1988 its most significant electoral victory came in the form of the mayorship of the city of São Paulo,[38] the country's largest and most economically powerful municipality, with a population of more than nine million (9,626,894 according to the 1991 census) and a municipal budget of nearly four billion for the 1991 fiscal year.[39] The PT municipal government under mayor Luiza Erundina de Souza—a woman from Freire's homeland of the impoverished North East, origin of the great majority of São Paulo's working class migrant population—had a profound impact on the educational reality of this enormous city. Given his pre-eminence and his close ties to the PT, Paulo Freire was the logical choice for Municipal Secretary of Education. Under Freire's initial leadership, during the four years of its administration (1989-1992),[40] the PT's educational efforts were oriented by three principles: participation, decentralization and autonomy.[41] These principles were geared towards the Party's goal of constructing a Popular Public School. The Popular Public School was defined by the PT Secretariat as follows:

> [It] not only is one to which all have access, but in whose construction every one participates, [it is a school] which truly attends to the popular interests which are of the majority; it is, therefore, a school of a *new quality*, based on commitment and solidarity, in the formation of class consciousness. Within [the popular public school] all agents, not only teachers, take on an active and dynamic role, experimenting with new forms of learning, participating, teaching, working, playing and celebrating. [42]

To begin the hard work of achieving this newly fashioned vision of the public school, at the outset, Freire's administration defined four areas of action.

1. The creation of concrete proposals for the **improvement of the quality of education** offered in the municipal schools through various programmatic and curricular changes. These included the reorganization of grade levels into three cycles and the introduction of new evaluation methods, continued evaluation and research to secure technical refinement, the provision for ongoing professional training and just remuneration for teachers, and the establishment of the Movement for the Reorientation of the Curriculum with the implementation of the Interdisciplinary Project as well as numerous other educational programs.

2. The advancement of the process of **democratization of the administration of municipal schools** through increased participation and social control of the system by creating institutional channels of communication and participatory methods of decision making as manifested in the systematic effort to make authentic the pre-existing School Councils (deliberative representative bodies).

3. The promotion of **a movement for the education of youth and adults** (i.e., *Movimento de Alfabetização de Jovens e Adultos,* MOVA) through the technical and financial support of existing social movements working in adult literacy training throughout the city.[43]

4. The **democratization of access** through the construction of new schools and renovation and expansion of existing facilities and fulfillment of basic infrastructure necessary for adequate student performance.

In its educational policy efforts the PT claims that its municipal administration attempted to break from the tradition of a politics of grandiose campaigns, isolated pedagogic experimentalism, or formulaic solutions to the complex problems of public schooling. Its approach to educational policy making was multifaceted—as the preceding points illustrate—and "above all, [the Secretariat insisted, it was an approach that implicated] a persistent predisposition to face the political resistance on the part of conservatives, which [was] not small."[44]

Teacher training constituted an area of primary concern for the PT administration, in as much as the Secretariat viewed teachers as the principal agents for the realization of its proposals for profound institutional and curriculum change in the schools. Hence, the administration created teacher formation groups as the key method for supporting their development and transformation. The specific nature of this administration's focus on teacher training is further elaborated as follows:

Here, distinct from a mere educational fad or pedagogic experimentalism, it was not a matter of training teachers in a new revolutionary method, but more an effort to patiently work towards the continuous reflection on their practices, the discovery of alternative approaches through the exchange of experiences, to have at their disposal the assistance of conceptually sophisticated educational thinkers, to gradually elevate the level of knowledge of the teachers, promote collective work as the privileged form of teacher formation, and afford the material conditions for all this to occur. In this manner the pedagogic innovations are appropriated, the curricular alterations fruitful, because the principal agents [of these changes], the teachers, are considered not objects of training, but elements that produce and re-elaborate knowledge.[45]

In summary, the educational policies that emanated from Secretary Freire's administration of the Municipal Secretariat of Education of São Paulo (MSE) embodied both the transformative pedagogical premises of Freire's own philosophy, including the experience of popular education in Latin America, and the socialist tenets of the Worker's Party's political platform which, since the Party's inception, promoted a public education in the interest of the working class sectors that make up the majority of the public school's clientele. Given the Party's origins in the labor unions and grassroots movements that flourished in the 1970s in opposition to a brutally repressive military regime, it is not surprising that its educational vision includes the association of non-formal and formal approaches to educating the poor and oppressed.[46] Freire's own contribution to the development of non-formal alternative educational methodologies as exemplified in his approach to the teaching of literacy skills to adults through consciousness raising or *conscientização* was therefore adopted in the formulation of a curricular reform program in the formal elementary schools under the jurisdiction of the Municipal government. It is the PT administration's initiation of the Interdisciplinary Project, as part of its over all effort to create a *Movement for the Reorientation of the Curriculum* which is a central focus of this book. The next chapter, however, will offer a broader perspective on the theoretical bases that we use to analyze the policies and characteristics of the PT's democratic socialist state.

Afterword: The Neoliberal Project

It is important to note, as an afterword to the above discussion of the progressive politics of education in Brazil and the role of the Popular State in the advancement of such socialist democratic proposals as those embodied in the PT administration of the municipal public schools under Paulo Freire's leadership, what the neoliberal response has been to these and other educational proposals from the Left. This is of particular relevance for the PT project given the fact that the PDS administration that won the 1992 municipal elections in São Paulo introduced its own project called *Controle da Qualidade Total* (CQT, Total Quality Control) into the municipal schools. The CQT proposal is based on Japanese managerial models for industry and is attributed to the contributions of North Americans' Edwards Deming (who developed the Deming Administrative Method working with the Japanese in the 1950s), and William Glasser (who applied Deming's managerial propositions of quality control to the more efficient and effective organization of schools in the United States). [47]

Although the CQT was presented with a significantly lesser degree of impetus and organization than the previous PT administration's policy efforts, its articulation as the PDS administration's basis for the orientation of its policies led to a critical affront on the CQT by those educators within the municipal school system who aligned themselves with the PT and the political-pedagogic principles that underscored the Inter Project. The prevalence of an antagonistic stance with regard to the CQT was evidenced in the title of the 5th Annual Congress of the SINPEEM (*Sindicato dos Profesionais de Educação no Ensino Municipal*—Syndicate of Professional Educators of Municipal Schooling) held in June 1994: "Que Qualidade é Essa?" (What quality is that?) This tension between the neoliberal proposal for a school of Total Quality and the concept of the Popular Public School emanating from the progressive forces in Brazil is one that extends to a national level and is linked to the partisan conflicts between the PT and the neoliberal parties which oppose its politicized conceptualization of the public school (namely in favor of the popular sectors in the country).

In turn, the neoliberal position regarding what needs to be done to improve public schooling in Brazil is ideologically linked to the neoconservative critique of schools that has emerged in the North (i.e., United States) in recent years. The neoconservative critique points to the shortcomings of a watered down curriculum and the incompetence of teachers without linking the so-called educational crisis to broader structural changes in the economy (i.e., industrial restructuring and globalization) and its impact on inner city populations (e.g., unemployment) and the general cultural trends characteristic of late capitalist postmodern society.

Concurrent to the rising tide of Conservativism against what is perceived as the failure of Liberal educational policies implemented in recent decades in the North, neoliberals in the South (i.e., Latin America) claim that the problems facing public schooling can best be addressed through the adoption of more efficient modes of school administration and curriculum planning. As a matter of clarification, in Latin America the particular political history of the region renders the term Liberal to mean that which adheres to the Classical Liberal tenets of the reign of the free market and the limitation of the role of the state in the organization of society and provision of services. Therefore, what is being termed as a "Neoliberal" trend in the public policy discourse is being articulated from the Right as it struggles to reconfigure its power from within the disastrous legacy of the corporatist, populist and authoritarian bureaucratic regimes that in the 20th century have constructed the Latin American State. In summary, the neoliberal project seeks to divest the state of its popular mandate to provide for the downtrodden and underprivileged in societies where the sharp social economic distinctions are so prevalent, isolating a small middle and even more minute upper class to a protected realm of privilege and increasingly concentrated wealth.

Taking a Brazilian critical pedagogic perspective, Tomaz Tadeu da Silva comments on the "new" neoliberal policies, pointing to the underlying agenda that they promote: "The so-called *Gestão da Qualidade Total* in education is a clear demonstration that the neoliberal strategy will not merely be content to orient institutionalized education to the necessities of industry nor to organize education in the way of the market, but that its aim is to attempt to reorganize the very interior of education, that is of schools and of classrooms, in accordance with the schemes of the process of work."[48] Tomaz Tadeu da Silva sees this project as one that not only has prescriptive policy implications—i.e., the privatization of schooling at all levels and the tailoring of education to meet the needs of industry by training students for the workplace—but as having profound ideological reverberations as well; that is, "to prepare students to accept the postulates of the liberal credo."[49] He identifies the fundamental aim of both the neoconservative and neoliberal projects in education in the North and South respectively as having as their central aim: [. . .] the creation of a space in which it becomes impossible to think of the economic, the political and the social outside of the categories that justify the social arrangements of capitalism."[50] He continues, "it is not irrelevant that this process of redefinition of the categories with which we think of the social space result in the translation of social and political issues into issues of public morality, [individual] behavior and social assistance [. . .] Within that redefinition, the solution of these issues is dislocated from the social, political and public sphere and resurrected in the realm of individual initiative."[51]

Along these lines, speaking at the 1994 SINPEEM congress, historian Antonieta Antonucci critiqued the PDS municipal government's adoption of the Total Quality model for São Paulo posing this question: "A quem serve esta qualidade total?" (Whom does this Total Quality serve?)[52] Recounting its historical roots in the Taylorism—which dominated Brazilian modernist discourse since the 1920s—Antonucci positions the QT project as an affront on the previous administration's effort to reconstruct the working conditions of teachers in the municipal system in more democratic and participatory ways. "Total Quality Control," she argues, merely "brings with it the illusion of participation" by aggressively enlisting educators to participate in "the molding of workers" in the interests of industry and capitalism. It does so with the messianic language of the undertaking of a "mission" coupled with the logic of technical rationality in reforming the school to more effectively and efficiently produce competent workers. In focusing on the virtues of order, morality and ethics in educational endeavors, it circumvents the critical social issues of schooling and fails to advance a proposal for pedagogic change and transformation of the broader structures of society. Accordingly, key actors in the PT reform project offer this argument against the adoption of market models to the context of schooling:

> In the area of education, the university transplants technical models of assistance which are limited to the resolution of problems and which call for the presence of the specialist. To consult, in this case, is the same as contributing a type of knowledge whose history begins and ends in the moment of its donation (or commercialization). Recall that the relationship between the technocrat and his client, a service to be rendered and a work contract, is an exercise in systematized knowledge in order to fulfill specific needs. If this model serves its function in the technical assistance to industry and commerce and industrial management systems and to the various segments that form the dynamic of the market, it is imperative that [this technocratic model] be reexamined, reformulated when the "commodity" is schooling and the "market place" education.[53]

In the words of a former NAE Inter Team member who returned to his teaching position after the PT administration, "The neoliberal project is counter to the vision of the Inter Project. The Inter Project had as its objective to elevate [students'] level of critical political consciousness of the world, to create a transformative reality and to become a subject of that transformation" (Interview, 1994).[54] The chapters that follow provide both theoretical and practical elaboration of the Inter Project, demonstrating exactly how it attempted to achieve such radical objectives.

Notes

1. Ruth Berins Collier and David Collier, *Shaping the Political Arena. Critical Junctures, the Labor Movement, and Regime Dynamics in Latin America* (Princeton, New Jersey, Princeton University Press, 1991). See also Carlos Alberto Torres and Adriana Puiggrós, "The State and Public Education in Latin America," Introduction to the special issue on Latin America of the *Comparative Education Review*, Vol. 39, No. 1, February 1995, pp. 1-27.

2. Atilio A. Boron, *The Formation and Crisis of the Oligarchical State in Argentina, 1880-1930* (Ph.D. dissertation, Harvard University, 1976).

3. Ruth Collier and David Collier, Op. Cit.

4. Adriana Puiggrós, *Sujetos, disciplina y curriculum en los orígenes del sistema educativo argentino* (Buenos Aires: Galerna, 1990). For an alternative explanation using a world systems framework, see the work of representatives of the institutionalist school. For example, John Boli and Francisco O. Ramirez, "Compulsory Schooling in the Western Cultural Context," in Robert F. Arnove, Philip G. Altbach, and Gail P. Kelly (Eds.), *Emergent Issues in Education. Comparative Perspectives* (New York: SUNY Press, 1992), pp. 25-38. See also Carlos Alberto Torres and Adriana Puiggrós, "The State and Public Education in Latin America," *Comparative Education Review*, Vol. 39, No. 1, February 1995.

5. Adriana Puiggrós, *Democracia y autoritarismo en la pedagogía argentina y latinoamericana* (Buenos Aires: Galerna, 1986); Adriana Puiggrós et al., *Escuela, democracia y orden 1916-1943* (Buenos Aires: Galerna, 1992).

6. UNESCO. *Evolución reciente de la educación en América Latina* (Santiago de Chile: UNESCO, 1974, mimeographed, pp. 167; 227.

7. UNESCO, Conferencia de ministros de educación y ministros encargados de ciencia y tecnología en relación con el desarrollo de América Latina y el Caribe. Venezuela, December 6-15, Caracas, Venezuela (Caracas: UNESCO, 1971, mimeographed).

8. UNESCO/CEPAL/PNUD, *Desarrollo y Educación en América Latina: Síntesis General* (Buenos Aires: Proyecto DEALC, 4 vols., 1981).

9. Ernesto Schiefelbein, *Financing Education for Democracy in Latin America* (Santiago de Chile: Unesco-OREALC, January 1991, mimeographed), p. 4.

10. Beatrice Avalos, "Moving Where? Educational Issues in Latin American Contexts," *International Journal of Educational Development*, 1986; Marlaine E. Lockheed and Adriaan Verspoor, *Improving Primary Education in Developing Countries: A Review of Policy Options* (Washington, DC: World Bank and Oxford University Press, 1991).

11. Fernando Reimers, "The Impact of Economic Stabilization and Adjustment on Education in Latin America," *Comparative Education Review*, Vol. 35, May 1991, pp. 325-338.

12. Of course, despite disparities in income distribution, and the fall in the GNP in the region, this decade considered "lost" for economic growth was extremely prosperous for several sectors of the Latin American bourgeoisie, particularly the segments associated with the state which have enjoyed fiscal incentives and specific protectionism in certain areas of the economy. It is important to emphasize that not everybody lost during the "lost decade," and that some fractions of the elites became even richer while several segments of the population grew poorer. That is the reason that Latin American societies are now if not more, at least as unequal than before but, as documented by a number of socio-demographic studies, poverty has increased dramatically. See Atilio A. Boron and Carlos Alberto Torres, "Pobreza, Educación y Ciudadanía," paper presented to the Conference on Educación y Desigualdad Social en América Latina, Toluca, México, Colegio Mexiquense, October 26, 1994.

13. Sergio Bitar, "Neo-Conservatism versus Neo-Structuralism in Latin America," *CEPAL Review*, 34, 1988, p. 45.

14. Raúl Laban and Federico Sturzenegger, *Fiscal Conservatism as a Response to the Debt Crisis* (Los Angeles and Santiago de Chile, manuscript, 1992).

15. See, for instance, United Nations Development Program, *Mitigación de la pobreza y desarrollo social* (Montevideo, Uruguay; UNDP project RLA/92/009/1/01/31, 1992, mimeographed). United Nations Development Program, *Desarrollo Humano y Gobernabilidad* (Montevideo, Uruguay: UNDP project RLA/92/030/I/01/31, 1992, mimeographed).

16. Gert Rosenthal, "Latin America and Caribbean Development in the 1980s and the Outlook for the Future," *CEPAL Review*, 39, 1989, p. 1.

17. The Aspen Institute, *Convergence and Community: The Americas in 1993, A Report of the Inter-American Dialogue* (Washington: The Inter-American Dialogue of the Aspen Institute, 1992).

18. Raimundo Moniz de Aragão, *A instrução pública no Brasil* (Rio de Janeiro: Editora da Fundação Getulio Vargas, 1985), p. 35.

19. For an excellent analysis of the impact of nationalism on the development of public education in Brazil, see Carmen Nava, "Patria, Patriotism and National Identity in Brazil: 1937-1974" (Ph.D. dissertation, University of California, Los Angeles, 1995).

20. Suano Helenir, "A Educação nas Constituições Brasileiras," in *Escola Brasileira: Temas e Estudos,* coord. Roseli Fischmann (São Paulo: Atlas, 1987), p. 176.

21. Ibid., p. 178.

22. Ibid., pp. 178-179.

23. Paulo Freire, "La misión educativa de las iglesias en América Latina," *Contacto*, IX/5, Mexico, 1972, p. 32 [Our translation].

24. Carlos Alberto Torres, *The Politics of Nonformal Education in Latin America* (New York: Praeger, 1990).

25. Maria del Pilar O'Cadiz and Carlos Alberto Torres, "Literacy, Social Movements, and Class Consciousness: Paths from Freire and the São Paulo Experience," *Antropology and Education Quarterly,* 25 (3), September 1994, pp. 208-225.

26. SME-SP, *Cadernos de Formação Nª 1—Um Primeiro Olhar sobre o Projeto, 3ª Série—Ação Pedagogica da Escola pela via da interdisciplinaridade* (February 1990), p. 15.

27. *Diário Oficial do Município de São Paulo* (October 15, 1992).

28. Moacir Gadotti and Otaviano Pereira, *Pra que PT: Origem, Projecto e Consolidação do Partido dos Trabalhadores* (São Paulo: Cortez, 1989), p. 41.

29. Ibid., p. 61.

30. Moacir Gadotti and Otaviano Pereira, *Pra que PT: Origem, projeto e consolidação do Partido dos Trabalhadores* (São Paulo: Cortez, 1989), p. 31.

31. "O PT brilha e também mete medo," *Veja* (June 15, 1994), pp. 38-47.

32. Ibid. p. 41.

33. Sue Branford and Bernardo Kucinkski, *Brazil: Carnival of the Oppressed* (London: Latin American Bureau, 1995), p. 12.

34. *O PT e Marxismo, Cadernos de Teoria & Debate* (São Paulo: Partido dos Trabalhadores, 1991).

35. Tarso Genero (vice mayor of Porto-Alegre), cited in Ibid. p. 45.

36. Margaret E. Keck, "Brazil's Workers' Party: Socialism as Radical Democracy," in *Fighting for the Soul of Brazil,* eds., Kevin Danaher and Michael Shellenberger (New York: Monthly Review Press), p. 241.

37. Manuel Castells writes of the Cardoso's victory over Lula the following: "Las paradojas de la historia han hecho que Cardoso, un intelectual de izquierda ayer y hoy, llegue a la presidencia apoyado por el centro y la derecha brasileñas, para cerrar el paso al legendario Lula, un gran dirigente obrero, respetable y respetado por todo el mundo, Cardoso incluido." "El intelectual presidente," *El País* (Madrid, November 14, 1994), p. 15. Translation: "The paradoxes of history have made it possible for Cardoso, an intellectual of the Left, yesterday and today, to arrive at the presidency supported by the Brazilian center and the right, in order to close off the passage of the legendary Lula, a great labor leader, respectable and respected throughout the world, Cardoso himself included."

38. São Paulo was among 36 municipalities that the PT won in the 1988 municipal elections.

39. Fundação Instituto Brasileiro de Geografia e Estatística (IBGE) cited in *Almanaque Abril* (São Paulo Brasil, 1994), p.79.

40. Although Paulo Freire began his administration of the Secretariat in January of 1989, he resigned from the post of Secretary of Education in May of 1991, and was replaced by his former Cabinet Chief, Mário Sérgio Cortella. Still, Freire's two year presence at the head of the Secretariat had a profound impact on the direction of the educational reforms it pursued. In his book *Educação na Cidade* (1991), a synthesis of Freire's speech at the time of his departure from the Secretariat is entitled:

"Manifesto á maneira de quem, saindo fica." [Manifesto in the manner of one who leaving, remains] in which he makes the following gesture of solidarity with the PT administration and the educators in the municipal schools: "Continue counting on me in the construction of a politics of education, of a school with another 'face,' more joyful, fraternal and democratic," p. 144.

41. SME-SP, *Balanço Geral da SME: Projeção Trienal* (December 1992), p. 14.

42. Gadotti and Pereira, Op. Cit., p. 192.

43. For a more detailed discussion of the PT policy effort in adult literacy see O'Cadiz and Torres, " Literacy, Social Movements, and Class Consciousness," Op. Cit.

44. Bittar Jorge, org., "A Educação que o PT Faz," *O Modo Petista de Governar. Cadernos de Teoria & Debate* (São Paulo: Partido dos Trabalhadores, 1992), pp. 56-57.

45. Ibid. p. 62.

46. Gadotti and Pereira, Op. Cit., p. 191.

47. Cosete Ramos, *Exelência na Educação: A Escola de Qualidade Total* (Rio de Janeiro: Quality Mark, 1992).

An active proponent for the adoption of CQT by public schools in Brazil, Cosete Ramos—at the time of publication of this book—formed part of a Central Nucleus of Quality and Productivity of the Ministry of Education in Brasilia. Also, cf. William Glasser, *Control Theory in the Classroom* (New York: Perennial Library, Harper and Row Publishers, 1986); *The Quality School—Managing students without coercion* (New York: Perennial Library, New York Harper and Row Publishers, 1990).

48. Tomaz Tadeu da Silva "A "NOVA" direita e as transformações na pedagogia da política e na política da pedagogia," *Paixão de Aprender*, No. 7 (Porto Alegre: Municipal Secretary of Education, June 1994), p. 41.

49. Ibid. p. 32.

50. Ibid. p. 33.

51. Ibid. p. 33.

52. The following accounting of Antonucci's arguments are culled from field notes taken by O'Cadiz who attended the SINPEEM Congress during her field research in 1994.

53. Adilson Odiar Citelli, Lígia Chiappini, Nídia Nacib Pontuschka, "Proposta de Ação," in Pontuschka org., *Ousadia no Diálogo: Interdisciplinaridade na escola pública* (São Paulo: Loyola, 1993), p. 220.

54. Interview, Marco Antonio Gouvêa, February 1994.

III

Redefining Relationships: The State, Education, and Social Change

Education as Social Movement: The São Paulo Experience

The debate surrounding the new educational policies launched by the PT administration in the municipality of São Paulo involves a number of crucial issues: What kind of state is being constructed? What kind of democracy is being asked for in a democratic-socialist project? What kind of education will eventually emerge from popular public education? Is it possible to establish working relationships between public sectors and social movements without the latter's co-optation and loss of autonomy? If tensions, ambiguity, and uncertainty are built into the very same dynamic of this relationship, how can a workable agreement be devised for long-term planning and execution of participatory educational policies? And, conversely, can the state provide the impetus for the development of an autonomous and independent social movement (e.g., the Movement for Curricular Reorientation within the schools)?

This chapter situates the *problematique* of relationships between reformist state policies in education, social change and the role of social movements. Although it may seem anachronistic to speak of socialist policies after the demise of the Soviet Union, the drastic changes in Eastern Europe, and general acceptance of the view that state political and economic planning has failed, the policies developed by the PT and Freire in Brazil still claim to have a democratic-socialist and anticapitalist rather than a social-democratic orientation. Yet it would be misleading to consider the PT as a homogeneous political party. On the contrary, as mentioned earlier, the PT contains five different tendencies and up to 15 factions, each reflecting political differences that are visible in debates regarding educational policies. In addition, state politics in Brazil are complex, particularly when the different roles of the federal, state, and municipal governments are considered. This chapter focuses exclusively on the local or municipal levels, which have become central to the process of political democratization in Brazil and other South American societies. If speaking of socialism may sound anachronistic, to discuss the role of the state as a prominent actor in shaping educational policy may appear esoteric, particularly in view of the strong drive for decentralization and privatization of educational services in Latin America and the state's diminishing role because of structural adjustment policies in the region.

Finally, the democratic process of policy making becomes even more complex when we consider the contributions of social movements, including their goals, modus operandi, and political rationality.[1] Yet it is precisely the tenacity and imagination that permeates the PT's policies that makes the current case of educational reform so compelling to study and so instructive to analyze. Thus, this chapter examines the basic premises and rationale of state formation and development that guided Freire's work as Secretary of Education. Particular emphasis is placed on the relationships between social movements and state policies in the educational process.

Education, the Democratic State, and Social Movements: Conceptual Foundations

Theory of the State and Education

On the basis of a historical-structural approach informed by critical theory, two major questions arise about São Paulo and the democratic-socialist administration of 1989-1992. First, to what extent can a theory of the state explain the formulation of educational policy by local and municipal governments? Second, to what extent can the class character of the municipal state apparatus permeate the educational policies advanced by an elected democratic-socialist administration?

The concept of the state that has become fashionable in political science is used here in two ways. First, it is used as a reaction against liberal-pluralist political approaches that for many decades worked within a "stateless" theoretical framework; and second, it is used in order to highlight the state's role as an actor in policy making. In this view, the state is seen both as a purposeful and relatively independent actor and as a terrain where public policy is negotiated or disputed.

At the highest level of abstraction, we propose to consider the state as a pact of domination and a self-regulating administrative system. Several related theories of the state have been advanced, including contributions by Claus Offe, Bruce Fuller, and Martin Carnoy and Henry Levin.

German political scientist Claus Offe argues that state-organized governance is a selective, event-generating system of rules; that is, a sorting process.[2] Offe views the state as the institutional apparatuses, bureaucratic organizations, and formal and informal norms and codes that constitute the "public" and "private" spheres of social life. In Offe's analysis, policy making in every capitalist state has a distinctive class character. The primary focus, then, is neither the interpersonal relations of various elites nor the decision-making process per se. The state's class character resides not in the social origin of policymakers, state managers, bureaucrats, or the ruling class but in the internal structure of the state apparatus itself, because of its necessary selectivity of public policy—a selectivity that is "built into the system of political institutions."[3]

Offe argues that state actors (in the ministries, parliaments, and political parties) constantly find themselves facing the dilemma that "many legally and politically sanctioned demands and guarantees remain unreconciled to exigencies and capacities of the budgetary, financial, and labor market policy of the capitalist economy."[4] For Offe, the state's role in shaping policy is confined mostly to the definition of themes, times, and methods; that is, the establishment of an institutional framework for processes of social power rather than specific outcomes. In so doing, state actors produce strategic calculations or rationalization strategies in dealing with social problems. Examples of such strategies include reliance on preventive rather than curative problem-solving strategies, organization of final rather than conditional policy programs, institutionalized assistance, and, in some areas, reprivatization. A structural selectivity is manifested in the state's strategies of rationalization to deal with the contradictions of welfare policies.

Offe's work has been interpreted by various scholars, among them Bruce Fuller whose work applies Offe's theories to an analysis of selected Third World countries. Fuller's interpretation of Offe's work assumes that the state is a totally independent mediator of conflict among various social classes and groups. Thus, in this approach, the state is a structure up for grabs that cannot be consistently controlled by a particular elite. Whereas Offe's structural analysis is based on critical theory, neo-Marxist, and neo-Weberian analyses of state-society relationships, Fuller's approach appropriates this analysis into a liberal-pluralist interpretation of the state as exemplified by his "signaling theory of schooling" and institutional theory. For example, Offe's forms of state action—allocation of material resources, administrative practices, and symbolic expressions—are taken by Fuller out of the context of a capitalist state that, given the contradictions of disorganized capitalism, must promote the private accumulation of capital and ultimately legitimate the political system. Thus, in Fuller's view, the state is seen as a bounded institution responsive to a mix of interests or interdependencies. In his final analysis, however, the state must acquire material capital and technical know-how, as it fights for legitimation and organizational efficacy required for its own survival. Thus, the state's fragility (in developing societies) and the contradictions it faces have more to do with fragile states competing with other modernizing institutions than with external and internal forces that erode state autonomy, particularly in the context of the globalization of world economies. Similarly, the state's inability to govern (including the ungovernability of democratic systems) occurs when it provides conflicting signals to communities. Therefore, Fuller's analysis virtually neglects the intrinsic contradictions of disorganized capitalism (i.e., those based on class, gender, race, and a myriad of distributional and moral conflicts) and the implications of the shifting political coalitions fighting over the symbolic and material distributions of goods and services.[5]

While theories of the state have left the relationships among federal, state, and municipal governance (and educational policies) considerably under-theorized, the democratic-socialist program and popular nature of the PT administration suggest a dual character of the capitalist state and its organizational forms. On the one hand, the state claims to be the official representative of the nation as a whole. That is why Max Weber views the state not only as the monopoly of force but also as a site for the exchange of services and community benefits, although Offe observes that this Weberian definition rests on the notion of formal authority of sovereign acts but tells us nothing about by whom and against whom this monopoly of force is employed.[6]

On the other hand, the state also becomes a terrain for struggle of national and sociopolitical projects. Brazilian sociologist Fernando Henrique Cardoso has suggested that the state should be considered "the basic part of domination that exists among social classes or factions of dominant classes and the norms which guarantee their dominance over the subordinate strata."[7] It does so as a pact of domination, as a corporate actor assuming the representation of popular sovereignty, and as the political authority that enforces democratic rule—that is, democracy as a system of political representation and political participation where subjectivities and rules are not reduced, in the end, to the effects of power, gender, race, and wealth.[8]

To clarify the role of the democratic state, we should distinguish between democracy as a method and democracy as practice. As a method, democracy is primarily political representation that includes regular voting procedures, free elections, parliamentary and judicial systems free from executive control, notions of checks and balances in the system, the predominance of individual rights over collective rights, and freedom of speech. As practice, democracy is associated with political participation by the people in public affairs. It is related to the power of the people (over any other regulatory institution, such as kinship or a bureaucracy), the idea of equal rights for all citizens, and, particularly in the U.S. Constitution, a political philosophy of egalitarianism.[9] In addition, democracy as practice implies power shifts in the interactions among individuals, both at the micro level (e.g., achieving nonexploitative gender relationships in families) and at the macro level (e.g., pursuing gender equality in social and economic exchanges).

When theories of democracy are considered, the notion of the state acquires new normative and political dimensions. It upholds universalistic, rational, and consistent laws that provide a level playing field. At the same time, the democratic state uses public policy to create a modern citizenship, separating the particular interests of individuals from the general will.[10] Taking a critical view of theories of the democratic state, Martin Carnoy and Henry Levin argue that public policy is a product of basic social conflict, a conflict that is played off in the state arena. In their research on the production of educational policy resulting from class conflict and social movements, advanced capitalist states appear as a terrain of social struggle. Carnoy and Levin argue that, to grasp the transformation of education, one needs to simultaneously understand changes in labor process and how these two processes mutually condition each other. For this approach, educational change is perceived as part of a larger social conflict resulting from inequalities of income and social power of capitalist production.[11] Despite the cultural and economic differences between advanced capitalist societies and dependent-development capitalist Brazil, Carnoy and Levin's approach may prove useful as a starting point for analysis.

Thus, conceived as an administrative system of political domination, the state can be understood as the totality of political authority in a society, notwithstanding the level (national, provincial, or local) at which it operates.[12] The democratic state, in its policies directed toward the constitution and reproduction of capitalism, protects the system of commodity production from various threats and guides its transformation. Concomitantly, it overcomes sectoral or factional short-term needs and disputes among individual capitalists or corporative groups.

But the state also reflects the dynamics of democracy. Basic human rights are protected by laws enacted and enforced by the democratic state.

In many democracies, the public sector has become the main source of employment for minorities and women in an attempt to advance civil rights. Health, welfare, and educational policies are particularly sensitive areas in efforts to satisfy the democratic aspirations of citizens. Thus, democratic states have also advanced the cause of egalitarianism and equity through welfare policies, the enforcement of progressive laws, and the employment of minorities and women.[13] In the Brazilian context, the major figures in the pursuit of democratic goals are grassroots organizations, social movements, and political parties such as the PT, which has extensive grassroots support. Whether these new educational policies promoted by social movements are politically feasible and workable, technically competent, and ethically sound will be discussed later.[14]

The State, Education, and Social Movements

By considering the relationships among grassroots organizations, social movements, and educational policies in São Paulo, we characterize the state as both a relatively independent actor and a contested terrain for public policy formation. First, some clarification of terms is necessary. Grassroots organizations are often defined in Latin America as private community-based organizations working to provide democratic leadership and improved economic opportunity for the poor through job creation, education, health care, and productive microenterprises.[15] Similar types of organizations in other regions might be non-governmental organizations (NGOs). Nongovernmental organizations (NGOs), which are usually defined by their autonomy from governmental control, normally refer to "a nonprofit organization having a principal fund of its own, managed by its own trustees or directors, and established to maintain or aid . . . activities serving the common welfare."[16] Nongovernmental organizations may or may not be grassroots organizations in Latin America.

Social movements refer to collective efforts to promote some type of change in power. For French sociologist Alan Touraine, social movements employ a type of conflictual action best characterized as defensive collective behavior. For instance, attempts by grassroots organizations and NGOs to ameliorate the impact of unemployment, housing shortages, and limited health-care or educational infrastructures can easily be classified as collective defensive behavior. Touraine also discusses a second type of conflict, in which conflicts modify decision making and become social struggles. If groups seek to change the social relations of power in cultural actions, ethical values, science, or production, they can be classified as social movements.[17] Thus, the feminist, the ecology, the peace, and the antinuclear movements are examples of social movements in contemporary U.S. society.

In Latin America and Brazil, social movements include the Christian Base Communities, neighborhood associations, the feminist movement, and ecological associations.[18] If we understand politics as a struggle for power, these social movements should not be interpreted exclusively in political terms, as they also represent cultural and moral practices centered on the construction of collective identities and spaces. They originate around certain demands and specific social relations, becoming increasingly autonomous from traditional institutions of political representation of interests. This is so, argues Ernesto Laclau—joining other proponents of social movement theory—because individuals no longer exclusively define their identity in relationship to the means and relations of production, but also as consumers, residents of a particular neighborhood, members of a church or gender groups, and participants in the political system.[19]

In fact, social movements may arise as alliances of grassroots and community organizations, NGOs, political parties, trade unions, church organizations, and even individuals such as intellectuals, artists, and others. Since new social movements challenge the increasing bureaucratization, commodification, and cultural massification of social life, they are the "expression of a more open and pluralistic form of democracy" striving to enhance "the diffusion of collective and participatory values and practices through an ever-widening range of sites of social struggle."[20]

The diversity and numbers of NGOs and social or popular movements in Brazil are impressive. In his research, Moacir Gadotti and his associates surveyed 91 nongovernmental organizations working on behalf of public schooling, and they also studied 89 organizations promoting popular education.[21] Gadotti reports that researchers at Brazil's Superior Institute of Religious Studies identified 1,041 nongovernmental organizations. Of this total, 556 were working for popular movements in 173 cities, 251 organizations were associated with women's movements, and 234 were involved with African-Brazilian movements. He argues there are other nongovernmental organizations not identified in this research, including ecologists, fishermen, the unemployed, religious communities, and indigenous peoples.

The praxis of social movements offers potentially fertile ground for a "conscientization" approach *à la* Freire. Social movements typically build on the knowledge base and previous struggles of people, taking into account their organizational capabilities and grievances. This allows for the building of programs *with* and *from* the communities rather than *for* them. From a critical perspective, a conscientization approach gets mixed reviews. According to Agneta Lind and Anton Johnston, "Freire provides an important source of critical reflection and inspiration for literacy practitioners, through his criticisms of domesticating and elitist approaches to literacy and his insistence on the experiences with the learners, teaching while at the same time learning from them. The conscientization approach does not, however, provide sufficient guidelines for a whole literacy strategy, and contains non-applicable elements, especially for large-scale government programs."[22]

These criticisms can be assessed in the context of Freire's experience as a policymaker in São Paulo, where literacy training and overall educational policies were based on a pedagogy of the oppressed and policy formation involved large-scale government programs. In São Paulo, however, a partnership between social movements and the municipal state was established, linking human resources from the movements with financial and technical resources from the state. In the case of the policies aimed at creating a dynamic model of the Popular Public School, the state intended to create the impetus for a reform movement within the municipal schools by organizing teachers and the school community—namely through the Inter Project effort, the *grupos de formação* (Teacher Professional Development Groups), and the School Councils—around the themes of democratization of administration, access and improvement of the quality of schooling. We will delve into the complexities of this latter and, we would say, more audacious political project to foster a social movement within the schools in subsequent chapters (IV, V, VI) in which we discuss in detail the Inter Project, its theoretical foundations and practical implications. In this chapter we focus on the former case of MOVA.

Questions about the class character of the municipal state and its bureaucratic behavior seem to haunt democratic and progressive educators trying to link state and social movements. For instance, Gadotti, one of Freire's close collaborators, argues that "social movements, even when dealing with progressive municipal administrations, adopt an attitude of "being tactically inside and strategically outside." In other words, social movements fighting for popular education or participating in developing social policies always keep one foot inside and the other outside the state.[23] Given the misgivings that these movements have concerning the state's nature and character in São Paulo, is it possible to establish a common framework for action or a set of guidelines to orient policy formation for both the municipal state and the social movements? And if it is possible, what kind of framework will emerge? And, as we later address, is it possible—as the PT administration in São Paulo set forth to do—for the state to create conditions that foster a social movement within the institutional setting of the schools?

Freire as Secretary of Education of the City of São Paulo: Historical Background

As stated above, educational policy making in São Paulo illustrates the tensions between the state's reproductive functions and the state as a site in the struggle for greater democracy.

Appointed by Mayor Luiza Erundina de Sousa in January 1989, Freire worked as Secretary of Education until May 27, 1991, when he resigned to resume his academic activities, lecturing, and writing. The team that worked with Freire continued to be in charge of policy formation, and his former chief of cabinet, Mário Sérgio Cortella, a professor of philosophy and theology at São Paulo's Pontifical Catholic University, was appointed as the new secretary of education until the mandate's completion in December 1992.[24] At the beginning of his tenure, Freire and his team implemented drastic changes in municipal education, including a comprehensive curriculum reform for grades K-8; new models of school management through the implementation of school councils that included teachers, principals, parents, and government officials; and the launching of a movement for Literacy Training (MOVA-São Paulo) built on participatory planning and delivery, in partnership with nongovernmental organizations and social movements.

Educational administration is a major undertaking in the city of São Paulo, as its population of 9.6 million makes it one of the world's largest municipalities.[25] São Paulo also is the financial center of Brazil, which has the world's tenth largest economy.[26] With a municipal budget of $2.75 billion dollars for 1989, $3.6 billion for 1990, $3.89 billion for 1991, $3.0 billion for 1992, and $5.5 billion for 1993, the city has also the nation's third-largest budget after the state of São Paulo and the federal government. Freire presided over 691 schools with 710,000 students and 39,614 employees (teachers, administrators, and service personnel), the latter constituting 30 percent of the municipality's total employees.

Analyzing a socialist administration ruling the financial and industrial center of capitalist Brazil poses many theoretical challenges. In addition, the personification of new educational policy in the figure of Paulo Freire offers a unique perspective of social struggles and conscientization.[27] Freire is not only an outstanding figure in the academic world but also one who has uniquely combined theory with practical experience in adult education. He became famous in the early 1960s as a result of his powerful experiences in literacy training, and his writings have now gone beyond mere techniques for literacy training to become a cornerstone of critical pedagogy worldwide.

Freire's work originally gained attention with writings that documented his earlier experiences with literacy training in northeast Brazil. His pedagogical work has been associated with the *Movimento de Educação & Base* (Movement for Grassroots Education), the Centers for Popular Culture, and base communities in Brazil.[28] Appointed in 1963 by the populist government of João Goulart to serve as president of the National Commission of Popular Culture and as coordinator of the National Plan of Literacy Training, his work in literacy training has had a profound impact on the character of citizenship in Brazil.[29] As the first director (1961-64) of the Cultural Extension Service of the University of Recife in Pernambuco, Freire was associated with the Catholic Left, and his ideas have been an inspiration for liberation theology in Latin America.[30]

Freire has also been involved with important literacy campaigns outside Brazil, including Guinea-Bissau, Sao Tomé and Principe, and Nicaragua, and his books are viewed as a source for educational innovation in many parts of the world. His new analyses about the role of liberatory pedagogy in advanced industrial societies are important subjects for debate and pedagogical thinking.[31]

But what is it about Freire's political philosophy of education that renders it so current and universal, placing him and some of the "generative themes" he proposed at the center of educational debates in critical pedagogy over the past three decades? Freire argues that human interaction rarely escapes oppression of one kind or another; by reason of class, race, or gender, people tend to be victims and/or perpetrators of oppression. He points out that class exploitation, racism, and sexism are the most conspicuous forms of domination and oppression, but he also recognizes subjugation on other grounds such as religious beliefs or political affiliation.[32]

Starting from a psychology of oppression influenced by the work of psychotherapists such as Franz Fanon and Erich Fromm, Freire has developed a "pedagogy of the oppressed." His goal is to use education to improve the human condition, counteracting the effects of oppression and ultimately contributing to what he considers the "ontological vocation of mankind."

Freire's *Pedagogy of the Oppressed*,[33] which has been influenced by myriad of philosophical currents including phenomenology, existentialism, Christian personalism, humanist Marxism, and Hegelianism, calls for dialogue and ultimately conscientization—critical consciousness or awareness—as a way to overcome relationships of domination and oppression.[34] Thus, notions of education for social participation, conscientization, and empowerment are central to Freire's political philosophy of education. It is not altogether unpredictable, then, that upon his return to Brazil in 1980, Freire became a member of the PT and emerged as one of its most noted intellectuals and educators. What acquires particular relevance in this case, however, is that Freire's work in this instance marks a distinct departure from past efforts implemented largely with adults in nonformal settings; the new educational model embodied in Freire's educational administration takes place in the context of municipal state policies dealing with public primary schooling in all content areas, nonformal education, and literacy training.

In the next sections we introduce the conceptual foundations of the PT's agenda for creating a new quality of public education, as embodied in initiatives for curriculum reform in the elementary schools, governance reform and the PT effort to promote adult and youth literacy in São Paulo.

Finding a Balance: State Policy-making and "Popular Public Schooling"

The challenges of recreating the state to reflect the socialist and democratic ideologies and goals of the PT, which were faced by Freire and others in the administration, have been explored above from a theoretical perspective. In this section, we briefly present the ways in which the Freire administration grappled with these fundamental challenges and questions related to class interests, state autonomy, independence of social movements and the dynamic and productive integration of the three.

The overall program of educational reform advanced by Freire's administration rests on the concept of Popular Public Schooling *(Escola Pública Popular)*. Originally, the concept of popular education (e.g., the "education of the people") was used in Latin America to define the model of public education conceived by liberal governments, particularly during the last three decades of the nineteenth century. Freire's revolutionary work with the *pedagogy of the oppressed* has radically transformed that original notion of popular education to one that arises from political and social analyses of living conditions among the poor and aims at engaging these groups in individual and collective processes of critical awareness and action.[35]

The contemporary debate on Popular Public Schooling in Brazil thus starts by acknowledging serious problems regarding the equality of educational opportunity in terms of access, permanence, and quality. For instance, out of nearly 88 million Brazilians 10 years and older, 25.5 percent were illiterate.[36] According to the 1980 national census, 33 percent (7.6 million) of the 23 million children from ages 7 to 14 were unschooled; among those attending schools, 27.6 percent (or 6.3 million) were placed in lower grades than their corresponding school age. On average, 46.3 percent of Brazilians have two years of schooling or fewer, considered inadequate to provide a level of functional literacy, while 75 percent of Brazilians five years and older have fewer than four years of school instruction. Once in school, as Plank has argued (see Chapter I), children's educational opportunities are quite limited with 15 percent of first graders and 19th percent of fifth graders leaving school and only 32 percent of children completing elementary school in the allotted eight-year period.

Educational constraints are further aggravated by pressing economic problems, poverty, and inequality. According to a study by economist Helio Jaguaribe, 64.7 percent of the economically active population lived below the poverty level (e.g., receiving two or fewer minimum salaries).[37] As the Inter-American Dialogue pointed out, poverty and institutionalized inequality are inextricably linked throughout Latin America: "In Ecuador, Peru, and Brazil, the wealthiest 20 percent of families earn 30 times more than the poorest 20 percent."[38]

It was in this context that Freire argued that the physical conditions of São Paulo's school buildings were even worse than the quality of municipal education itself. Hundreds of classrooms were completely dilapidated, with unusable desks and chairs.[39] An evaluation after Freire's first year in office revealed the extent of the problem. At the beginning of his mandate, 654 of the 691 municipal schools were in poor physical condition, including 400 that had serious problems. There was a deficit of 35,000 student chairs and desks, and the Secretariat's inability to pay prevented the completion of approved repairs to school buildings. In the first 11 months, public funds were appropriated for repairing 26 schools, and renovations began in 20 schools. Ten new school buildings initiated by the previous educational administration were completed, and nine other school buildings were under construction. Finally 500 new student desks and chairs were provided, and more than 6,274 desks and chairs were repaired.[40]

Also contributing to educational inequality in Brazil is the prevalent practice of school tracking. There are parallel systems of elementary and secondary schools: a thriving private sector occasionally subsidized by the state serving a middle-class constituency, and public education for the children of poor and working-class families.[41] Advocates of Popular Public Schooling denounce official policies to privatize public services. They argue that the erosion of quality in public education creates growing discontent, helping a number of educational entrepreneurs to profit from the malaise of public schooling. In this context, the working class and peasants face two choices: either to enter a "demoralizing public schooling or total exclusion."[42]

In his book *Uma só escola para todos* [One School for All], Gadotti documents debates among radical Brazilian scholars about the notions of unifying popular schools or public popular schools. He attributes the origins of this debate to the work of Freire and other prominent intellectuals, many of them associated with the PT including Florestan Fernandes, Luiz Eduardo Wanderley, and Marilena Chaui.[43] Similarly, this notion of Popular Public Schooling is associated with PT proposals advanced in several "democratic" municipal administrations, including Campinas, Diadema, Porto Alegre, Rio Grande do Sul, Santos, and São Paulo.

Institutionalized racism, unbalanced disciplinary practices, or irrelevant curriculum content may push working-class children and youths out of the system. The goals of Popular Public Schooling or popular public education include improvements in the equality of access and retention, the prevention of school dropouts, and the enhancement of structural and organizational routines. Children from the popular sectors find the institutionalized cultural capital of schools awkward or at odds with their own cultural experience. As French sociologist Pierre Bourdieu argues, all human activity involves the accumulation of cultural capital on the basis of specific "habitus." The notion of habitus refers to an internalized, permanent system of beliefs or meanings, resulting from an individual's interaction with his or her family and immediate environment or community. Different social activities and roles produce different cultural capitals, which are hierarchically articulated along class and (in Brazil) racial lines. In addition, they are very often related to elite educational credentials.[44]

Thus, proponents of Popular Public Schooling believe drastic improvements are needed in the quality of education. Children from the working class should be taught to appreciate their own cultural capital and be exposed to learning strategies based on their own habitus. At present, they must constantly adapt to a dominant, middle-class cultural capital and habitus. There is also a need to adapt the supply of schools to the demands and needs of working-class students, many of whom also work part- or full-time.

Further, Popular Public Schooling is a concept that links education and hegemony in Brazil. Advocates of Popular Public Schooling criticize public education for its low quality and authoritarianism. They link its reform to control of educational planning and implementation by popular forces, meaning community groups and social movements. The democratic management of schools is another central feature of popular public education. This goal which calls for autonomy in planning, management, and control of school operations, with inputs from students, parents, social movements, teachers, principals, and state education officials, implies a strong critique of technocratic planning and the notion of technical expertise devoid of any democratic control or input.

Hence, advancing a highly politicized notion of the role of schooling in Brazilian society allowed the PT-MSE to fathom the possibility of the public school becoming an instrument for the transformation of society by

the popular classes: the Popular Public School. Secretary Freire elaborates
on the notion:

> A *Popular Public School*, is not only that which provides access to all, but
> also one in which all can participate in its construction, one that authenti-
> cally addresses the popular interests which are the interests of the major-
> ity; and therefore, it is a school with a *new quality*, based on commitment,
> on a posture of solidarity, forming the social and democratic conscience.
> [. . .] The first step is to conquer the *old school* and convert it into a center of
> investigation, pedagogic reflection and experimentation with *new alterna-*
> *tives* from a popular point of view [italics in text].[45]

In the Freirean perspective, the objective is to link education with a
historical project of social emancipation: educational practices should be
related to a theory of knowledge. Consequently, education appears as the
act of knowing rather than a simple transmission of knowledge or the assumption of society's cultural baggage. Since knowledge and power are
considered to be intimately related, cultural traditions and practices in
schooling, for example, are suspected of concealing relations of domination. Thus, critical appropriation of knowledge by the working class also
implies a criticism of the culturally arbitrary.

The term "culturally arbitrary" is used here in reference to school knowledge and how schools produce and distribute unequal cultural capitals. In
the present analysis, however, it should be considered descriptive rather
than analytic. The notion of the culturally arbitrary, a product of the new
sociology of education, refers to each class having its own culture whose
contents are arbitrary. Since class relations are unequal, a dominant class
may exercise "symbolic violence" in the school curriculum by imposing its
cultural capital—that is, a system of meanings reflecting a particular cultural heritage, language, and patterns of reasoning, including intellectual,
moral, and aesthetic perceptions. Similarly, but from a different theoretical
perspective, Jurgen Habermas argues that "bourgeois culture"—based on
principles of possessive individualism and oriented toward achievement
and exchange value—is transmitted through socialization in families and
schools. Demonstrating that the curriculum is problematic and that school
knowledge reflects human interests represents a main contribution of cultural reproduction models, yet it is dangerous to carry these models too
far.[46] This is particularly true when, according to Habermas' analysis, processes of social change in contemporary capitalist societies transform key
principles constitutive of bourgeois culture. This will make the "culturally
arbitrary" notion problematic. For instance, the notion of a bourgeois culture and the ideology of fair exchange can no longer account for the legiti-

mation of liberal capitalist systems when an ideology of achievement is challenged by the increasingly uncertain connection between formal education and occupational success or when the orientation to exchange value is progressively undermined by the growth of social groups that are excluded from the social life of wage labor yet are subject to relations of capitalist domination.[47]

Essentially, Freire's proposal is an education for liberation:

> Education will be liberating as long as it sponsors the conscious and creative reflection and action of oppressed classes about their own process of liberation. To assume its hegemony, the people (*o povo*) need an education of quality. They need the tools, appropriation of knowledge, methods, and techniques to which their access today is restricted to a privileged minority. This implies the systematic and critical appropriation of reading, writing, and mathematics, and the scientific and technological principles. Even more so, this implies the appropriation of methods of acquisition, production, and dissemination of learning: research, discussion, argument, the use of the most diverse methods of expression, communication and art.[48]

In summary, the notion of Popular Public Schooling challenges the need for growing privatization of public services, arguing instead for increased investment in public education and improved access and quality (i.e., *democratização do accesso*), while at the same time relating school effectiveness to the educational and social needs of children and youth from the popular classes. Finally, by linking public schooling with popular movements, this project emphasizes democratic—as opposed to authoritarian or technocratic—control of educational resources, planning, and implementation (i.e., *democratização do gestão*). The implementation of Popular Public Schooling includes a major movement for curriculum reform, new forms of school governance, and a program of literacy training, which are briefly introduced in the following sections and discussed in detail in the remaining chapters.

The Movement for Curricular Reorientation

The central characteristic of Popular Public Schooling is education as the practice of freedom, in São Paulo the curriculum reform became a centerpiece of the Secretariat's strategy for creating an emancipatory educational paradigm and practice. From such a paradigmatic perspective, schools should not only be a place for the critical reconstruction of knowledge and critique of society but also a center for the production of popular culture.[49]

The curriculum reform movement—of which the Interdisciplinary Project was its primary impetus—is based on the following principles: (a) it is a collective construction based on participation; (b) it should reflect diverse experiences, with a fundamental respect for the autonomy of each school; (c) it should highlight the link between theory and practice, with a methodology of action-reflection and new action (praxis) in curriculum; and (d) it should include a model of continuing teacher training, with a critical analysis of the curriculum in practice. The methodology of curriculum reform starts with a process of action, reflection, and then new action developed collectively by teachers, students, parents, members of school councils, and educational specialists from the Municipal Secretariat of Education, schools, and universities, by using interdisciplinary approaches and the contributions of social movements.[50] Three phases (related to Freire's original method) are defined in this process of curriculum reform: (a) *problematization,* including a critique of the current curriculum and a discussion of innovative ways to change it; (b) *organization,* including the systematization of responses to a questionnaire discussed in the schools and to the findings of the first phase of problematization; and (c) *design and implementation* of a new *interdisciplinary curriculum via the generative theme.*

Curriculum reform starts with administrators and teachers learning how to listen to their students. Using an interdisciplinary approach, educators must also draw out key generative themes centered on the knowledge of the students, as well as teachers' knowledge. For instance, housing was a generative theme selected by a school in São Paulo's Perus region during the first semester, with this issue to be studied in all subjects, from physical education to mathematics. In the second semester, transportation was selected.[51]

The curriculum reform process started in 1990 with 10 pilot schools, one in each Nuclei of Educational Action (NAE). It was then implemented in 100 additional schools (10 associated with each pilot site). By the end of 1992 the project had extended to approximately 100 schools and was expected to gradually spread throughout the system. Simultaneously, a number of other educational programs were initiated in 1989, including the *Grupos de Formação* (Formation Groups or teacher professional development groups), *Projeto Gênese* (computers for the classroom) and *Projeto Não Violencia* (anti-violence work with adolescents). The *Grupos de Formação,* for instance, promoted teachers' training through regular meetings to discuss their educational practices and offered teachers opportunities to engage in discussions with a number of scholars and to read theoretical and philosophical texts.

The radical reform process initiated by the PT-MSE was not free of conflicts and contradictions, however. To this effect, Freire describes a conversation with a school principal in which, after a few moments of discussing the principal's attitude, she became angry and exclaimed, "Yes, yes, yes, I am authoritarian, and I will continue to be." Then Freire said to her, "Look, I know that you are authoritarian. I would like to ask you very lovingly to begin to be less authoritarian in this administration. But really I cannot impose on you the taste of democracy."[52] The principal remained in her post.

Governance Reform: The School Councils

The Municipal Secretariat of Education operates through collectives of directors, with school councils at the base. For every 40 school councils, delegates are selected to participate in a higher school council within each Nuclei of Educational Action. The coordinators of each NAE meet in the Intermediate Collegiate, and representatives of this group participate in the Central Collegiate, which includes the Secretary of Education, the Chief of Cabinet, the Coordinator of Coordinadora dos Núcleos de Ação Educativa, the Technical Director (who oversees curriculum reform), the Chief of the Administrative Division, and the technical and planning advisor to the Secretary.

Freire described the school council, an entity created by an earlier municipal administration but never fully implemented, in the following manner:

> The school council is the representation of some power, it has some power, not only the power of the director of the school, the head of the school. It is constituted by teachers, representatives of the parents, and also of the people (staff) of the school and the students. For example, I constantly am admitting some people to work inside the school. I sign the document, but the approval comes from the council; it is not myself who chooses the person. School councils are one of the serious attempts we are doing to democratize the school and to decentralize power.[53]

For the school council to function democratically, the draft of the *estatuto do magisterio municipal* (statue of the municipal teaching profession) proposed that principals, vice-principals, and pedagogical directors be elected by each school community. People with the appropriate qualifications could be elected to these positions for two years.[54] They could then be reelected for an additional two years. However, after this second term, they could not have run for office again until a two-year period had elapsed. This, in effect, would have forced school administrators to return to classroom teaching every four years. All parents, children of 10 years and older, administrative staff (including janitors, maintenance, and security), and faculty were eligible to vote under this proposal. The parent and student votes were to have accounted proportionately for 50 percent of the total, with staff and faculty votes accounting for the remaining 50 percent. To remove school officials from the school council before the end of their mandates would have required a petition signed by 50 percent of the school community's eligible electors.

After lengthy discussions involving union officials, teachers, and administrators, the draft of this statute was overwhelmingly rejected, as all three groups vehemently opposed elected positions. They also opposed new provisions that would have forced teachers working in both the state and municipal systems of education to accept full-time employment in only one of them. A new statute, which incorporated most of the teacher union's concerns, was drafted and decreed as Municipal Law 11.229 of June 26, 1992.[55]

Freire recognizes that his first proposal was flatly defeated. However, he argues that this defeat "does not show that we were politically mistaken, but that the municipal educational system is politically backward."[56] Freire attributes the rejection of the original draft to Brazilian corporatism.[57]

The Literacy Training Movement (MOVA-São Paulo): Literacy Training as Cultural Politics?

The dilemmas in the relationships among social movements and the state are clearly evident in the Literacy Training Movement, known as "MOVA-São Paulo." The initial idea that the municipal government collaborate with existing social movements in fomenting an organized literacy movement within the city was announced by the Secretariat in October 1989 when Freire first took office as Secretary of Education: MOVA was launched the following January, with the goal of making 60,000 people literate. Consequently, MOVA's structure grew out of an agreement between the democratic popular administration and a number of social movements in São Paulo concerned with issues such as land tenure, housing, health, and education.

Given this unique compact, it is important to explore the nature of the relationship between MOVA and the municipal government (i.e., the Secretariat of Education). Interviews with some of the leaders of the social movements who collaborated with the Secretariat in MOVA emphasized the historical process of education as an instrument of popular struggle. When asked "how is the relationship between social movements and State (particularly the Municipal Secretariat of Education) carried out under the PT administration?" they responded:

"When was the last time that we participated in something so beautiful?!"

"The government of Ms. Mayor Luiza Erundina is an administration oriented towards the popular masses . . . she already worked here in the region [the impoverished periphery of the city] . . . this government opened up a space to our movements."

"The movement, MOVA, was built upon the basis of Paulo Freire's ideas. Past experiences such as MOBRAL and the Suplência [adult night school] do not reach the quality of MOVA. [MOVA] works with our reality, investigating the reality of the community. . . . MOVA is the conquering of our rights, it is not a mere 'opportunity' handed down to us."

"Under the PT administration, for the first time a new experience reached the population of the city, together [the municipal government and social movements], despite the difficulties confronted, have tried to get it right."[58]

When asked what is the future of MOVA (given the possibility of change in municipal governments)[59] and of social movements in Brazil in general, one MOVA activist insisted: "As long as there are people there will be a movement."[60] In all its simplicity, this statement demonstrates the inherent grass-roots nature of the PT's political organization and anticipated the fluid, albeit at times conflictual, relationship between the state and social movements which the PT administration in São Paulo achieved.

Still, maintaining a productive and mutually satisfactory relationship between the so-called popular municipal administrations and social movements presents major challenges. The social movements argue that their participation should not preclude the state from investing in activities (be they adult education or schooling) in which the social movements are collaborating. For social movements, the challenge is to form partnerships with the state without being co-opted, thus preserving their political and pedagogical autonomy while achieving higher levels of organization and social practice. These dilemmas were well expressed during a 1990 forum held in São Paulo to discuss the partnership between the public sector and social movements in adult education:

TABLE 3.1 Municipality of São Paulo: Full-Time and Part-Time Teachers' Salaries, Daytime and Nighttime Teaching (in Cruzeiros), August 1992.

			Neighborhoods			
	Central (1)	Intermediate (2)	(1)/(2) (in %)	Peripheral (3)	(2)/(3) (in %)	(1)/(3) (in %)
A. Full-time day teaching	2,110.366 (406.19)	2,743.475 (528.04)	30.0	3,165.548 (609.28)	15.4	50.0
Part-time day teaching	1,160.701 (223.40)	1,477.256 (284.33)	27.3	1,688.292 (324.95)	14.3	45.4
Full-time day teaching/ part-time day teaching (in %)	45.0	46.1		46.7		
B. Full-time night teaching	2,743.475 (528.04)	3,376.585 (649.90)	23.1	3,798.658 (731.14)	12.5	38.5
Part-time night teaching	1,477.255 (284.33)	1,793.810 (345.26)	21.4	2,004.847 (385.87)	11.8	36.0
Full-time night teaching/ part-time night teaching (in %)	46.1	46.9		47.2		
Full-time day teaching/ full-time night teaching (in %)	30.0	23.1		20.0		
Part-time day teaching/ part-time night teaching (in %)	27.3	21.4		18.7		

Source: Prefeitura do Município de São Paulo, Secretaria Municipal de Educacao, Assessoria Financeira, unpublished data, August 1992.
Note: U.S. dollar equivalents are in parentheses. Full-time teacher (*Jornada de Trabalho Integral*) = 30 hours/week (EM-O4A [beginning teacher]); and part-time teacher = 20 hours/week (EM-041 [beginning teacher]). Full-time teacher with higher education = 30 hours/week (EM-O4A [beginning teacher]). Location of neighborhoods: (1) central = more desirable or safer location; (2) intermediate; and (3) peripheral = poorest neighborhoods, shantytowns, neighborhoods with security problems, etc.

The material and pedagogical support that municipal administrations offer to popular groups that promote adult education should happen under two basic conditions: that this support will not imply that the public municipal administration is withdrawing from offering quality adult education programs, and that this support to popular groups be given under conditions that respect and preserve the political and pedagogical autonomy of these popular groups. . . . There are still doubts if this modality of relationships between the municipalities [*prefeituras*] and the popular movements will not result objectively in a mechanism of institutionalization and loss of autonomy of the popular movements, and co-optation by the state. This is a controversy that only the passing of time and practical experiences will be able to resolve.[61]

This articulation between the public sector and social movements represents a fundamental principle of literacy training and educational policy formation in São Paulo. In describing this relationship, Freire argued that "the Secretariat does not want to absorb the movements, but neither does it want to simply give away funding." He added that "we are not afraid of the tensions that may arise from this arrangement. We want to learn together how to deal with the conflict. We respect the pluralism, but also we have our own agenda. If the movements do not accept our pedagogical model we will consider it a breach of contract."[62]

Within the general context of this state-social movement relationship, an analysis of MOVA's organizational structure sheds important light on factors influencing various domains of its relationship with the Secretariat. In principle, MOVA was a federation of movements coordinated by an institution called "The MOVA Forum," which included approximately 50 leaders ranging in average age from 18 to 24 years. Many of these individuals were lower- and middle-class university students, some of whom were connected with Christian Base Communities or more traditional church organizations.

Within the Secretariat a central coordination team included pedagogues, administrators, sociologists, and journalists, with a general coordinator reporting directly to the Secretary. Because of personality conflicts and tensions among social movements and the municipal administration, this coordinator position had been occupied by five different individuals since the coordination team was created to act as a liaison between the Secretariat and the Forum.

There were 49 social movements that had signed agreements with MOVA when it started in February 1990 with 320 classrooms or *núcleos de alfabetização* (literacy training nuclei), each containing 20-30 students (6,400-9,600 students overall), with a goal of reaching 1,200 classrooms by the end of the year. Although it is difficult to assess whether that figure was reached, it is clear that many students dropped out. For instance, by May 1990, 12,000 students were registered in MOVA, and it was expected that 9,000 would conclude their program of literacy training. By the time Freire resigned as Secretary in May 1991, MOVA had 640 classrooms, with 29,000 students. Just over a year later, in July 1992, there were 18,329 students enrolled in MOVA, served by 887 *monitores* (literacy trainers) and 130 supervisors working for 78 social movements that had signed collaboration agreements with the Secretariat.

A coordination team *(nucleo coordinador)* organized the training workshop (30 hours) to train the monitors. Teachers (also called "literacy trainers" or "monitors") were selected by the social movements, which also recruited the students. The key responsibilities of the Secretariat were to design pedagogical content and methods to be used by the nuclei in their literacy training classes, to train the selected teachers, and to finance the process, including paying monitors' salaries.

Monthly training of MOVA monitors was organized for Saturdays and Sundays from January to March 1990. After May, new and longer training sessions were designed. At these sessions the Secretariat disseminated pamphlets *(cadernos de formação)*, which communicated the political-pedagogic principles to individuals active in the movement as well as offering concrete methodological orientation. Furthermore, regular (usually weekly) meetings among literacy workers of each literacy nuclei associated to MOVA were realized under the guidance of a professional pedagogic coordinator (provided by the Secretariat). This pedagogic orientation within the MOVA infrastructure was aimed at promoting a scientific approach to literacy teaching, while allowing for debate around teaching practices as well as issues of political content and organization to take place between participants at all levels of the movement, on the premise that "knowledge and pedagogic know-how is a historical process: continual, collective and profoundly personal."[63] A principal goal for learners within MOVA was that they conclude the first grade (i.e., acquire basic literacy skills) and be prepared to enter the second grade of regular schooling for adults.

Given these objectives, a logical question follows: *What was MOVA's method of literacy training?* Within the context of a PT administration and a Secretariat of Education headed by Paulo Freire, it might be expected that MOVA's literacy training methodology would closely resemble Freire's previous experiments. The second coordinator of MOVA points out a number of differences, however. First, there is no Freirean method, but only a theory of knowledge. Second, this theory of knowledge is coupled with a political vision and some literacy training techniques, but MOVA would not necessarily use all the techniques such as the generative word or the thematic investigation. Third, MOVA's method also incorporates the work of Emilia Ferreiro, an Argentine linguist and pedagogue living in Mexico, who has developed a new "constructivist" understanding of the process of literacy, especially in children, on the basis of research in psychology by Jean Piaget. Finally, MOVA's method incorporates dialectic logic and contributions from linguistics, including Lev S. Vygotsky's notion of an "interior discourse."

In addition to genetic psychology, the contribution of Vygotsky's work in sociolinguistics to MOVA's method is recognized. Discussing Vygotsky's importance from a whole-language perspective, Yetta Goodman and Kenneth Goodman hint at some commonalties between Freire and Vygotsky: "In a broader sense Freire was recognizing that learners learn best when they are free to control their own learning. This liberation is neither romantic nor abstract. Teachers cannot liberate pupils from society or from the constraints of social transactions. But they can remove the artificial controls of traditional schooling. They can encourage pupils to enter freely into speech and literacy events, authentic social transactions, in which language is a tool for communication."[65]

Departing from behaviorist models, a basic premise in Ferreiro's psychogenesis-of-knowledge approach is that "to understand children we must hear their words, follow their explanations, understand their frustrations, and listen to their logic."[66] These premises suggest that the achievement of learning results from the same activity of learners known in Piagetian genetic psychology as "assimilation."[67] Thus, "rather than being concerned with whether children know how to speak, we should help them become conscious of what they already know how to do, help them move from 'knowing how' to 'knowing about' a conceptual knowing."[68]

This approach is compatible with Freire's attempt to discover generative themes and words for literacy training. Likewise, a constructivist approach shares Freire's criticisms of traditional education—"banking education" in Freire's terminology—which, being teacher centered, understands that learning depends on and is derived from the instructional methods.

On July 15, 1990, the Secretariat organized a conference where Secretary of Education, Paulo Freire, discussed with the MOVA monitors (approximately 500 were present) and the elected regional representatives of the associated nuclei specific matters of methodological importance to the literacy movement. In his "dialogue" with the MOVA activists present at the congress, Freire reflected upon his past experience in adult literacy work and emphasized the political nature of his proposal in contrast to a technical, linguistic perception of his methodology. As such, he argued for the development of new insights into the literacy process, to assist in the passage from the theoretical to the practical and to overcome the limitations of past experiences. He states, "the keys of the most recent investigations, are exactly the keys to the dominion of science so that we can facilitate the learning of the reading of the word, in the sense that we approach the people with a greater rigor in our own comprehension of the world that must be." Freire identified Emilia Ferreiro's work as one of those valuable keys to opening up new approaches to the comprehension of knowledge. He pointed out to the audience, however, that "Emilia does not surpass Paulo Freire; Emilia needs to be incorporated into Paulo Freire." Having elicited laughter from the audience, Freire went on to maintain with all seriousness that such a merger between the two pedagogic philosophies is a necessity for the popular classes. He asserted, *"As classes populares precisam de que Paulo Freire e Emilia se incorporam"*: (It is a necessity [in the interest of the popular classes] that [the theories of] Paulo Freire and Emilia [Ferreira] be incorporated together). Rejecting the notion of the irrelevance of academic theory to the interests of popular sectors, Freire concludes, "The popular classes need theory, that theory only need be placed in the service of their real interests, and remain dominated by a popular political orientation: science in their interest."[69]

A former MOVA coordinator defines the program's method as basically 80 percent Freire and 15 percent Ferreiro, with the remainder from other influences.[70] Thus, a cursory review of the literacy training material will show that Freire's epistemology, the notion of education as the act of knowing; Freire's and Vygotsky's perception of knowledge and culture as inherent to the praxis of individuals and communities; and Freire's theoretical perspective on the relationships among politics, power, and education all seem to influence the design of MOVA's method, as does Ferreiro's psychogenesis of language. Despite the Secretariat's theoretically sophisticated and well outlined approach to literacy training, the second MOVA coordinator emphasized that the PT Secretariat did not impose a so-called Freirean method or any other for that matter: "We propose, but do not impose [. . .] We cannot obligate our nuclei of literacy training to strictly follow a specific methodology."[71]

At the same time, this former coordinator is also critical of Ferreiro's contribution, particularly her positivism and her assumption that there is no apparent loss of knowledge or regression in individuals who have achieved cognition. This individual also faults Ferreiro's approach for its very limited perspective of the relationships between education and politics. Along these lines, at the MOVA Congress, Maria Jose Vale Ferreira (one of MOVA's pedagogic directors) spoke to the need for more concrete strategies for reaching the abstract goals of critical consciousness raising in association with "the political struggle of popular movements" as expressed in the movement's rhetoric: "We must make those words a reality," Ferreira emphatically stated. She also made an appeal to members to overcome "unconstructive internal divisions" (which became apparent in heated sectarian political debates that emerged as the Congress progressed).

Summary

Through each of the three major areas of initiative briefly highlighted above—the Movement for Curricular Reorientation, the institution of School Site Councils, and MOVA—the PT-MSE, working as an activist and democratic-socialist state, attempted to create a new dynamic between a state institution and forces for social change (e.g., social movements). In the case of the Movement for Curricular Reorientation and the institutionalization of the School Site Councils, the PT-MSE actually structured conditions and experiences that, it hoped, would lay the groundwork for raising community awareness about and involvement in teaching and learning issues. It was intended that ultimately such heightened access to schools and school issues would foment the momentum necessary for community organizing, or even a grassroots social movement, around the quality of public education and the creation of Popular Public Schools. MOVA represented the complement to the previous examples, which were, in a sense, situations in which the PT-MSE tried to galvanize support for a broad-based social movement around primary education. With MOVA, the PT-MSE itself played a supportive role vis à vis existing adult/youth literacy movements rather than an initiating role. This was clearly the more challenging situation, though as our analysis reveals, the relationship was ultimately a mutually respectful one, despite recurring tensions and obstacles.

The next chapters analyze the theoretical foundations of the Freire administration's major policy initiatives for primary education and provide preliminary highlights of some of the achievements and challenges experienced by educators as they implemented these new reforms. Their full experience is studied in more detail in the case studies of Chapter VI.

Notes

1. Fernando Calderón Gutiérrez and Mario R. dos Santos, "Movimientos sociales y democracia: Los conflictos por la constitución de un nuevo orden," in *Los conflictos por la constitución de un nuevo orden*, ed., Fernando Calderón Gutierrez and Mario R. dos Santos (Buenos Aires: Consejo Latinoamericano de Ciendas Sociales [CLACSO], 1987), pp. 11-32; Rolland Paulston, "Education as Antistructure: Nonformal Education in Social and Ethnic Movements," *Comparative Education*, 16, no. 1 (March 1980), pp. 55-66; Susan Eckstein, ed., *Power and Popular Protest: Latin*

American Social Movements (Berkeley and Los Angeles: University of California Press, 1989); Jane S. Jaquette, ed., *The Women's Movement in Latin America* (Boston: Unwin Hyman, 1989); Emilie Bergmann et al., *Women, Culture and Politics in Latin America* (Berkeley and Los Angeles: University of California Press, 1990).

2. Claus Offe, "Structural Problems of the Capitalist State: Class Rule and the Political System: On the Selectiveness of Political Institutions," in *German Political Studies*, ed. K. V. Von Beyme (Beverly Hills, CA: Sage, 1974), p. 37.

3. Ibid., p. 37; see also Claus Offe, *Contradictions of the Welfare State* (London: Hutchinson, 1984).

4. Op. Cit.

5. Bruce Fuller, *Growing-Up Modern: The Western State Builds Third-World Schools* (New York: Routledge, 1991), esp. pp. 12-24, 108. It is instructive to read Offe's analyses of how, in the context of disorganized capitalism, relations of social power are translated into political authority and, conversely, how political authority transforms power relations within civil society. See Claus Offe, *Disorganized Capitalism* (Cambridge: Polity, 1985).

6. Max Weber, *Economia y Sociedad* (Mexico: Fondo de Cultura Económica, 1969), pp. 210-15; Offe, *Contradictions of the Welfare State*, p. 88.

7. Fernando Henrique Cardoso, "On the Characterization of Authoritarian Regimes in Latin America," in *The New Authoritarianism in Latin America*, ed., David Collier (Berkeley and Los Angeles: University of California Press, 1979), p. 38.

8. This definition borrows elements from Thomas McCarthy's criticism of Michel Foucault's unidimensional notion of power. See Thomas McCarthy, "The Critique of Impure Reason: Foucault and the Frankfurt School," in *Rethinking Power*, ed., Thomas E. Wartenberg (Albany, NY: SUNY Press, 1992), pp. 121-49.

9. See Carlos Alberto Torres, *The Politics of Nonformal Education in Latin America* (New York: Praeger, 1990), pp. 102-5. A fascinating discussion about notions of democracy in Marx and Weber in the context of capitalism and modernity is found in Derek Sayer, *Capitalism and Modernity: An Excursus on Marx and Weber* (London: Routledge, 1991).

10. Martin Carnoy, *The State and Political Theory* (Princeton, NJ: Princeton University Press, 1984).

11. Martin Carnoy and Henry Levin, *Schooling and Work in the Democratic State* (Stanford, CA: Stanford University Press, 1985), pp. 24, 76-110; Carlos Alberto Torres, *The Politics of Nonformal Education*, pp. 138-40; Martin Carnoy and Joel Samoff, *Education and Social Transition in the Third World* (Princeton, NJ: Princeton University Press, 1990).

12. Hans N. Weiler, "Compensatory Legitimation in Educational Policy: Legalization, Expertise, and Participation in Comparative Perspective," Report no. 81-A17 (Institute for Finance and Government, Stanford University, Stanford, CA, September 1981). In São Paulo, the articulation among the state at the local, state,

and federal levels will pose additional complexities for the analysis. However, these are not addressed in the present study.

13. In the context of policies of financial austerity and structural adjustment, investment in public works and social sectors associated with investment in human capital (mainly education and health) has fallen, in some cases significantly. Structural adjustment loans sponsored by the International Monetary Fund and the World Bank impose a number of conditions, including reduced government spending, real devaluations to promote exports, tariff reductions, and attempts to increase public and private savings by reducing public consumption, and particularly employment in the public sector. The withdrawal of state investment has resulted in the increasing privatization of public schooling, "both through parents bearing a growing proportion of public education costs and, as the quality of public education fills, through the flight of those who can afford private education." See Daniel A. Morales-Gómez and Carlos Alberto Torres, "Introduction: Education and Development in Latin America," in *Education, Policy, and Social Change: Experiences from Latin America*, ed., Daniel A. Morales-Gómez and Carlos Alberto Torres (Westport, CT, and London: Praeger, 1992), p. 5.

14. Scott Mainwaring and Eduardo Viola, "New Social Movements, Political Culture and Democracy: Brazil and Argentina in the 1980s," *Telaso*, 61 (Fall 1984), pp. 17-54.

15. Inter-American Foundation, *1990 Annual Report* (Rosslyn, VA: Inter-American Foundation, 1990).

16. F. Emerson Andrews, *Philanthropic Foundations* (New York: Russell Sage, 1956), cited in *Philanthropy and Cultural Imperialism: The Foundations at Home and Abroad*, ed., Robert F. Arnove (Bloomington: Indiana University Press, 1980), p. 4.

17. Alan Touraine, *The Voice and the Eye: An Analysis of Social Movements* (New York: Cambridge University Press, 1981).

18. Scott Mainwaring and Eduardo Viola, "New Social Movements, Political Culture and Democracy: Brazil and Argentina" (Notre Dame, IN: Kellog Institute for International Studies, University of Notre Dame, 1984); David Slater, ed., *New Social Movements and the State in Latin America* (Amsterdam: Centrum Voor Studie en Documentatie Vans Latijns Amerika [CEDLA], 1985); Elizabeth Jelin, "Movimientos sociales en Argentina: Una introducción a su estudio," *Cuestión de Estado* 1 (September 1987), pp. 28-37; Carlos R. Brandao, *Lutar com a palavra* (Rio de Janeiro: Graal, 1982).

19. Ernesto Laclau, "New Social Movements and the Plurality of the Social," in Slater, ed., pp. 27-42. See also Henry Pease García et al., America Latina 80: Democracia y movimiento popular (Lima: Centro de Estudios y Promoci—n del Desarrollo, DESCO, 1981); Calderón Gutierrez and dos Santos, Op. Cit.; Norbert Lechner, ed., Cultura política y democratización (Santiago, Chile: Facultad Latino americana de Ciencias Sociales, CLACSO, and Instituto de Cooperación Iberoamericana, 1987).

20. David Slater, "Social Movements and a Recasting of the Political," in Slater, ed., p. 6.

21. Moacir Gadotti et al., *A força que temos* (Pontificia Universidade Catolica de São Paulo, Sao Paulo, 1989, mimeographed). For the dilemmas of social movements and the unique experience of the PT, see Tilman Evers, "Identity: The Hidden Side of New Social Movements in Latin America," in Slater, ed., p. 55.

22. Agneta Lind and Anton Johnston, *Adult Literacy in the Third World: A Review of Objectives and Strategies*, Education Division Document no. 32 (Stockholm: Swedish International Development Authority, October 1986), p. 63. For a discussion of Freire's experiences with literacy training in Guinea Bissau, see Carlos Alberto Torres, "From the 'Pedagogy of the Oppressed' to 'A Luta Continua: the Political Pedagogy of Paulo Freire," in *Paulo Freire: A Critical Encounter*, ed. Peter McLaren and Peter Leonard (London: Routledge, 1992), pp. 119-45.

23. Moacir Gadotti, "The Politics of Education and Social Change in Brazil: A Critical View from Within" (paper presented at the American Education Research Association annual meeting, Chicago, April 4-7, 1991, mimeographed), p. 12.

24. See the following interviews conducted by Mario Sergio Cortella: "O homen que substituio Paulo Freire," *Aconteceu* 576 (April 10, 1991), p. 14, "Aqui não inauguramos paredes," *Folha Dirigida/Nacional* (December 24-30, 1991), p.I.d., and "São Paulo acaba com seriacão e fortalece conselho," Nova Escola (April 1992), p. 50.

25. Instituto Brasileiro de Geografia e Estatistica (IBGE) cited in Almanaque Abril (São Paulo, Brasil, 1994), p. 79.

26. For the period September 1990-91, Brazil's GNP of $375.15 billion ranked tenth in the world after the United States ($5.2 trillion), Japan ($2.9 trillion), Germany ($1.3 trillion), France ($1 trillion), Italy ($872 billion), Great Britain ($834 billion), Russia ($650 billion), Canada ($600 billion), and China ($393 billion). See "Indicadores Econ6micos Internacionais," *Folha de São Paulo* (April 19, 1992), p. 3.

27. The Portuguese word *conscientização*, translated as "conscientization" or "critical consciousness," was defined by Freire as follows: "The French prise de conscience (to take consciousness of) is a normal way of being a human being. Conscientization is something which goes beyond the prise de conscience. It is something which is starting from the ability of getting, of taking the prise de conscience. Something which implies to analyze. It is a kind of reading the world rigorously or almost rigorously. It is the way of reading how society works. It is the way to understand better the problem of interests, the question of power. How to get power, what it means not to have power. Finally, conscientizing implies a deeper reading of reality [and] the common sense goes beyond the common sense"; Paulo Freire, videotaped conversation with Carlos Alberto Torres in *Learning to Read the World* (Edmonton: ACCESS Network, October 1990). Reproduced in French in Paulo Freire, *L'education dans la ville* (Paris: Paideia, 1991). See also Carlos Alberto Torres,

"From the 'Pedagogy of the Oppressed' to 'A Luta Continua': The Political Pedagogy of Paulo Freire," McLaren and Leonard, eds. (n. 22 above), pp. 119-45.

28. Celso de Rui Beisiegel, *Politica e educação popular: A teoria e a pratica de Paulo Freire no Brasil* (São Paulo: Editora Atica, 1982); Moacir Gadotti, *Concepção dialética de educação: Um estudo introdutório* (São Paulo: Cortez-Editora Autores Associados, 1986); Thomas J. La Belle, "From Consciousness Raising to Popular Education in Latin America and the Caribbean," *Comparative Education Review*, 31 (May 1987), pp. 201-217; Scott Mainwaring, *The Catholic Church and Politics in Brazil, 1916-1985* (Stanford, CA: Stanford University Press, 1986), pp. 45, 66.

29. The importance of literacy training for citizenship building and the constitution of the popular sectors in Brazil cannot be underestimated. It has been argued that "since until 1983 only the literate could vote in Brazil, the desire for literacy programs should be understood as a mechanism for increasing the number of voters, which would politically sustain the regime in power. To this extent, the figures are impressive: in the early 1960s, out of a total population of 25 million, northeastern Brazil had 15 million illiterates; in 1964, the year of the coup d'etat, in the state of Sergipe alone, literacy training added 80,000 new voters to the 90,000 already existing. In Pernambuco, the total of voters went from 800,000 to 1 million"; Carlos Alberto Torres, *The Politics of Nonformal Education in Latin America* (New York: Praeger, 1990), p. 40. From a different theoretical and political perspective than Freire, the Movimento Brasileiro de Aabetização (MOBRAL) attempted to affect the character of Brazilian citizenship. For instance, see Philipe R. Fletcher, "National Educational Systems as State Agencies of Legitimation" (paper presented at the 1982 Western Regional Conference of the Comparative and International Education Society, Stanford University, October 22-24, 1982, mimeographed); Hugo Lovisolo, *Educação Popular: Maioridade e conciliação* (Salvador, Bahia: Organization of American States, Universidade Federal de Bahia, and Empresa Gráfica de Bahia, 1990).

30. Emmanuel de Kadt, *Catholic Radicals in Brazil* (New York: Oxford University Press, 1970); Marcio Moreira Alves, *O Cristo do Povo* (Rio de Janeiro: Editera Sabiá, 1968); Ruben Alves, "Towards a Theology of Liberation" (Ph.D. dissertation, Princeton Theological Seminary, 1969); Carlos Alberto Torres, *The Church, Society, and Hegemony in Latin America: A Critical Sociology of Religion in Latin America*, trans. Richard Young (Westport, CT: Praeger, 1992).

31. Freire has been a catalyst, if not the prime "animateur," for pedagogical innovation and change. The importance of his work is expressed in the fact that his most important books (e.g., *Pedagogy of the Oppressed* [New York: Herder & Herder, 1970]; *Education for Critical Consciousness* [New York: Seabury, 1978]; *Pedagogy in Process: Letters to Ginea-Bissau* [New York: Seabury, 1978]) have been translated into many languages including German, Italian, Spanish, Korean, Japanese, and French. *Pedagogy of the Oppressed*, which has been translated into 18 languages, has more than 35 reprints in Spanish, 19 in Portuguese, and 12 in English. See Ira Shor, ed.,

Freire for the Classroom: A Sourcebook for Liberatory Teaching (Portsmouth, NH: Boynton/Ceok, 1987); Ira Shor and Paulo Freire, *A Pedagogy for Liberation: Dialogues on Transforming Education* (Amherst, MA: Bergin & Garvey, 1987); McLaren and Leonard, eds., Op. Cit.; Ira Shor, *Empowering Education: Critical Teaching for Social Change* (Chicago: University of Chicago Press, 1992); Peter McLaren and Colin Lankshear, eds., *Politics of Liberation: Paths from Freire* (London: Routledge, 1994).

32. A generative theme is an existential and crucial daily life situation for members of a given "oppressed" community. When a generative theme is discovered through thematic investigation and then codified, it becomes a knowledgeable object mediating between knowing subjects and it then leads to the discovery of "generative words" (which are in turn selected on the basis of their syllabic complexity and richness), the basis for the Freirean literacy training method.

33. Freire, *Pedagogy of the Oppressed*, p. 19.

34. Moacir Gadotti, *Convite a leitura de Paulo Freire* (São Paulo: Editora Scipione, 1989); Beisiegel; Carlos Alberto Torres, "A dialetica hegeliana e o pensamento lógico-estrutural de Paulo Freire: Notas para uma analise e confronta são dos pressupostos filosóficos vigentes na dialetica da pedagogia dos oprimidos e do pensamento Freireano em geral," *Revista Sintese* 3 (April-June 1976), pp. 61-78, *Lectura critica de Paulo Freire* (Mexico City: Gernika, 1978), *Educación y concientización* (Salamanca, Spain: Ediciones Sigüeme, 1980), and Carlos Alberto Torres, *The Politics of Nonformal Education*, Op.Cit.

35. Torres, *The Church, Society, and Hegemony*, pp. 117-97.

36. Moacir Gadotti, *Uma só escola para todos: Caminhos da autonomia escolar* (Petropolis: Vozes, 1990), pp. 165-167; Secretaria de Planejamento da Presidencia da República, Fundação Instituto Brasileiro de Geografia e Estatistica IIBGEl, *Censo demografico: Dados gerais-migração-instrução-fecundidade-mortalidade: 9 recenseamento geral do Brail-1980*, vol. 1, tomo 4, no. 1 (Rio de Janeiro: IBGE, 1983), pp. 114-67; Secretaria de Administrao Geral, Ministerio da Educação, *A Educação no Brasil na decada de 80* (Brasilia: Sistema Estatistico da Educação and Ministerio de Educação e Cultura/SAG/CPS/CIP, December 1990); IBGE and Unicef-Fundação Centro Brasileiro para a Infancia e Adolesencia, *Perfil estatistico de criancas e mães no Brasil* 1 (Rio de Janeiro: IBGE, 1990).

37. See Gadotti, *Uma só escola para todos*, p. 166.

38. Aspen Institute, *Convergence and Community: The Americas in 1993: A Report of the Inter-American Dialogue* (Washington, DC: Aspen Institute, December 1992), p. 43.

39. Paulo Freire, interview with Carlos Torres, São Paulo, February 17, 1990.

40. Secretaria Municipal de Educação, "Boletim 9: Canal de comunicação entre a secretaria municipal de educação e a comunidade escolar" (São Paulo, December 11, 1989, mimeographed).

41. David Plank and Richard Pelczar, "Democratic Politics, Constitutional Reform, and Basic Education in Contemporary Brazil" (paper presented at the annual

meeting of the Comparative and International Education Society, Atlanta, GA. March 1988); David Plank, "Public Purpose and Private Interest in Brazilian Education," *New Education* 12 (1990), pp. 83-89.

42. Fórum de Políticas Municipais de Educação de Jovens e Adultos, *Educação de jovens e adultos: Subsidios para elaboração de politicas municipais* (São Paulo: Centro Ecumenico de Documentação e Informação, 1990), p. 10.

43. Gadotti, *Uma so escola para todos*, pp. 15-101,143-183.

44. See Pierre Bourdieu and J.C. Passeron, *Reproduction in Education, Society and Culture* (London: Sage, 1977); Pierre Bourdieu, *Distinction: A Social Critique of the Judgement of Taste* (London: Routledge, 1984), and Pierre Bourdieu *Coisas Ditas* (São Paulo: Editora Brasiliense, 1990).

45. SME-SP, *Cadernos de Formação Nᵃ 1—Um Primeiro Olhar sobre o Projeto*, 3ª Série—Ação Pedagogica da Escola pela via da interdisciplinaridade, February 1990, p. 15.

46. Linda M. McNeil, *Contradictions of Control: School Structure and School Knowledge* (New York: Routledge, 1986), p. 165.

47. Thomas McCarthy, *The Critical Theory of Jurgen Habermas* (Cambridge, Mass.: MIT Press, 1979), pp. 372-374.

48. Fórum de Políticas Municipais, p. 20 (n. 42 above).

49. Secretaria Municipal de Educação, "O movimento de reorientação curricular na secretaria municipal de educação de São Paulo," documento 1 (São Paulo, 1989, mimeographed), p. 1. The process of reforming curriculum is termed "Curriculum Reorientation through Interdiscplinarity."

50. Ibid., p. 3.

51. Joaquim de Carvalho, "Pedagogia de Paulo Freire chega a mais cem escolas," *O Estado de São Paulo* (July 24, 1990), p. 12.

52. Paulo Freire, videotaped conversation with Carlos Alberto Torres in *Learning to Read the World* (n. 28 above).

53. Paulo Freire, videotaped conversation with Carlos Alberto Torres, São Paulo, May 1990.

54. After 60 years of operation for the municipal educational system, no statute for the teaching profession had been implemented. Freire told us in 1991 that he considered it important to correct this omission. Proposed qualifications for school printpals were three years of seniority in the municipal education system and proper teaching credentials. *Estatuto do magisterio municipal: Minuta do anteprojeto de lei* (São Paulo: Secretaria Municipal de Educacão de São Paulo, March 1991), p. 44.

55. Key principles of this statute, the first ever for municipal education in the city of São Paulo, included monthly salary adjustments tied to inflation (garantia de piso salarial profissional); changes in working conditions, including the creation of a Jornada de Trabalho Integral (i.e., full-time equivalent [EYE] positions of 30 hours a week, including 20 contact hours and 10 additional hours for extraclassroom activities); guaranteed part-time equivalent positions of 20 hours a week,

with the possibility for those part-time teachers with tenure to opt for a position; and implementation of a conselho de escola (school council) as a deliberative organ comprising the principal, teachers, teachers' aides, students, and parents.

56. Paulo Freire, conversation with Carlos Alberto Torres, São Paulo, July 2, 1991.

57. Ibid. For a discussion on corporatism and education, see Daniel A. Morales-Gómez and Carlos Alberto Torres, *The State: Corporatist Politics and Education Policy Making in Mexico* (New York: Praeger, 1990).

58. Interviews conducted by Pilar O'Cadiz in São Paulo, September 1992.

59. In October, 1992, the PT lost the municipal elections to the *Partido Democratico Social* (PDS, Democratic Social Party), a conservative party lead by Paulo Maluf who subsequently became mayor of São Paulo.

60. Interview by Pilar O'Cadiz, October 1992.

61. Fórum de Políticas Municipais (n. 41 above) p. 18.

62. Paulo Freire, interview with Carlos Alberto Torres, São Paulo, February 21, 1990.

63. *Reflexões sobre o Processo Metodológico de Alfabetização—MOVA-SP Caderno, 3*, (São Paulo: Secretaria Municipal de Educação de São Paulo, 1990), p. 6.

64. Lev S. Vygotsky, Thought and Language (Cambridge, MA: MIT Press, 1962), and *Mind and Society*, ed., M. Cole, V. John-Steiner, and E. Souberman (Cambridge, MA: Harvard University Press, 1978).

65. Yetta M. Goodman and Kenneth S. Goodman, "Vygotsky in a Whole-Language Perspective," in *Vygotsky and Education: Instructional Implications and Applications of Socio-Historical Psychology*, ed. Luis C. Moil (New York: Cambridge University Press, 1990), p. 238.

66. Quoted in Yetta Goodman, "Preface to the English Edition," in *Literacy before Schooling*, by Emilia Ferreiro and Ana Teberosky (Portsmouth, NH: Heinemann, 1982), p. xii.

67. For Piaget, cognition is an organizational structure that involves cognitive adaptation. In its dynamic form, intellectual development is characterized by three functional invariances: organization, assimilation, and accommodation. The nature of assimilation is that every cognitive act of a subject involves a kind of cognitive structuration or restructuration of the external object to the systems of meanings already internalized by the subject. Thus, the process of assimilation appears in three forms: cumulative repetition, generalization of the activity with the incorporation of new objects of knowledge, and motor recognition. See Jean Piaget, *The Origins of Intelligence in Children* (New York: International University Press, 1952).

68. Ferreiro and Teberosky, p. 285; Emilia Ferreiro, ed., *Los hijos del analfabetismo: Propuestas para la alfabetázción escolar en América Latina* (Mexico: Siglo XXI, 1989).

69. From recording of Freire's speech at the MOVA Congress, July 15, 1990.

70. Cited in Maria del Pilar O'Cadiz, "Social Movements and Literacy Training in Brazil: A Narrative," in *Education and Social Change in Latin America*, ed., Carlos Alberto Torres (Melbourne: James Nicholas, 1994).

71. Ibid.

IV

Creating the Popular Public School: Theoretical Foundations and Policy Initiatives

Democratization of Administration and the Creation of a Movement for Curriculum Reform

Why a Popular Public School?

In 1964 Paulo Freire was stripped of his post as President of the Commission in Popular Culture and forced into exile. He fled Brazil in the midst of a military clamp down to purge the government of the cadre of social activists appointed by then-President João Goulart. For the next 16 years, Freire lived abroad, contributing his many talents and celebrated ideas to a range of literacy and educational campaigns in countries around the world.

In 1980, Paulo Freire returned to Brazil. As was his custom, he approached his homecoming with a reflective attitude. His response to the onslaught of reporters who sought initial words of wisdom from one of their internationally renowned thinkers was: *"Vim para aprender o Brasil, e, enquanto estiver no processo de reaprendizagem, de reconhecimento do Brasil, nao tenho muito o que dizer. Tenho mas o que perguntar."*[1] Nine years later, Freire's appointment as Secretary of Education in São Paulo symbolized a coming of age of the Brazilian Left—grown up from the radical populism that nurtured its naive idealism in the 1960s, having now reached a political maturity borne of the harshness of two decades of persecution and exile, mitigated by the tempered Marxism of European democratic socialism—and a full circle journey for Paulo Freire.

In many respects Freire can be regarded as an intellectual and spiritual grandfather of the generation that now heads the Worker's Party's loosely joined if not tenuous coalition of Marxist intellectuals, organized labor and radical grass roots social movements. His appointment to the post of Secretary of Education of São Paulo, Brazil's industrial and financial capital, signaled the historical contemporaneousness of his thought and reaffirmed the validity of its tenets for educational practice. Though Freire's ideas had been consistently read and experimented with throughout the world, his presence as a central player in the formal educational structure of his country marked a major milestone for the prospects of democratization in Brazil. In addition, his appointment as Secretary of Education rekindled the pedagogic passions of those who had long been inspired by his thoughts and ignited the liberatory flame of young educators who had just been born when he was exiled.

The efforts of the PT-MSE under Freire's leadership fanned these flames with five primary policy objectives that furthered their radical, political-pedagogic reform program:

1. increased access to schooling;[2]
2. democratization of school administration;
3. an improved quality of instruction;
4. education for working youths and adults; and,
5. the formation of critical and responsible citizens.[3]

In order to achieve these broad and ambitious policy objectives, the administration set out to formulate and implement several specific educational reform projects including, but not limited to, the Movement for Curricular Reorientation (with the Interdisciplinary Project as the linchpin), Continuing Professional Education Groups or *Grupos de Formação* (for teachers, pedagogic coordinators, and school directors), the Genesis Project (a computer instruction program), and MOVA (the Movement for Youth and Adult Literacy). [4]

The theoretical foundations for three aspects of the PT's overall reform agenda are considered in this chapter: democratization of school administration, an improved quality of instruction, and the formation of critical and responsible citizens.[5] Though these are articulated as distinct policy goals, in reality they are inter-related and inter-dependent and have as their primary vehicle the creation of a Popular Public School.

From the perspectives of procedure, content and historical context, the reforms that the Municipal Secretariat of Education initiated during the PT's tenure departed dramatically from those offered by previous administrations. They called for democratization of schools in a society just beginning to emerge from 25 years of military rule. Their theoretical foundation drew from a Freirean vision of education as liberatory praxis combined with the principles of constructivism, challenging most of the technicist and modernist orientation of policies preceding them. They required active involvement in the development of curriculum on the part of educators who were accustomed to using "teacher-proof" instructional packages. They attempted to empower educators by providing more autonomy than they had ever experienced but simultaneously required much broader and more intense participation from them. They offered interested educators opportunities to work collaboratively with their colleagues and with students and parents, despite their profound lack of experience and limited training in such dynamics. Finally, they made an explicit political choice to place public education at the service of poor and working class communities. In doing so, the PT's reforms pushed all involved to examine more critically their own lives in relation to the education of Brazilian children, and poor children in particular.

These ambitious and radical new policies and programs emerged against a backdrop of a host of challenges and obstacles. First, the PT's electoral mandate gave them a short period of four years within which to develop and implement their reforms. In addition to this limited reform period, the PT was challenged by the overall state of public education in the city. A few examples illustrate the sorry situation. In 1989 it was estimated that over one million pre-school and primary school age children in São Paulo were not enrolled in schools, due to limited capacities. A junior teacher earned slightly more than a domestic servant. Grade retention and drop out rates were disturbingly high. Because the previous administration did not offer certification exams, thousands of teachers were working under temporary contracts, resulting in significant understaffing at many schools and unnecessary staff turnover. Sixty percent of all school facilities required major structural and cosmetic repairs due to collapsed ceilings, exposed electrical wiring, and faulty plumbing. The district owned two trucks which serviced the distribution needs of a system that covered 1,500 square kilometers. Compounding this situation, the PT administration faced a multi-million dollar deficit in the educational budget upon its inauguration into office.[6]

As we have described previously, a unifying notion in the PT's efforts to meet the aforementioned goals was the construction of a Popular Public School in which the institution of public education becomes an instrument for the transformation of society by the popular classes. The conceptualization of a Popular Public School emerged out of decades-long, intense theoretical debate which has taken as its primary line of inquiry the following: what and how do we teach the poor, the children of the illiterate, the disenfranchised and the least empowered in a society of harsh inequities and virtually insurmountable obstacles to social mobility through education? The roots of this theoretical debate can be found in various pedagogical, sociological, and anthropological theories originating both within and outside of Brazil and reaching a point of tentative closure within a particular context, the municipal schools of São Paulo and the particular historical moment of the PT's tenure (1989-1992).

Through its efforts to democratize educational decision making in the city and through other projects oriented around the democratization of access to education, the creation of an alternative pedagogic proposal, and the promotion of literacy training for youths and adults, the PT sought to build a broad based campaign in defense of a Quality Public Schooling.[7] Freire's Cabinet Chief, Moacir Gadotti, describes what is meant by "quality" in this particular context and how the administration set forth in pursuit of that new quality of schooling from a practical perspective:

> Quality for us is not to return to an old quality, it is to generate a new quality from within a new social political economic and historical perspective in which we believe. Therefore, it is a critical formation in allegiance with a technical formation, and for that we invited the universities to work with us (150 professors from various campuses).[8]

Thus, in keeping with the democratic principles of the Workers Party and the *Equipe Paulo Freire* (Paulo Freire's Team, made up of leading educators and university specialists working at the Secretariat level), democratic participation and collective construction were key operational terms of the administration. *Democratization of the administration of the municipal schools* —a principle policy objective of the PT-MSE—implied a curriculum reform process that called for the participation of the school community in the construction of a purposeful education project. It follows then that the second policy objective of the PT-MSE, *the improvement of the quality of education offered in the municipal schools,* would take on the characterization of a political mobilization effort as much as a project for pedagogic transformation. Finally, the *formation of critical and responsible citizens* was a natural outcome of the previous two goals, where the improved quality of education would help students to develop the knowledge base and skills for this citizenship and the experience of democratic schooling would give them the necessary empirical foundations.

Why a Movement for Curriculum Reform?

The remarkable distinction which sets the PT's reform agenda apart from other major school reform and improvement efforts is the dual political-pedagogic focus of the administration's efforts and its attempts to create a reform process defined as a political/educational movement. The underlying factor behind the idea of a multifaceted *movement* versus a rigidly defined *reform* program was a consciousness on the part of the PT educators in the Secretariat that they may only have four years (or less if one considers transition time between administrations) to carry out their efforts to impact the educational reality of the city's children and the pedagogical minds of the teachers working in its schools (they were ultimately correct about this timeline). To this end and in an effort to avoid the perception that the Secretariat was imposing its political-pedagogic agenda on the schools, the PT-MSE opted to create a grassroots movement within the schools to advance their proposal for radical educational reform. This of course would take place under the impetus and guidance of a "popular state," represented in the PT municipal government. However the PT-MSE intention was that the reform effort ideally take root at the level of the schools so as to develop enough autonomy to continue evolving beyond the Workers Party's hold on power in the municipal government (i.e., after the next municipal elections). For this reason, their principal elementary level initiative, the *Movement for the Reorientation of the Curriculum* (MRC), rather than representing a neatly packaged and highly contrived reform project, essentially aimed at provoking the rethinking and reshaping of relationships between teachers, students and administrators of the municipal schools of São Paulo, in order to lay the groundwork for the on-going critical reflection on pedagogical practices and the establishment of a continual long-term process of curriculum renovation. To accomplish the difficult work of transforming values, attitudes, norms and even organizational culture, the PT-MSE proposed a working model of a curriculum reform project: *the interdisciplinary curriculum via the generative theme* or Inter Project. The Inter Project was presented to teachers as a viable option for coordinated pedagogic action under the general MRC rubric.

Also in accordance with the democratic goals of the PT-MSE, schools that did not opt into the Inter Project developed independent proposals for a variety of educational projects (e.g., parent participation projects, cultural and curriculum enrichment activities such as school newspapers, theater groups, marching bands, etc.) which also received Secretariat technical and logistical support. According to Secretariat documents, by January 1992, 326 pre-schools and elementary schools were involved in the implementation of special projects.[9]

In addition, the PT-MSE promoted numerous other projects such as: *Projecto Gênese* (44 schools carried out this program using computers as an integral part of their educational program); *Programa Sala de Leitura* (a program for the establishment Reading Rooms at 90 percent of the elementary schools with a traveling collection of 400 books for the remaining schools); AIDS and Sex Education projects; *Projecto Não Violencia* aimed at addressing the educational needs of the most marginalized sectors of the city's youth and street children, and at the prevention of their delinquency.

The following sections describe the administrative reforms initiated by the PT-MSE and elaborate on the theoretical foundations of the Secretariat's main policy effort, the Inter Project.

Transforming the Central and Regional Administration of the PT-MSE

While the content of the PT's programs drew heavily from Freire's lifelong body of critical pedagogical work—both in theory and practice—it would be far from the truth to assert that the educational reform project put forth by the PT-MSE under Freire's leadership was solely his brainchild or the mere reflection of Freire's legendary persona. Initially—as indicated above—it was the product of an intensive collective effort among a core team of colleagues (i.e., *Equipe Paulo Freire*) from the University of São Paulo, the Pontifical Catholic University of São Paulo and the State University at Campinas whom Freire invited to the Secretariat to work on developing an overall educational program for his administration to advance. Eventually, program development and policy implementation was shaped in large part by educators in regional administrations and by educators and students at the school site. This gradual shift of the locus of innovation grew out of a commitment to one of the overarching principles of the PT-MSE: democratization of school administration. This democratization of the administration of the municipal schools implied substantial procedural reforms.

At the level of the central office, the PT-MSE introduced several innovations. First, the managerial corps underwent a significant transformation. Under Freire's administration, concerted efforts were made to recruit active teachers into the administrative ranks, while still allowing them flexibility to stay in the classroom. In addition, the PT administration reduced an over staffed bureaucracy by sending 183 administrators back into the schools as teachers. This restructuring of Secretariat personnel reflected the administration's premise that "the place of educational planning is at the school site." Consequently, Gadotti estimates that "97 percent of Secretariat personnel worked directly with schools."[10] As a result, policy development efforts were shaped by the classroom experience which still constituted a vivid frame of reference rather than a romanticized abstraction for many central office personnel. In addition, the inclusion of classroom teachers at the level of policy development provided unencumbered feedback channels—central office personnel involved in developing components of the reforms also participated in their implementation in the classroom. Thus, information about the viability and effectiveness of reform components was easily transmitted back to the policy table for refinement. The overall result of this new administrative core was a dynamic experience of integrating theory and practice.

The central administration also made attempts to democratize its interactions with regional administrative offices. In prior administrations, employees at the regional offices, formerly called *Delegacias Regionais de Educação Municipal* (Regional Delegacies for Municipal Education) or DREMs, served as the managerial police force of the central office. Their contact with schools was limited to a monitoring role, checking to make sure that all regulations and procedures were properly followed. Their relationship with the central office was defined by the completion and submittal of surveillance reports from schools. Under the PT, these dynamics changed quite noticeably. The structure and purpose of the regional administrations was substantively transformed. The PT administration abolished these DREMs and replaced them with 10 *Nucleos de Ação Educativa* (Nuclei for Educational Action). The Nuclei for Educational Action (NAEs) allowed for a more democratic structure in the orientation and supervision of the municipal schools and a more decentralized system of technical assistance and support.[11]

Personnel at the regional administrations, or NAEs, were increasingly recruited from the teaching ranks under the PT-MSE. More importantly, the role of regional personnel changed from one of monitoring compliance to one in which they acted as facilitators and resource people for schools undergoing reform. In addition, regional personnel were treated as partners of their colleagues at the central office. In fact, their insights and experiences at reforming school sites played a crucial role in shaping and refining the different educational reforms proposed by the PT-MSE. The administrative structure of the municipal school system under Freire's administration is illustrated in Figure 4.1.

The PT-MSE also attempted to redefine the traditionally hierarchical relationship between central office and school site. Rather than strengthening the strong arm of centralized control, the PT sought to expand the autonomy of school sites, while also providing support to build their capacity for program development and decision-making. This was accomplished primarily through the re-introduction of School Site Councils. These councils served as mechanisms for increasing family and community participation in school decision-making processes. They drew representatives from the teaching staff, the administrative staff, the students, and the school

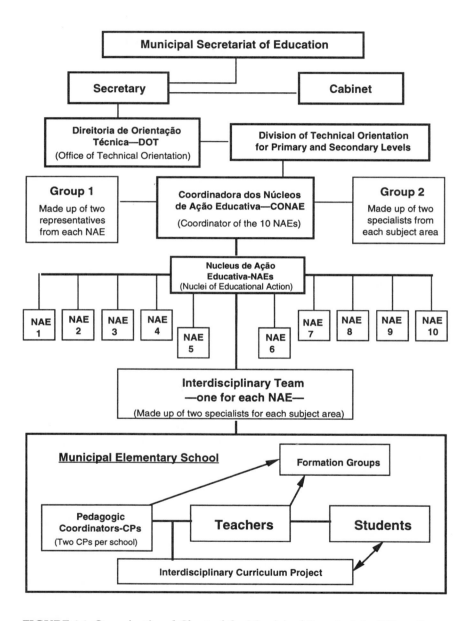

FIGURE 4.1. Organizational Chart of the Municipal Secretariat of Education: Components Involved in the Interdisciplinary Process

community (including parents and other community members). Their primary responsibilities covered budget and personnel issues, although some curricular issues were also attended to on occasion.

More importantly, however, the PT-MSE redefined schools' relationships to policy development and implementation. First, schools voluntarily participated in PT-MSE programs such as the Interdisciplinary Project, rather than participating in response to administrative fiat, as had historically been the case. With each of the initiatives launched by the PT, schools had the option of choosing participation in PT-MSE programs. It is important to point out, again, that schools were also provided with the option of not selecting an PT-MSE program but choosing instead to develop their own unique program, while still receiving technical assistance from the Secretariat. Thus, voluntary participation and buy-in from school faculties was the first step in the mobilization of this movement.

Once a part of the movement, other processes were in place to ensure its solidification. First, a central source of curriculum content was seen as being derived from the community in which the school was located. Second, students and their families were active participants in deciding what aspects of their community life should be included in the curriculum. Third, community resources became important tools for instruction. Through these three components, the PT-MSE laid the groundwork for creating localized centers of educational improvement that not only included students and staffs in school but also were energized by a substantial relationship with school communities. At each point, regional administrative resources were available in the form of technical and material support, training opportunities, and professional development courses.

At each NAE an Interdisciplinary Team (or Multidisciplinary Teams as they sometimes called themselves) was charged with coordinating the Inter Project at the schools in their corresponding regions. A pair or team of mentors was assigned to each school and typically attempts were made to place mentors at schools based on a match between the school's profile and needs and the mentors' experience in content areas, in similar geographical regions and with similar student populations. NAE staff visited schools anywhere from once a week (at the minimum) to daily (most common at the pilot sites). NAE mentors' involvement at school sites covered such activities as regular meetings with teachers and pedagogic coordinators to discuss progress with curriculum development, pedagogical issues, and special projects associated with the elaboration of the Inter Project. The NAE staff as a group also were responsible for developing courses for teachers in their region on various educational and professional issues, organizing conferences, and scheduling networking events among schools. To do this, NAE staff also spent much of their time conducting research on such diverse topics as child psychology and organizational behavior; their findings were then funneled into publications and other resources for teachers and optional enrichment courses offered to teachers.

These varied responsibilities marked a significant change in the scope of services provided by regional administrators. Under the PT-MSE their role became one primarily dedicated to assisting schools and providing practical and theoretical resources. They in turn were coordinated by the central entity, CONAE (*Coordenadora dos Núcleos de Ação Educativa*), made up of two groups: Group 1 was composed of two representatives from each NAE; and Group 2 formed by two specialists from each subject area that worked to develop guidelines for teachers as they developed their interdisciplinary curriculum. Though the CONAE provided orientation to the NAE staff, in reality this was also a dialectic relationship, built on an open communication structure where reflection, critical analysis, experimentation and risk-taking were strongly encouraged. The CONAE was clearly a policy-making body, but it performed its duties with full and honest information and in dialogue with the practitioners in the field—both the school staffs and the NAE staffs.

Through the PT's efforts, then, came a bold marriage between the critical theoretical tenets of a popular educational tradition, historically carried out in nonformal settings, and the immense bureaucratic body and setting of São Paulo's municipal school system. This marriage was predicated on vows to fundamentally change the nature of this bureaucracy by democratizing the very procedures and processes from which it drew its authority and sustenance. The explicitly political nature of the PT's reform agenda invigorated many educators who saw themselves on the educational front in the battle to transform the entrenched authoritarian relations of power that permeated Brazilian society. Taking on a project for the democratization of schooling in Brazil, they hoped to join in a broader societal movement to dismantle the edifice of power and privilege that had been erected by the military regime upon the foundations of the slavocratic society of the Imperial era, the nationalist fervor of the Republics and the liberal developmentalist demagoguery of the populist period. With the support of an activist state, they hoped for the demise of a system structured to reproduce educational failure, putting students of public schools at a gross disadvantage to the children of the upper and middle classes attending private schools. Hand in hand with this struggle was the fight to better the working conditions of teachers whose salaries, training and logistical support declined from bad to worse during the 1980s decade of economic disarray. The PT's tactic of building a social movement around education reform reflected in its central concepts and guiding principles the essence of a radical cultural politics and a revitalized notion of democracy, civic participation and public responsibility.

Democratization of School Administration:
The School Councils

The PT's curriculum reform holds as its core ethos the democratization of schooling and the creation of a critical citizenry prepared to take part in the movement to democratize Brazilian social and political life. From the perspective of the PT administration, the public school is one of the few public spaces left to the popular classes in Brazil and consequently represents an important arena for the construction of a democratic culture in the country. With regard to the central role of schools in this process, sociologist Francisco Weffort—currently Minister of Culture for the Cardoso administration—writes:

> If the public school, especially the elementary school is primarily a school for the formation of citizens, if the public school gives such a central contribution to the process of formation of citizens and the process of the formation of a democratic culture, it is fundamental that the community participate in the administration of the school."[12]

Similarly, the PT-MSE argued that "educational democracy is mainly . . . the sharing of educational policy decision making with parents, students, functionaries and educators."[13]

To fulfill this objective the PT administration resurrected the *Conselho de Escola* (School Council) a deliberative body that had been created by a previous administration but never fully implemented. According to Article 41 of the Common Regiment of the Municipal Schools, the School Councils are made up of elected representatives of teachers, students, parents and functionaries which are "charged with discussing, defining and elaborating a School Plan, that translates for the reality of each school site the guidelines of the educational policies of the municipality."[14] To further institutionalize this process of democratizing decision making throughout such an enormous school system, each regional administration, or NAE, was to establish a Regional Council of Representatives of the School Councils (CRECEs, *Conselhos Regionais de Representantes de Conselhos de Escola*) which was to elaborate a Regional Educational Plan.

If they could establish effective and strong School Councils through the municipal system the PT believed that it could contribute in a concrete and lasting manner to the democratization of other aspects of municipal life. In an illustrated pamphlet produced by the Secretariat to disseminate the existence and purpose of the School Councils to parents, Gizelda [a cartoon character in the shape of a piece of chalk—*giz* means chalk in Portuguese] explains: "Through the School Council we can express an opinion about a service that the government provides the population. This is a way in which we can participate in the administration of the city. As such, the Council is a space for the organization and conquest of better living conditions . . . that is why they should remain in any administration."[15]

In addition to viewing the School Councils as a means of building a critical citizenship, the PT also envisioned the School Councils as an opportunity to galvanize public support for its educational policies. To this effect, in the same bulletin a cartoon teacher explains to parents and students attending a school council meeting: "I think that it is necessary to do a different kind of work in the school that takes into account the reality that we live. In this way, the work that we would do with the students would make sense in their lives." In response to the teacher's proposal, a cartoon father raises his hand and asks, "But how do issues such as health services; transportation; and security of our neighborhood have anything to do the school?" Interestingly, it is precisely such issues that became the "generative themes" around which schools involved in the Inter Project built their interdisciplinary curriculum. Clearly, the administration intended to make the School Councils a central instrument in its pedagogical reforms and political project to mobilize communities through democratic participation. Evidence of such an effort is presented in Chapter VI in the narration of a school council meeting that took place at one of the school sites included in this study.

The organization and activation of the School Councils was carried out unevenly through out the municipal schools system, reflecting the distinct characteristics of the different school communities. School Councils carried out a range of roles, from being a forum for addressing basic school building maintenance problems to debating the school's educational program to actually voting and determining the appointment of school administrators. In schools implementing the Inter Project, the School Council often did serve as a means to communicate and discuss with the community the educational methods and principles behind the Project.

As elaborated in the previous chapter, despite the administration's efforts to increase the impact of this body on the governance of the schools, the power of the School Councils to elect top school administrators (principals, vice-principals, and pedagogical coordinators) was curtailed when a statute drafted by the administration was struck down by union officials, teachers and administrators who opposed such an electoral process.[16] Furthermore, the smooth articulation between the CRECEs, social movements and schools was not so easily or quickly achieved and in reality parents, school functionaries and, to an even lesser degree, students had little part in the debates that evolved around the legislation of the Statute of the Teaching Profession (*Estatuto do Magisterio Municipal*), Regional Educational Plans, and Budgeting and other significant administrative issues. Nonetheless, the School Council was legally established as a deliberative body within a revised version of the statute that was passed as the Municipal Law 11.229 of June 26, 1992.

Subsequently, the administration set out to create better conditions for the articulation between the NAE, CRECE and School Councils through the organization of electoral campaigns for School Council representatives and investment in the training of School Council members as well as involving NAE personnel in the facilitation of Council meetings. They planned to work on improving communication with social movements by scheduling Plenary meetings and Congresses in order to guarantee their participation in the discussions on resource allocation and school programming. Through the School Councils and Regional Councils, the PT sought to bring more players into the fold of the educational policy making process.

Curriculum Innovation: The Interdisciplinary Project

Freire and his colleagues ventured out from the loftiness of the university and the stifling desk of the bureaucrat into the squalor of the favelas and the wobbly desk of the student. To be sure the bold strides made with such initiatives as the Inter Project brought on definite qualitative changes in the municipal public schools during the PT's tenure. In the words of one its principal theorists, "We were able to create in theory and in practice a new conception of the elaboration of a participatory curriculum in which the various teams involved—professors, specialists of the PT-MSE, university advisors—in constant and systematic interaction with one and other, constructed together the path to follow."[17]

Creating a quality education in service of the working classes and city's poor was to be achieved through direct transformation of affective factors (e.g., teachers' attitudes and beliefs) and practical factors (e.g., curriculum content, instructional strategies), supported by the simultaneous democratization efforts at the site, regional and central administrative levels. The PT envisioned the Popular Public School emerging from a complex and organic process that went far beyond a mechanistic approach to changing instructional delivery or adding extra chapters to a textbook. Several theoretical concepts undergird the construction of this Popular Public School.

In fact, those involved in formulating the PT's reform efforts operated within the framework of the following five principles:

1. Reconceptualization of the knowledge production process;
2. Redefinition of the content areas covered in school curriculum;
3. Reorientation of the understanding and use of school curriculum;
4. Transformation of the relationships between educators and those being educated;
5. Transformation of the role played by schools in students' lives and in communities.[18]

For the educators behind the PT reform efforts, the democratization of the public school necessarily implied a reconsideration of the way the knowledge and culture of the children in the schools was to be treated within the institutional setting of the classroom. Thus, Freire's general notion of problematization took precedence over the notion of knowledge as concrete and crystallized. Knowledge, it was agreed among the formulators of the reforms, constituted a collectively constructed and historically situated creation of subjects within the structural, ideological and psychological conditions of their individual and collective existence. Consequently schooling was perceived as a conflictive process of negotiating the various knowledges, "falas" (discourses) and realities of the educator, learner and the communities from which they come and in which the school exists. The goal is that the triangulation between dialogue—reflection—practice, or Freire's notion of praxis, leads to creating educational experiences that resonate with the poor and working class children of São Paulo's schools and develop their critical awareness of their conditions and the ability to transform those conditions.

This meant that curriculum reform was not merely a reformulation of the technical aspects of teaching and the means by which the curriculum is organized, but that curriculum content was central to the reform effort. One of the principal planners of the Project articulates how they focused on the issue of knowledge in the curriculum. She explains:

> The process of appropriation of knowledge by the educatee should permit that [s/he] learn to think in order to formulate hypotheses, to dominate information, transform and construct concepts and form interpretations. To achieve this, the school can not neglect [or scorn] the knowledge brought by the student. To the contrary, the validation and consideration of [his/her] social, cognitive, affective and cultural experience should be

the point of departure for the pedagogic work [of the school] in order to move beyond that experience as a synthesis and not to negate it. To ignore or negate the experience of the educatee makes difficult his intimacy with the new bodies of knowledge [s/he meets in the classroom] and results in [his/her] revering the professor and the school, constructing from that point on a relationship of power from which the knowledge is transformed into more of an instrument of competition than one of cooperation.[19]

This passage illustrates well the philosophy behind the PT administration's effort to devise a method of developing a curriculum that systematically made the reality and culture of the student the basis upon which the educational experiences generated in classroom settings evolved. In order to better understand how the PT educators went about carrying out their political-pedagogical vision, it seems appropriate here to identify the core elements and the theoretical underpinnings of Inter Project.

Generative Theme and the Curriculum

At the foundation of the PT's theoretical framework for educational reform is the Freirean model of problematizing pedagogy and his notion of the generative theme. Freire developed the concept of the generative theme in the early 1960s during his work with pre-literate adults in rural Northeastern Brazil. This concept was somewhat reworked for an urban, formal, and mass education system involving primary grades. The PT-MSE presented the concept of the generative theme to educators in this way:

. . . the generative theme . . . is one path towards getting to know, understand, and intervene critically in a particular studied reality. . . . [It] presupposes a methodology that believes in the growth of the individual through collective work, discussion, problematization, questioning, conflict, [and] participation . . . in the appropriation, construction, and reconstruction of knowing. . . . [It] is the interdisciplinary point of encounter for all of the areas of knowledge.[20]

Generative themes are based on real life situations, problems and concerns of the learners. In the Popular Public School generative themes are the building blocks for the construction of a locally relevant curriculum,[21] which at the same time relates that local reality to a broad range of individual, community and societal problems ranging from peer group relations in the school, to public transportation, to air and water contamination in an industrial city like São Paulo. Thus it represents an effort to make the curriculum more relevant to the urban poor students of São Paulo while at the same time working to educate a critical and participatory citizenry.

At the same time, the generative theme perhaps represents one of the more problematic and controversial elements of the PT's curriculum reform project. In fact, from the very beginning of the administration's policy planing meetings with university specialists a fierce debate ensued and persisted throughout the experience—from the Secretariat and NAE level to the school sites—regarding the feasibility of organizing an educational program for elementary students around a single generative theme.

These concerns along with the political-pedagogic position assumed by the educators designing the PT project consequently led them to engage in a process of reevaluation of the curriculum and how it was developed. In effect,

> [t]he reevaluation of the curriculum, understood from a broad perspective, can make possible that the selection of content matter, that [ultimately] always occurs in the school, results from a conscious process in which action and reflection are combined. . . . In constructing and developing its own curriculum the school can only enrich its experience if it operates from a dialogical perspective which makes the community an object of investigation as well."[22]

Therefore, the PT-MSE elaborated the following process for identifying generative themes that maintained the integrity of their goals while also addressing some of practitioners' concerns.

As the initial step in implementing the Project, the school community, assisted by an Inter-Team (Secretariat personnel from the newly formed NAEs), engages in a *Levantamento Preliminar* (preliminary investigation) or *Estudo da Realidade* (Study of the Reality) to discern the "significant situations," i.e., social-cultural-political circumstances of the daily lives of the students which make up their "life-world."[23] The "significant situations" are culled from the fragmented individual lived experiences of the community which emphasize the individual over the collective and hence offer limited explanations or solutions for the social phenomena and problems to which they make reference. The "significant situations" are those which persistently emerge in the discourse of the community and therefore represent a collective dimension as opposed to the strictly individual experience. They may even reflect a certain degree of systematization and organization at the level of "popular knowledge," allowing for their linkage with other shared notions that may not necessarily appear at the time of the preliminary investigation. Staff at a school collects data for this Study of the Reality of a school community through a variety of methods including observations, interviews, casual conversations, and surveys.

From these "significant situations" teachers work collaboratively to derive a different generative theme each semester for the entire school to use as the basis for the formulation of an interdisciplinary curriculum. According to Delizoicov, a key university expert behind the Project, "The generative themes, once discovered will indicate pertinent academic content. This entails a new approach to the selection of culture, dictated not by the inertia of tradition but on the basis of necessity, be it of a concrete reality or an imagined one."[24] Such a foundation in the reality of the students allows for an interdisciplinary approach to the systematized universal knowledge which schools traditionally are charged with transmitting while encouraging the construction of new knowledge in the interests of the popular sectors. Hence, the generative theme is a means by which both the appropriation and construction of knowledge can occur. Each area of knowledge, in turn, contributes to the learning process with specific topics that pertain to the generative theme discovered in the community's own comprehension of its reality.

The Study of the Reality, therefore, is intended as an initial step to engaging educators and students in a process of critical reading of their world and should be part of a continual effort to "study and approximate concrete situations to the knowledge that can explain [those situations] and help to overcome them."[25]

Knowledge and the Interdisciplinary Curriculum

Central to the PT educational project is the concept of *interdisciplinaridade*, that is, taking on an interdisciplinary approach to the organization and production of knowledge. Such a guiding concept had important ramifications for the reorientation of the curriculum.

The Inter Project's innovation is precisely its coupling of the Freirean vision of collective construction of knowledge leading to transformative consciousness through dialogic exchange with the idea that the comprehension of reality is best achieved through an interdisciplinary approach to the organization of knowledge in the curriculum in the context of formal schooling of elementary children. *Interdisciplinaridade* [from which the Project's label "Inter" is derived] refers to the notion that the curriculum should not divide knowledge into separate subject areas but that all knowledge is interrelated. Specifically with regard to the Inter Project, the Secretariat's literature argued that such an interdisciplinary curriculum model was in the process of formulation and that the theoretical foundations of *Interdisciplinaridade* would evolve based on the practical experience of the schools in the Project.

The lynchpin of the proposed interdisciplinary curriculum once more was provided by Freire. His notion of the generative theme as the basis for the development of a liberating educational praxis in the context of adult literacy training was seized and refashioned for the schooling of elementary children: hence, the *interdisciplinary curriculum via the generative theme*. One of the distinctive features of the Project is that it proposes a curriculum planning process which takes the following principle as its basis: that "the various sciences should contribute to the study of certain [generative] themes that orient all of the work of the school." [26]

In this regard the PT-MSE introduced interdisciplinary curriculum via the generative theme as the mediating factor in this process of knowledge exchange. It provides a kind of unifying focus in the struggle for the educator to find a nexuses with specific areas of knowledge and an equilibrium between the general and the specific in an otherwise free-flowing dialogue. In the words of a university researcher and subject area specialist advising the Secretariat:

> The Project of *Interdisciplinaridade* does not remain merely in the "critique of the school" but presupposes changes that have to do with a broader conceptualization of teaching, the school, of education and of the relationship between the areas of science and knowledge. One of the fundamental principles of that conceptualization is that the student be led to perceive the existing links between the diverse areas or disciplines of knowledge. At the core of the Project, then, is the idea that learning is not a monolithic bloc to be distributed piecemeal to students, but is an entirety that is constructed through the continual teacher-student interaction. [27]

Such a dialogical approach to teaching, "leads to a kind of teaching that reads in the alienated discourse [of students] not a succession of errors, but a complex expression of other visions of the word with their own intricate web of values and singularities." [28] Hence, the process being set into motion is one of a continual and joyful—as Freire would have it—critical reading of the world.

In addition to Freire's contribution to the theoretical foundations of the Inter Project, the work of several other scholars such as Bachelard, Gusdorf, Piaget and Rogers [29] has been influential. Brazilian scholars such as Marcio D'Olne Campos, Demétrio Delizoicov, Ivani Fazenda, Antonio Faundez, Luis Carlos de Freitas, Hilton Japiassú and Marta Pernambuco have also played pivotal roles in the development of Brazilian literature on the interdisciplinary nature of knowledge and its relevance for curricululm planning.[30] These authors' elaboration of the concept of *Interdisciplinaridade* has served as a point of reference for the conceptualization of the PT's Inter Project. In particular, D'Olne Campos and Pernambuco worked directly with the Secretariat as advisors to the Project in the formulation and publication of texts dealing with the theory and methods of "*Interdisciplinaridade* by means of the Generative Theme" and as instructors in seminars and workshops to introduce these complex theoretical concepts to teachers working in the municipal schools of São Paulo.

According to Project coordinators, the interdisciplinary approach signifies "an inversion of the whole mechanical process of inculcation of compartmentalized content. It presupposes a new epistemological organization of knowledge, collectively and historically constructed and reconstructed, never closed or finished."[31] The intention is to generate a curriculum that moves beyond an encyclopedic approach to the organization of knowledge as generic and discrete, divorced from human social formations, history and culture, to one that facilitates the interdisciplinary interpretation of reality in a way that more adequately addresses the "social-natural complex," working toward what Faundez conceives as the "substitution of a fragmented Science for a unified Science."[32] This constant striving to overcome the contradictions among the distinct areas of knowledge allows for the evolution of a macro vision of men and women in the world and ultimately points to an interdisciplinary ontological comprehension of men and women's being and acting in the world.[33] A main theoretical undercurrent to this interdisciplinary approach is the idea of a new curriculum paradigm that incorporates critical theory in the development of a "critical science of the curriculum."[34]

This interdisciplinary approach to curriculum building differs markedly from the standard interdisciplinary notion of simply minimizing the rigid boundaries between the disciplines; instead, it speaks from critical perspective to the way knowledge is produced in society and how this process can contribute to either merely reproducing relations of power or to the creation of new knowledge and to the transformation of society. In this way, although the Project attempted to move teachers away from the traditional practice of isolating the disciplines, it did respect the specificity of each area of knowledge. Hence, from a critical perspective, the different knowledge areas serve as reference points in a continual and collaborative process of investigation around a particular theme of social-historical relevance. Each subject area specialist, therefore, has an important role in contributing to the curriculum planning process and to the provision of a "multifaceted" view of the totality of reality.[35]

Accordingly, the literature disseminated to educators in the municipal school system by the Secretariat explicitly rejected the static notion of knowledge. Such a notion is embodied in what Freire has identified as the "banking" method in which knowledge is conceived as a defined object of linear transmission from educator to learner.[36] Instead, the Secretariat advanced the concept of knowledge as "not a simple copy or description of a static reality" but as continually evolving out of the historical context of social life of both the educator and educatee. Education therefore is "a dynamic and permanent act of knowledge centered in the discovery, analysis and transformation of reality by those that live it."[37]

Beyond these broad principles, the Secretariat never pretended to offer a definitive approach to the design of an interdisciplinary curriculum. They preferred to view the Project as being in perpetual state of evolution and sought to gradually fine tune the model based on the educational activity of the schools experimenting with the Inter Project and the ongoing theoretical work of Secretariat Personnel (e.g., subject area specialists informed by the theorists and literature mentioned above). As a product of this ongoing effort, a series of pamphlets entitled "*Visão da área* " (subject area perspective, i.e., Mathematics, History, Geography, Portuguese Language, Physical Education, Science and the Arts) were published in January of 1992 . These publications included a brief history of the discipline in the context of Brazilian education and guidelines for teachers on how to integrate the specific content of each area of knowledge into the interdisciplinary curriculum. Theoretical mimeographed texts by the aforementioned authors (especially by Marta Pernambuco) and the "*Visão da área*" pamphlets and other Secretariat produced literature served as the materials studied by teachers in what were called *Grupos de Formação* (Formation Groups) or Professional Development Groups (discussed in subsequent sections).

Dialogue as Pedagogy

In a widely distributed publication, the Secretariat openly challenged teachers to "acts of boldness: to work in a project of an interdisciplinary nature that presupposes a physical and intellectual disposition to read, research, listen, hear, discuss, teach and learn; and that also supposes a disposition for dialogue; and that does not hide criticisms, self critiques, tensions, conflicts, but that seeks to continually deal with them."[38] Dialogue, hence, appears as a primary feature of the reform effort.

By establishing this dialogical approach to teaching, the PT-MSE indicated its preference for active as opposed to passive learning, as is exemplified in the Freirean concept of education for critical consciousness. Indeed, the dialogical method of educational practice, developed fully within the theoretical body of Freire's work and the history of experiences in Freirean approaches to literacy training throughout the world, was a corner stone of the São Paulo experience. In this regard, the principal policy makers firmly promoted the idea that dialogical relations should become the modus operandi of the municipal school system from the Secretariat to the classroom. At the administrative level dialogue was seen as the means to develop more democratic relations between the educational actors involved and as the methodology for engaging administrators, teachers, students and community in a collective process of knowledge exchange and knowledge construction.

In the classroom, "[t]he establishment of *dialogicidade* (or a dialogic nature) within the relations between students and teachers can permit the establishment of connections and axes between the new knowledge that is intended to be learned and that which the educatee brings in as his own baggage." Hence, within the Freirean model which reforming schools adapt, the student is conceived as a subject as opposed to an object (mere recipient) in the process of knowing, and the curriculum organized in such a way as to avoid the false dichotomy between theory and practice and the fragmentation of knowledge into artificially discrete disciplines. Methodologically, then, teachers would use the pedagogical strategies of dialogical teacher/student interaction and cooperative learning among students. This represents a particularly complex approach to education given the density and social-cultural-political diversity of the São Paulo's metropolitan milieu.

The act of engaging in dialogue is defined as "navigating through the sea of sufficient similarities so as to establish a communication of the sufficient differences, in an effort to avoid repeating one another in a dialogue that turns into a monologue."[39] Dialogue as pedagogy—from this perspective—requires a predisposition on the part of the educator to relinquish his/her status as the sole bearer of knowledge and to recognize the validity of the positions and perceptions of the other subjects involved in a given educational context. The educator's job, therefore, is to secure an interactive space for competing discourses in the classroom to emerge and evolve. Ira Shor aptly describes the practical features of a dialogic pedagogy from a Freirean perspective:

> Dialogue is simultaneously structured and creative. It is initiated and directed by a critical teacher but is democratically open to student intervention. Co-developed by the teacher and the students, dialogue is neither a freewheeling conversation nor a teacher dominated exchange. Balancing the teacher's authority and the students' input is the key to making the

process both critical and democratic. Dialogic teachers offer students an
open structure in which to develop. This openness includes their right to
question the content and the process of dialogue, and even to reject them.[40]

Consequently, this meant fundamentally changing the traditionally
hierarchical teacher/student relation. Yet it also had a specific pedagogic
purpose related to the Inter Project's emphasis on the social construction
of knowledge and the desired intersection of the universe of systematized
knowledge and the realm of popular knowledge. As shall be elaborated in
subsequent sections, the Project also offered continual opportunities for
educators themselves to constantly exchange their experiences in the classroom through dialogue amongst themselves and therefore learn from each
other as well (i.e., *grupos de formação*, workshops, conferences).[41] In effect,
"dialogical negotiation," was the principal means to both planning and
implementing an interdisciplinary curriculum via the generative theme.

Constructivism with a Freirean Twist

Beyond the Freirean elements outlined above, many of the pedagogical tenets advanced by the Secretariat were based on the constructivist theories of cognitive development of Ferreiro and Vygotsky, which view the
acquisition of language and knowledge in general as mediated by social
and affective factors.[42] Emilia Ferreiro, in particular is widely read among
Brazilian educators and is known for her indictment of traditional mechanistic approaches to teaching children literacy which disregard the notions
of language that they bring with them when they initiate their schooling.
Her fundamental contention is that children, in their acquisition of literacy
skills, undergo a process of cognitive development (according to Piaget's
theories) that follows a similar path to the anthropological and historical
process of the construction of written language: this process begins with
the child's very first experiences with oral and written language. For
Ferreiro, the fallacy of most approaches to teaching is the presupposition
that children only learn when taught, hence the systematic effort to control
that learning process based on a second erroneous assumption: learning is
determined by the teaching methods imposed.[43] Consequently, Ferreiro
argues for an epistemological reflection on the psycho-pedagogic foundations of our educational practices. Such a reflection necessarily takes for
granted the idea that no pedagogy is neutral, all are founded on a precon-
ceived notions of knowledge and the processes by which learners acquire
knowledge. She establishes the need to search for creative and flexible approaches to literacy teaching, while allowing for the child's own innate

needs and instinctual discoveries to manifest themselves and guide our pedagogical actions.

From the point of view of adult literacy training, Paulo Freire explains the compatibility of his own thinking with that of Ferreiro as follows:

> If before adult literacy training was treated and carried out in an authoritarian manner, centralized in the magical comprehension of the word, a word donated by the educator to the illiterates; if before the texts generally offered for reading to students covered up much more than they revealed about reality, now, on the contrary, literacy learning as an act of knowing, as a creative act and as a political act, is an effort to read the world and the word.[44]

Speaking to a group of literacy workers, in 1989, Secretary of Education, Paulo Freire reflected upon his experience in adult literacy work and emphasized the political nature of his proposal as opposed to a strictly technical, linguistic adoption of his methodology. As such, he argued for the development of new insights into the literacy process, to assist in the passage from the theoretical to the practical and to overcome the limitations of experience. He asserted, "The keys to the most recent investigations, are precisely the keys to the dominion of science so that we can facilitate the learning of the reading of the word, in the sense that we approximate ourselves with *o povo* [the people], with greater rigor in our comprehension of the world that must be." Further establishing the link between his own political philosophy of education and Ferreiro's constructivist theories of cognitive development and literacy acquisition, Freire insisted that the work of Emilia Ferreiro be considered as one of the keys to a new comprehension of knowledge.

Similarly, the educators behind the Inter Project in the schools understood knowledge as collectively constructed, they believed that teachers should not be isolated in their classrooms but should work collaboratively across the disciplines to create an interdisciplinary curriculum. Working collectively teachers can find ways to link thematically the content from the different areas of knowledge to the social-cultural reality of the students. This approach to curriculum planning eschewed the use of single subject text books and teacher proof lesson plans in favor of a more creative process, albeit more uncertain one, in which teachers continually conduct research using new and varied sources of knowledge, bringing information into the classroom and structuring learning activities so that students also have opportunities to contribute their own knowledge sources.[45] Marta Pernambuco illuminates the Freirean influence on this approach to curriculum planning and student learning when she writes:

Paulo Freire, in demonstrating that the student is an educatee that together with the educator recaptures in the classroom the process of production of knowledge, points us to dialogue as the most excellent of instruments by which that knowledge is produced. Initiated always from the universe of the student, from what for him is significant, from his manner of thinking, from the knowledge that he brings from his social group, it is in the school's capacity to make possible his overcoming that initial vision, giving him access to new forms of thinking which constitute the basis of systematized contemporary knowledge.[46]

The Inter Project—following constructivist learning theories advanced by Piaget and Vygotsky and as they have been more recently applied to the understanding of literacy acquisition of poor children in Latin America by Emilia Ferreiro—operated on the premise that children learn best by engaging in cooperative group activity guided by an adult educator charged with mediating the dialogic negotiation between the cognitive structure and socially acquired knowledge of the student and the accumulated historical, scientific and artistic knowledge that is organized into the different disciplines.[47] Consequently, knowledge was not an object to be intellectually attained by individual students in varying degrees of accuracy, but instead conceived as being in a process of continual construction throughout the various stages of the learning process.

Within the Inter Project, however, this process was construed as a very structured one: beginning with the initial phase of the problematization of reality; followed by the organization of the knowledge registered in the initial stage through reference to specific content areas; and finally the knowledge is synthesized in the application of knowledge phase with the realization of concrete activities aimed to demonstrate student comprehension of specific content and construction of new knowledge. These pedagogical concepts form the theoretical foundation of the Inter Project. They are explained in detail and illustrated with concrete examples of curriculum programs and dialogic classroom practice in the two chapters that follow.

Teacher Training for the Transformation of the Curriculum: The Role of the *Grupos de Formação* and the Pedagogic Workshops

In order to work towards its ambitious goals, the PT-MSE developed an elaborate and intensive implementation process that focused keenly on reorienting teachers' attitudes and behaviors and developing new pedagogy and understanding. This process focused on six key elements. The first element involved a week long series of introductory seminars held either at the University of São Paulo in conjunction with the Directorate of Technical Orientation (DOT) staff and university professors (from University of São Paulo, University of Campinas, and the Pontifical Catholic University of São Paulo) or at the Nuclei of Educational Action (NAE) facilitated by DOT and NAE staff. The second element concentrated on the creation of *Grupos de Formação* (Formation Groups) or Professional Development Groups which offered regular opportunities for dialogue, exchange, and reading for teachers through the provision of ten paid hours of meeting time per week at schools. In addition, periodic meetings by grade levels and subject areas for teachers in the same region as well as an annual week-long district-wide conference were organized. The third element utilized challenging theoretical texts with which to orient reflection and discussions (including two series published by the DOT: Stories from the Field and Formation Notebooks). The fourth element centered on regular technical assistance and coaching from NAE staff (two NAE staff were assigned to each school and each NAE also had specialists in the different subject areas). The fifth element offered regular opportunities for professional development courses (including workshops dealing with using media, journal articles and literature to develop classroom reading materials, the use of Socratic questioning, the contributions of Afro-Brazilians, Sexuality in the Classroom, etc.). The sixth and final element focused on a curriculum development process (i.e., the Interdisciplinary Project) which was supported by the previous five elements.

The six components of the PT-MSE's professional development plan coordinated nicely to provide a learning process that emphasized reflection on what was known (teacher's own classroom practice and their students' realities), the use of theory to expand upon what was known, and distinct opportunities (organization and application of knowledge) to experiment in the transformation of these realities. Furthermore, each of these activities occurred through collective efforts, where teachers forged new partnerships with each other and other stakeholders in the school community (e.g., students, parents, administration).

In actuality, the main focus of the teachers' efforts was on the Interdisciplinary Project and the primary vehicle for this Project were the *Grupos de Formação* or Professional Development Groups. These groups, organized around a series of facilitated meetings, gave teachers opportunities to reflect upon their pedagogic practice, explore educational theories and develop their professional skills in a collective and permanent process. In a document summarizing the state of public education upon the 1989 election victory, the PT argued although ". . . all teachers do theory and practice," education remained a profession in which teachers ". . . walked a solitary road, resulting in a practice which had crystallized and was never modified, whose theory was neither made explicit nor questioned."[48] Thus, the Professional Development Groups constituted an important mechanism for addressing this situation.

In a document entitled *Em Formação* (In Formation), organized and published under the initiative of teachers of the Professional Development Groups associated with NAE-6, the purpose of these groups is given further definition:

> The existing power structure in schooling ends up expropriating knowledge from the educator, changing [her] into a mere executor of programs and activities. The space [created in schools by the *grupos de formação*] constitutes a political-pedagogic space in as much as the act of distancing oneself from the alienating daily reality of the school is fundamental for reflecting upon that practice, allowing [teachers] to return to that reality with *bons olhos* [fresh eyes].[49]

The establishment of these groups was given genuine weight and importance as teachers were compensated for 10 hours worth of group meetings per week. The PT-MSE viewed this time as providing educators with:

> . . . a necessary space for reflection on their practice and knowledge . . . and moments for exchange that validate the social, affective and cognitive being. . . . The basic link for this construction is the routine, but a lively rather than static routine. . . . Observation, recording, reflection, synthesis, evaluation, and planning are the methodological instruments to be utilized in these Professional Development Groups.[50]

This weekly allocation of professional development hours was designed to provide teachers with an opportunity to engage in the several different types of activities. Briefly, these activities included: (1) operationalization of Project phases (i.e., collect or analyze data from the Study of the Reality, develop generative theme, design application of knowledge exercises, etc.); (2) reading and discussion of theoretical texts supplied by the PT-MSE and other materials found in journals, libraries, etc.; (3) discussion of classroom practice and its relation to the theoretical questions posed in texts; and (4) independent research by teachers into areas of interest at their school. The Secretariat was successful in instituting this professional development system on a wide scale. By 1991, 294 schools organized their own Professional Development Groups involving 4,000 teachers. Also 68 percent school principals and 94 percent of the Pedagogic Coordinators in the municipal school system were involved in Professional Development Groups under the co-ordination of the NAEs.

In addition to the ongoing teacher training through Professional Development Groups and the allocation of remunerated professional development hours, the CONAE organized workshops on numerous topics aimed at advancing the Secretariat's goal of transforming the educational methods and curriculum of the schools. This was also a way to tap the knowledge resources both within and outside the municipal system (i.e., university experts). Besides university professors, Secretariat personnel and School administrators, or teachers themselves could organize and lead workshops. Workshops were advertised in the *Diario Oficial Municipal* (the municipal government's daily bulletin) so teachers could register in advance to participate in them. They took place at school sites or at the NAE offices and lasted anywhere from one to several days. In some cases, these courses and presentations occurred during school hours and teachers could request release time to attend them. The range of offerings available to teachers included:

- Lectures by noted educators such as Ivani Fazenda and Emilia Ferreiro (whose works were typically read in Professional Development Groups);
- Regional and district wide conferences that offered opportunities to present and share work being done in schools by grade level and subject area;
- Opportunities to take students on field trips and outings to regional parks, ecological reserves, and plays and musicals.
- Workshops introducing the use of various technologies for instructional purposes such as video tapes (e.g., of movies), video taping (e.g., video production), computers and theater;
- Workshops by NAE/DOT staff addressing issues connected to the Inter Project such as how to use media, journal articles, and other resources to develop classroom readers, using student's errors as learning tools, and using Socratic questioning and reflection as pedagogic strategies;
- Workshops dealing with topical issues such as Sexual Orientation and Working with Sexuality in the Classroom, Contributions of African Brazilians, and Human Rights Education.

Hence, workshop topics ranged from dealing with highly charged social issues to offering practical pedagogic orientation. For example, the objectives in the workshop "Slavery, Segregation, Discrimination and Prejudice" lead by a Pedagogic Coordinator and teacher from NAE-9, were to

(1) demystify the traditional vision of slavery and abolition; (2) review the history of race related institutions and laws; (3) demonstrate the different forms of racial violence that exist in the world, comparing Brazil, the United States, and South Africa. At one of the workshop's four sessions, entitled "Looking is not always seeing," teachers learn "how to use illustrations in didactic books as material rich in content" to be applied to the discussion of race relations in the class room.[51] On the other hand, a workshop entitled "Games and the Teaching of Physics" organized by NAE-6 and led a by a professor involved in Physics Education Project at the University of São Paulo aimed to "(1) provide teachers with didactic-pedagogic resources for the teaching of Physics in a fun manner; (2) give teachers the opportunity to construct creative didactic material, preferably at low cost, to facilitate the concrete and accurate learning of physics at the preschool and elementary school level."[52]

Evidence in the literature suggests that the policy development process must draw on teachers' knowledge and provide a comprehensive learning environment to allow practitioners to make the personal and professional changes necessary for policy implementation. At the same time, we know that introducing such new dynamics and procedures into organizations and institutions is highly problematic for myriad reasons including their bureaucratic nature, inappropriate site conditions, insufficient resources, and the necessity of a comprehensive learning process to support changes in practice and procedure.

The PT-MSE attempted to address many of these challenges by creating the conditions by which teachers could engage in a meaningful learning process that also overlapped with policy implementation. Through the very elements of curriculum development and other activities such as the Professional Development Groups, the MSE designed a learning process for educators that clearly focused on their professional lives and enhancing their understandings of and actions in it. Professional learning was completely situated within the context of the classroom and school site, and resources were devoted to providing the opportunity to create a community of learners, experts, and apprentices (e.g., 10 paid hours of meeting time and regular assistance from NAE mentors). Reflection and discussion formed the foundation of this learning process and each activity was situated so as to become a regular and consistent part of the teachers' professional reality. The main purpose of this learning process was for educators to reflect, understand, and reshape their theoretical and practical professional foundations in an effort to enable them to engage with their students in a collaborative effort to develop new knowledge and identify avenues for transforming real life situations.

Several observations can be made about this learning process for teach-ers. First, it focused on the teachers' professional lives and conditions. The core of the Inter Project was not centered on raising test scores, increasing high school graduation rates, or improving college placement. The essence of the Project was the students' learning process and the collaborative con-struction of knowledge among students and teachers. The ER that the teach-ers conducted constituted an essential component because it allowed teach-ers to see and analyze critically the diverse situations that shaped the the-matic map for their professional universe.

Second, although the reflections were often personal and originating from an individual perspective, this activity occurred in a group. Through the sharing and discussion of these reflections on practice with other col-leagues came an eventual collective understanding of a particular phenom-enon or situation. This intersubjectivity resulted in individual transforma-tion as well as mutual familiarity and the construction of a collective knowl-edge base among peers. Third, this reflection and problematization of the teachers' realities was informed by a critical reading and interpretation of the theoretical foundations of educational practice. The reading of theo-retical works by such authors as Vygotsky, Dewey, and Piaget offered the framework for reflection, dialogue, and the reconstruction of knowledge and understanding of both theory and practice. Finally, these activities oc-curred in an environment in which technical assistance was available through NAE mentors and teachers received material support (e.g., publi-cations, compensation, enrichment courses, etc.). Taken together, these el-ements provided an environment conducive to the type of deep and pro-found un-learning and re-learning that was necessary for most teachers to implement the radical educational agenda promoted by the PT-MSE.

Additional Initiatives

In the space of what was effectively three years (PT-MSE inauguration occurred in 1989, elections were held again in November 1992), the PT-MSE attempted to transform the municipal school system in a bold and fundamental way. As described in detail above, the major initiative was the Inter Project, which involved additional related components including Teacher Professional Development Groups, the reorganization of regional administrative units into NAEs, and the empowerment of School Coun-cils. Planning for the PT administration had occurred well before its inau-guration in 1989 and within one year, the PT-MSE was ready to initiate 10 pilot schools into the Inter Project. NAE staff worked exclusively with these 10 pilot schools during the 1990-91 academic year and then, in 1991-92 the

Project was opened up to an additional 100 interested schools. This policy decision represented a gamble and a trade off: rather than firmly institutionalize the Inter Project in 10 schools, the PT-MSE chose to expand the Project, opting, in a way for breadth rather than depth.

During the 1992-93 academic year, two additional policies—the institution of the *ciclos* or cycles and the creation of the *Jornada Tempo Integral* (JTI) or the integrated daily meeting time—were enacted by the PT-MSE and had serious implications for its curriculum reform project. Instead of the primary schooling being comprised of a continual series of eighth grade levels the eight years were divided into three cycles: the first three year cycle was comprised of what were formally the first, second and third grades; the second three year cycle corresponded to the former fourth, fifth and sixth grades and the last two year cycle included the seventh and eighth grades of the former *seriação*. The rationale behind the *ciclos* was to transform the criteria for evaluating student progress and thus avoid unnecessary repetition of grades and ultimately address the problem of high drop out rates at the upper grade levels of elementary schooling. Children were no longer to be graded every trimester on a 10-point scale. A less strict semester grading system was put in place that served to provide a general sense of how students were progressing in their school work. Teachers had only three grading options *P (plenamente satisfatório)* (completely satisfactory); *S* (satisfactory) and *NS* (not satisfactory). As a result, students within a cycle were automatically considered eligible for promotion to the next grade level and could only be held back the last year of a cycle if they were considered by a evaluation team as too ill prepared to advance forward. This "automatic promotion" was the source of much dispute and discontent among the municipal school teachers. Many were uneasy about promoting students who they felt were not ready to move on to the next level. Moreover the consensus among those opposed to the *ciclos* was that students lost motivation to apply themselves in their work since they knew that they would automatically pass to the next grade level at the end of the school year. Consequently, a year following the PT's tenure the new Secretariat (under the *Partido Democratico Social,* the so-called Social Democratic Party) conducted a referendum which resulted in the municipal schools reverting back to the old system of *seriação,* or organization by grade level.

The JTI or integrated daily meeting time was a professional development opportunity made available to all certificated teachers in the last year of the PT's administration. This initiative created a secured space for the teachers at a school to engage in and be compensated for 10 hours of meeting time per week. The primary purpose of such dedicated time was to encourage exchange and collaboration among the school staff around key instructional and curricular ideas. Though an excellent idea in the abstract, the JTI disrupted many schools' efforts related to the Inter Project. In some of the less committed schools, the JTI served as a disincentive to participating in the Inter Project. Unfortunately, there were some school staffs that opted to engage in the Project in part because of the additional resources that accompanied it, mainly increased technical support and paid meeting times. Once the JTI became ubiquitous for certificated teachers, these schools had less of a reason to follow down the often-challenging path of curricular transformation. On the other hand, many schools that enthusiastically embraced the Inter Project also saw the JTI as a roadblock to their efforts at curricular transformation. In particular, many of these schools had teachers on staff that were not certificated but had been actively involved in the implementation of the Inter Project from its outset. Because the JTI was limited to certificated teachers only, these teachers, though active Project participants, basically faced a choice of continuing on in the Project on a volunteer basis or giving up Project participation (for many, this became essentially a financial decision where taking on additional classes was necessary to make up for the additional income that was previously furnished by extra meeting time). Several school staffs pointed to the JTI as fundamentally changing the dynamic of the Project at their school.

Summary

Paulo Freire's appointment as Municipal Secretary of Education in São Paulo was greeted with skepticism by many. How could his literacy ideas, developed over 25 years earlier with pre-literate adults in non-formal education settings, be applied in the Information Age to a formal elementary educational system that included almost one million students? In this chapter the metamorphosis of Freire's ideas has been detailed, demonstrating that while significant new ideas have been added, the core of Freire's education for liberation has remained solidly intact. The Movement for Curricular Reorientation, primarily through the Inter Project, constitutes the primary focus for the creation of the PT's Popular Public School. This school has all of the elements so celebrated in Freire's work: the dual role of student and teacher as subjects and objects in their learning and subsequent reading of the world; the necessary democratization of student/teacher relations; the dialectic interaction between popular, lived knowledge and universal, systematized knowledge in service of critical consciousness; the orientation of curriculum content around the realities of the school community; and, the construction of an educational project that fully embraces its political nature.

Equally important, this school is constructed on a comprehensive transformation of the role of teaching and learning, recreating it as a fundamental element in community movements for quality education. In addition, this nascent movement benefits from a sophisticated and complex network of administrative and technical assistance. Moreover, such assistance duplicates the democratic and political principles evident in the Popular Public School. With the democratization of policy and decision-making at all levels of the municipal bureaucracy—from the School Councils, to the NAEs, to the Secretariat—the political and liberatory agenda of the classroom reforms is mirrored by similar efforts in other important aspects of the system. As a result, there is coherence on all levels.

Notes

1. Translation: I came to *re* learn Brazil, and as long as I am in the process of *re*learning, *re*knowing Brazil, I do not have much to say. I have more to ask." Moacir Gadotti, Paulo Freire, Sérgio Guimarãoes, *Pedagogia: Diálogo e Conflito* (São Paulo: Cortez: Autores Associados, 1989), p. 15.

2. In 1989, approximately one million pre-school and primary school age children could not enroll in schools due to limited school capacities (Paulo Freire, *Pedagogy of the City* (New York: Continuum, 1993), p. 151.

3. Secretaria Municipal de Educação, *Cadernos de Formação: Um primeiro olhar sobre o projeto* (São Paulo: Secretaria Municipal de Educação, May - June 1990).

4. The organizational structure of primary schools in São Paulo includes the school director (a mostly administrative position), two pedagogic coordinators (who work directly with teachers), teachers, and support staff (secretaries, cooks, maintenance staff).

5. For more information on the PT-MSE's policy efforts in adult literacy training, see Pilar O'Cadiz, "Social Movements and Literacy Training in Brazil: A Narrative," in *Education and Social Change in Latin America*. Carlos Alberto Torres (ed.) (Albert Park, Australia: James Nicholas, 1995); Stromquist, Nelly; 1996, *Literacy for Citizenship Gender and Grassroots Dynamics in Brazil* (Albany, NY: SUNY Press); Carlos Alberto Torres, "Paulo Freire as Secretary of Education in the Municipality of São Paulo," *Comparative Education Review*, vol. 38, no. 2, May 1994.

6. This information has been synthesized from PT-MSE, *Construindo a Educação Publica Popular: Caderno 22 Meses* (São Paulo: Secretaria Municipal de Educação, 1990).

7. PT-MSE, *Diretriezes e Prioridades para 1991*, p. 13-14.

8. Interview with Moacir Gadotti, PT-MSE Cabinet Chief (July 1989).

9. PT-MSE, *Diretrizes e Prioridades para 1992, 1ª Série—Construindo A Educação Pública Popular*, Vol. 4, January 1992, p. 10.

10. Ibid.

11. After 1992, the new PDS administration abolished the NAEs and reinstituted the DREMs.

12.Francisco Weffort, "Escola Participação e representação Formal," *Paixão de Aprender*, June 1994.

13. PT-MSE, *Diretrizes e Prioridades para 1991. 1º Série—Construindo a Educação Pública e Popular*, Vol. 3, February 1991, p. 12.

14. Ibid.

15. PT-MSE, *Aceita um Conselho?*, April 1990.

16. Carlos Alberto Torres, "Paulo Freire as Secretary of Education in the Municipality of São Paulo," *Comparative Education Review*, Vol. 38, No. 2 (May 1994), p. 202.

17. Demétrio Delizoicov and João Zanetic, "A proposta de interdisciplinaridade e o seu impacto no ensino municipal de 1º grau" in Pontuschka, org., p. 14.

18. Secretaria Municipal de Educação, *Professional Development Notebooks No. 3* (São Paulo: Secretaria Municipal de Educação, 1991), p. 2.

19. Maria Selma de Morães Rocha.

20. Secretaria Municipal de Educação, *Cadernos de Formação: Grupos de Formação. Uma (Re)Visão da Educação do Educador* (São Paulo: Secretaria Municipal de Educação, 1991), p. 9.

21. Giroux points out that "educational relevance" for "critical literacy" must be distinguished from the traditional liberal pedagogic view of curricular relevance which "makes an appeal to a pedagogy responsive to the individual interests of the student in order to motivate him or her." According to Giroux, from the perspective of critical pedagogy, a more socio-political and economic connotation is given to the concept of *relevance* of the curriculum. He explains that unlike the liberal conceptualization of relevance, "[c]ritical literacy responds to the cultural capital of a specific group or class and looks at the way in which it can be confirmed, and also at the way the dominant society disconfirms students by either ignoring or denigrating the knowledge and experiences that characterize their everyday lives." Henry Giroux "Public Education and the Discourse of Crisis, Power and Vision." In *Excellence, Reform and Equity in Education: An International Perspective* (Comparative Education Center, Faculty of Educational Studies. State University of New York at Buffalo and Ontario Institute for Studies in Education, Toronto, September, 1984), p. 106.

22. Maria Selma de Morães Rocha.

23. "By every day life world is to be understood that the province of reality which the wide-awake and normal adult simply takes for granted in the attitude of common sense. By this taken-for-grantedness, we designate everything which we experience as unquestionable; every state of affairs is for us unproblematic until further notice" (A. Shultz, 1957). "It is the unquestioned ground of everything given in my experience, and the unquestionable frame in which all the problems I have to

deal with are located" (Luhmann, 1977). Both cited in Jurgen Habermas, *The Theory of Communicative Action*, vol. 2, *Lifeworld and System: A Critique of Functionalist Reason.*Translated by Thomas McCarthy. (Boston: Beacon Press, 1987), p. 130.

24. Delizoicov and Zanetic, in Pontuschka, org., Op.Cit., p. 10.

25. PT-MSE, *Estudo Preliminar da Realidade*, Cadernos de Formação N^a 2, 3^a *Série—Ação Pedagogica da Escola pela via da interdisciplinaridade*, February 1990, p. 59.

26. Demétrio and Joao Zanetic, "A proposta da interdisciplinardade . . .," in Pontuschka (org.), p. 13.

27. Beatriz Helena Marão Citelli, "Cruzando Linguagens" in Pontuschka, org. p. 95.

28. Beatriz Helena Marão Citelli, "Cruzando Linguagens," in Pontuschka (org.) 1993, p. 100.

29. Works translated into Portuguese and cited in Secretariat literature include: Gaston Bachelard, *Epistemologia* (Rio de Janeiro: Zahar Ed., 1971). Georges Gusdorf *Les sciences de l'homme sont des sciences humaines* (Université de Strasbourg, 1967), *Professores para quê?* (Lisboa: Moraes, 1970). Jean Piaget, *Seis Estudos de Psicologia* (Rio de Janeiro: Forense-Universitária, 1964), *Psicologia e epistemologia* (Rio de Janeiro: Forense, 1971). *A epistemologia genética* (Petrópolis: Vozes, 1972), *Para onde vai a educação?*, 8th ed. (São Paulo: Jose Olympio, 1988), *Linguagem e Pensamento da Criança* (São Paulo: Martins Fontes, 1989); Carl Rogers, *Tornar-se pessoa* (Lisboa: Moraes, 1973), *De pessoa para pessoa; o problema do ser humano* (São Paulo: Pioneira, 1976). Gadotti notes "the valorization of *dialogue and interdisciplinariness* in the acquisition of knowledge" as a common denominator among Rogers, Piaget and Gusdorf. *Pensamento Pedagogico Brasileiro* (São Paulo: Atica, 1987), pp. 68-69.

30. Examples of this literature include: Demitrio Delizoicov, D. *Concepção Problematizadora para o Ensino de Ciências na Educação Formal*, Masters Thesis (São Paulo: USP 1982). Antonio Faundez, "Dialogo e Multidisciplinaridade" (mimeograph n.d.). Ivani Fazenda, *Integração e interdisciplinaridade no ensino brasileiro* (São Paulo: Loyola, 1979). Luis Carlos de Freitas, "A questão da Interdisciplinaridade: Notas para a reformulação dos cursos de Pedagogia" (mimeograph) FE/UNICAMP, 1988. Hilton Japiassú, *Interdisciplinaridade e patologia do saber* (Rio de Janeiro: Imago, 1976); *Introdução ao Pensamento Epistemológico* (Rio de Janeiro: Livraria Francisco Alves, 1986); Antonio Joaquim Severino, "Subsídios para uma Reflexão sobre novos caminhos da Interdisciplinaridade," in *Serviço Social e Interdisciplinaridade: dos Fundamentos Filosóficos á Pratica Interdisciplinar no Ensino, Pesquisa e Extensão*, org., Jeanente L. Martins (São Paulo: Cortez, 1989).

31. NAE-6, *Realidade e Conhecimento* (mimeographed text), 1990, p. 1.

32. Antonio Faundez, "Diálogo e Multidisciplinaridade," in *Seminário Nacional do Programa Integração da Universidade com o Ensino de 1ª Grau* (mimeograph), cited in Ibid., p. 2.

33. Demétrio Delizoicov and João Zanetic, Op. Cit., p. 13.

34. Maria Nelli Silva, *A Construção do Curriculo na Sala de Aula: o professor como pesquisador* (São Paulo: E.P.U., 1990), cited in PT-MSE, *Tema Gerador e a Construção do Programa: uma nova relação entre currículo e realidade,* Caderno de Formação N° 3, Series 3—*Ação Pedagógica da Escola pela via da interdisciplinaridade,* March 1991, p. 11.

35. Delizoicov and Zanetic, Op. Cit.,p. 13.

36. Paulo Freire, *Pedagogy of the Oppressed,* 26th edition. Translated by Myra Bergman Ramos (New York: Continuum, 1970), p. 62-63.

37. PT-MSE, *Estudo Preliminar da Realidade—Resgatando o Cotidiano,* Caderno de Formação N° 2, *3ª Série—Ação Pedagógica da Escola pela Via da Interdisciplinaridade,* p. 17.

38. Ibid. p. 60.

39. Marta Pernambuco,"Quando a troca se estabelece: a relação dialógica," in Pontuschka (org.), Op. Cit., p. 24.

40. Ira Shor, *Empowering Education: Critical Teaching for Social Change* (Chicago: University of Chicago Press, 1992), pp. 85-86.

41. PT-MSE, *Tema Gerador e a Construção do Programa: uma nova relação entre currículo e realidade,* Cadernos de Formação N° 3, *3ª Série Ação Pedagógica da Escola pela via da Interdisciplinaridade,* 1991, p. 30.

42. PT-MSE, *Um primeiro olhar sobre o projeto,* Cadernos de Formação Nª 1, Series 3—*Ação Pedagógica da Escola pela via da interdisciplinaridade,* February 1990, pp. 31-53. Cf. L. S. Vygotsky, *Mind in Society* (Cambridge, Massachusetts: Harvard University Press, 1978). Emilia Ferreiro, "A Representação da linguagem e o processo de Alfabetização," *Cadernos de Pesquisa,* N° 52, February, 1985, and *Reflexoes sobre Alfabetização,* Translation Horácio Gonzales (et al.) (São Paulo: Cortez: Autores Associados, 1988). Works translated into Portuguese and cited in Secretariat Literature: L. S. Vygotsky, *Pensamento e Linguagem,* 2nd ed. (São Paulo: Martins Fontes, 1989); *Formação social da Mente,* 3rd ed. (São Paulo: Martins Fontes, 1989).

43. Emilia Ferreiro, *Reflexões sobre alfabetização* (São Paulo; Cortez: Autores Associados, 1986), p. 67.

44. Paulo Freire, *A importância do ato de ler: em três artigos que se completam* (São Paulo: Cortez: Autores Associados; 1987), p. 35.

45. PT-MSE, *Em Formação,* NAE-6, 1990, pp. 11 and 30.

46. Marta Pernambuco, "Quando a troca se estabelece: a relação dialógica" in Pontuschka, Op. Cit., 1993, p. 24.

47. SM- SP, *Tema Gerador e a Construção do Programa,* March 1991, p. 30.

48. PT-MSE, *Cadernos,* 1989, p. 9.

49. PT-MSE, *Em Formação,* NAE-6, 1990, p. 11.

50. PT-MSE, *Cadernos de Formação. Uma (Revisão da Educação do Educador* (São Paulo: Secretaria Municpal de Educação, 1990), pp. 9-11.

51. *Diario Oficial Municipal,* September 17, 1992.

52. Ibid.

V

Reorienting the Curriculum: The Interdisciplinary Project

Creating a New Pedagogic Paradigm: The Interdisciplinary Curriculum Via the Generative Theme

The Interdisciplinary Project (Inter Project) both embodied the notion of the Popular Public School and operationalized the goals of democratization of school administration and improvement of educational quality. Through the introduction of this bold proposal for a new pedagogic paradigm, the PT-MSE sought to create the conditions for the generation of a movement for curriculum transformation within the municipal schools. Hence, the Inter Project signified the principal impetus of this socialist state's conceptualization of the Movement for the Reorientation of the Curriculum (MRC). To do this the PT-MSE concentrated on teachers as focal actors and key entry points for its ambitious reforms. To collaborate with teachers in a program that had such serious implications for classroom practice was clearly the only strategy to use. At the same time, it was a tremendously risky proposition. The PT-MSE's objective was to radically change this situation by bringing teachers through a process that would allow them to identify, understand, and critique the underlying theories of their profession while also changing their practice into one that was reflective and dynamic. This process was the development and implementation of the Interdisciplinary Project.

The Inter Project was not generated from the desk of an educational bureaucrat, nor was it modeled after the latest foreign pedagogical fashion. It is the fruit of the decades of intense theoretical debate that has taken as its primary line of inquiry, what and how do we teach the poor, the children of the illiterate, the disenfranchised and the least empowered in a society of harsh inequities and virtually insurmountable obstacles to social mobility through education. This theoretical debate, evolving out of various pedagogical, sociological, and anthropological theories originating both within and outside of Brazil,[1] reached an important point of evolution within this particular context of the municipal schools of São Paulo during the Workers' Party tenure (1989-1992). Specifically, the project for an *interdisciplinary curriculum via the generative theme* sought to establish a dialectic relationship between the common sense notions of the community and the universe of systematized knowledge, and therefore signified a direct strategy for achieving one of the PT's more politicized pedagogic goals: that the school become a space for the validation and re-creation of popular knowledge and for the appropriation and production of new knowledge geared toward the critical formation of students from the perspective of the critical comprehension and transformation of social reality.[2]

Within the Inter Project, therefore, Freire's proposal for the problematization of knowledge took precedence over the notion of knowledge as finite and crystallized. His administration's ambitious project sought to radically modify traditional conceptualizations of knowledge and to involve the educator in the rethinking of curriculum practice. Four principles guiding this effort are identified as follows:

1. collective construction through a broad participatory process in the decisions and actions regarding the curriculum;
2. respect for the principle of autonomy of the school through the salvaging of valid practices and localized experiences;
3. valorization of the unity of theory-practice, that translates into a constant action-reflection-action on the part of educators and educatees and other individuals involved in the educational process and the daily life of schools; and
4. permanent formation of educators, on the basis of an ongoing critical analysis of the curriculum in action at the school.[3]

A key part of this reconceptualization of the foundations of curriculum construction proposed through the Inter Project was the consideration of "reality as the central factor in the construction of a program and the selection of content [in addition to the idea that] knowledge be sought as an element of comprehension of that same reality."[4] Whereas it is often the content of the text books or the specific subjects teachers feel most prepared to teach that ultimately determine curriculum content, with the Inter Project, teachers were required to undergo a more complex analytical process in deciding what content they were to teach. This process was inextricably linked to the Freirean notion of reflective praxis, with the determination of the generative theme and the subsequent steps to be taken in the organization of the program becoming a continual and systematic endeavor—one of reflective pedagogical praxis—on the part of the collective of the school's teaching staff. In effect, the work of curriculum construction was to become a part of their daily life as teachers.

As a result, the curriculum no longer represented frozen bits of knowledge to be delivered piecemeal and memorized by students according to a static plan of pedagogic action: the curriculum was to become more dynamic, continually evolving, subject to re-evaluation and revision. Rooted in the rich soil of the students' culture, the generative theme served as the trunk of the tree of knowledge which grew out of this process of curriculum construction, cultivated with the initial investigation into the reality of the community, its branches extending into the different areas of knowledge searching out the necessary connections to better comprehend that reality from which they parted. Yet this was not a haphazard occurrence; the proposal for curriculum construction under the Inter Project followed specific methodological steps to guide the process.

The Inter Project provided a four-phased framework for the interdisciplinary and democratic development of curriculum via the generative theme. The first phase involved the engagement of school staff in a deliberate and informed process through which they considered participation in the Interdisciplinary Project. An affirmative decision then required the submission of a proposal detailing the work they expected to do as participants in the Project. The second phase involved the *Estudo da Realidade* or Study of the Reality (ER), a product of which was the school's generative theme. In the third phase, teachers organized the content and methods of their various disciplines around the generative theme; this was called the *Organização do Conhecimento* or Organization of Knowledge (OC). In the fourth phase, teachers designed exercises, activities, and projects through which students applied their knowledge—known as the *Aplicação do Conhecimento* or Application/Assessment of Knowledge (AC). Once the initial phase was concluded—basically consisting of the school's collective process of electing to participate in the Project—the construction of the school's instructional program followed a process structured by the subsequent three essential pedagogic moments: ER; OC; AC. The curriculum planning process and specific instructional activities that evolved from such a methodological approach are described in more detail below.

The Methodological Moments in
the Process of Curriculum Construction

These three methodological moments—ER; OC; AC—permeated all pedagogical instances of the Inter Project. In other words, these moments not only signified the manner in which teachers were trained to carry out their curriculum construction efforts but also offered guidelines for instructional practice, and furthermore, constituted the framework for conducting the analysis of any given situation or topic in a variety of contexts (e.g., in the analysis of texts in teacher formation meetings, in the orientation of discussions at school council meetings, and even in structuring the evaluation of the Project by school personnel in staff meetings). But most importantly, these moments marked the steps taken in the implementation of an interdisciplinary curriculum project on both the broad level of general curriculum development and the specific context of classroom activity. In this regard the methodological moments can be considered an overarching characterization of the Secretariat's intervention in the way schools functioned and the manner in which teachers thought and acted, and students learned.

Pernambuco specifies the importance of this fundamental framework for the practice of an interdisciplinary curriculum via the generative theme: "The *pedagogical moments* are a means of organization used to guarantee a systematic practice of dialogue."[5] Again, dialogue is pointed out as a key feature of the Inter Project, highlighting the Project's promotion of a reflective curriculum praxis.

The implementation of the pedagogic moments as a curriculum planning and teaching methodology varied from NAE to NAE and from each school site depending on the different interpretations and applications made of the general Project guidelines that emanated from the Secretariat's central Directorate of Technical Orientation (DOT). These guidelines oriented but did not completely direct the work of the Nuclei of Educational Action and the educators involved in the initial development of the Project at the ten different pilot sites. Effectively, the Inter Teams at each NAE were granted a fair amount of autonomy in devising strategies and approaches to the Project's dissemination to the schools within their respective regions. Table 5.1 illustrates each of these three phases, while Figure 5.1 outlines the process of program construction [specifically as it was elaborated by the Inter Team of NAE-6, where most of our research was carried out]. We now examine more closely the processes that evolve at each moment, the required conditions and the outcomes sought with this methodological approach.

TABLE 5.1 Phases in the Interdisciplinary Project

Study of the Reality	Organization of Knowledge	Application of Knowledge
Problematization	Selection of content areas	Implementation of the program that has been organized
Discussion and stories of the students, educators, and community	Reality and systematized knowledge	Evaluation and planning for the transformation of the student, educator, and community
Visits	Educator's approach and attitudes	Knowledge: action, appropriation and (re)construction
Interviews	Cognitive and affective requirements	Tools: natural and built environments, games, magazines, books, etc.
Questionnaires	Notions	
Significant situations	Concepts	
Thematic Design	Hypotheses	
	Presuppositions	
	Theories	

Source: Nucleo de Ação Educativa 5, São Paulo Municipal Schools, 1992.

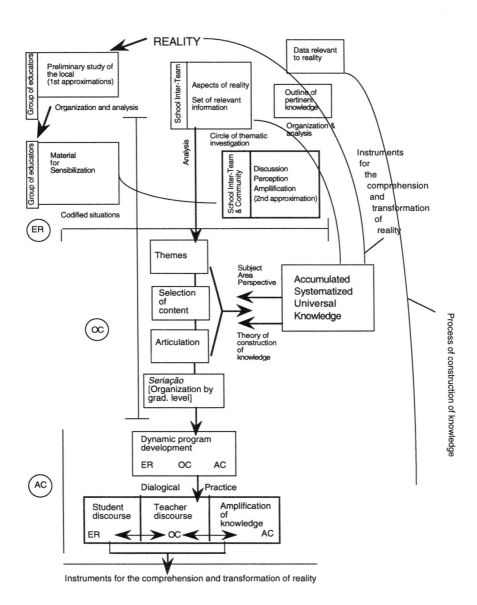

FIGURE 5.1 The Process of Curriculum Construction. *Notes:* Elaborated by the multidisciplinary team of NAE-2 based on interpretations of Chapter 3 of Paulo Freire's *Pedagogy of the Oppressed;* excerpts of the master's thesis of Demétrio Delizoicov; and material produced by Delizoicov with Martha Pernambuco; modifications realized by the multidisciplinary team of NAE-6.

Study of the Reality : The First Phase of Curriculum Development (*Estudo da Realidade, ER*)

Once a school opts into the Project, the first phase of curriculum development requires that the school community, assisted by an Inter Team (Secretariat personnel from the newly formed NAEs), engage in a preliminary investigation of its reality (the initial ER or *Levantamento Preliminar*) to discern what are the "significant situations" or social-cultural-political circumstances of the daily lives of the students which make up their "lifeworld."[6] Schools organize the data collected during this *Levantamento Preliminar* into a school "dossiê" or profile that depicts as accurately as possible the local reality of the school and remains open to additional contributions resulting from continual investigations and educational work carried out in future studies subsequent to this initial ER.

During this investigative stage, educators become participant observers of the local reality of the school. This moment, according to the Secretariat, has a special significance in the project to build a *Popular Public School*: because ". . . participating subjects, the investigator and the investigated, both readers of their realities [in the Freirean sense], can help each other reciprocally, from the perspective of a two way action: the improvement of the quality of education offered by the school revitalized by its relation with society and the development of a critical consciousness on the part of the "community," whose living and working conditions the school helps to read and transform."[7] In this light, educators are not to approach the community with a set of preconceptions that they seek to confirm, but remain open to learning about the community in ways they may not expect. Similarly, the community may be surprised by the sudden interest taken in its experience by an institution that historically has been conceived as a distributor of knowledge to a community considered as lacking in knowledge and culture. To counteract traditional knowledge/power relations reproduced in schools, the Inter Project requires the community within and outside the school to engage in a continual process of knowledge exchange and collaborative construction of new knowledge.

Interviews and surveys of students, parents, and local residents, therefore, constituted the principal means of data collection during the ER phase of curriculum planing, which was supplemented by polls of neighborhood businesses, clinics, and other agencies, and general recorded observations, in addition to secondary documentation such as statistical data on the area (e.g., demographic information, income statistics), news articles and other relevant literature. Authors cited in the *Study of Reality, Caderno de Formação* N° 2—a series produced by the Secretariat to guide educators in the Project— establish the theoretical foundations for the proposed data collection as based on "participant action research" and general tenets of "ethnographic and qualitative research."[8] As an example, the investigative team charged with collecting data from both the "school community" and the "local community" may ask residents about their neighborhood, what it is like to live there and what they believe the needs of the community are. The objective is to get at the collective and individual perceptions of the problems facing the community, its history, and the aspirations, hopes and dreams of its residents.

The Secretariat suggests—following a framework of linguistic analysis—that there be distinguishable among the *falas* [or discourses] collected from the community: (1) statements that reflect an opinion or defend a particular point of view; (2) views that reveal either a static or a more dynamic vision of the world; (3) statements that reveal different levels of consciousness about one's place in the world; (4) discourse of a symbolic nature (e.g., metaphors, comparisons).[9] The PT-MSE reasoned that if attention is given to the collection of such diverse representations a more complete configuration of the reality of the school and community can be registered and analyzed.

Once the data is collected and registered, the next step is to codify or "categorize" the particular *falas* (i.e., registered interviews of different individuals in the community), as well as additional data collected such as photographs, videos, demographic statistics and other information from formal documents on economic, political and socio-cultural characteristics of the region. The process of categorization must be "collective and interdisciplinary" in order to achieve a balance between objectivity and subjectivity and to effectively link the particular to the social creating a rich and broad vision of that reality.[10] Through this collective analysis the interdisciplinary team identifies not only the explicit situations illustrated in the data but also discerns issues, concerns, and problems implicit in the community's registered discourse.

For example, as part of its policy development process, the PT-MSE itself conducted an ER of the municipal school system which included surveying students. Out of these student-generated data, the PT-MSE identified the following categories of students' concerns:

1. **Function of the School** (perceived and desired), includes *falas* [student discourse] regarding the acquisition of knowledge, knowledge as instrumental for participation in the literate society; social mobility; formation of attitudes; social cohabitation; preparation for work; provision of other services, involving assistance to students and protection and recreation.

2. **Physical Structure** (perceived and desired) includes *falas* regarding building structure, conservation, security, and hygiene.
3. **Curricular Structure** (perceived and desired) divided into subdivisions such as: content-fragmentation, relevance to the daily life of the student, issues related to the application of knowledge, suggestions made by students for the inclusion of other content; methodology; evaluation; teacher-student relations; student-student relations; student-technical team relations; student-school functionaries; school- community relations grouping together aspects related to financial participation, following of school performance; participation in school decision making, socialization of school resources, human resources, material resources; organization of the school; structuring of the system of school discipline.[11]

In orienting the schools' efforts to carry out their respective ERs, the Secretariat emphasizes several concurrent processes: (1) record the micro level issues relevant to a specific community as they emerge during the investigative team's preliminary analysis of the collected data; (2) identify the related macro issues from the broader social context; (3) link these two sets of issues in order to discern the "significant situations" or those themes that persistently emerge in the discourse of the community and therefore represent a collective dimension as opposed to the strictly individual experience.[12] The following guidelines are offered to educators engaging in the analysis of the data collected:

1. Know the history of the "community" being studied.
2. All the persons involved in the analysis should read all the material collected and be involved in its interpretation.
3. The group should conduct discussions, taking into account individual readings and analyses, regarding the limitations of the data collected and information obtained at any given moment.

To this end, the PT-MSE further suggests that the team construct broad categories that allow for the organization of data in a way that makes evident the more significant tendencies and elements present in the community discourse. The validity of different categories is tested by the quantity of data that fall within each one. The more information that falls within a particular category, the more precise that category. Some data, it is pointed out, may not fall within any of the categories and therefore the group must evaluate the categories and determine whether new categories need be developed altogether, or the data itself determined insignificant. Following these guidelines, a dialectic comprehension of reality is pursued in as much as the categories identified serve to orient the analysis of data at the same time that the data orients the definition of categories, which in turn signal to the investigative team those situations most significant for a given community.[13] This qualitative analytical process is central to the curriculum building effort within the Inter Project.

In summary, the locus of teachers' efforts was in developing the generative theme for the school for a particular timeframe (e.g., a semester). Thus, the Study of the Reality took teachers on a collaborative venture as they collected data on their school community. Upon completing the Study of the Reality, the teachers assembled and analyzed these data, pulling out issues of significance to the community. From these "significant situations" teachers work collaboratively to derived a generative theme reflective of a fundamental issue or conflict in the school community that can orient the entire school in the formulation of an interdisciplinary curriculum. According to the PT-MSE, such a foundation in the reality of the student allows for an interdisciplinary approach to the systematized universal knowledge which schools traditionally are charged with transmitting while encouraging the construction of new knowledge in the interests of the popular sectors.

As a result of this interactive and dynamic process of collective analysis, a set of significant situations are identified and a consensus is reached as to the generative theme around which to construct the curriculum. Although many generative themes may be possible, the group comes to an agreement given the particularities of the socio-historical context of the school and its community and perhaps the current events of the day. For instance, one school determined "elections" as the generative theme because of the fact that the municipal elections were taking place that semester and the entire city was being inundated by campaign propaganda. As community groups, families, students and teachers debated the merits and shortcomings of the candidates and their respective political party platforms the elections became the most significant aspect of the daily life of the students in the school. This initiation of a dialogue between school and community/educator and educatee in the ER stage necessarily leads to the second and third moments in the curriculum development process and classroom practice in the Inter Project.

Organization and Application of Knowledge
(Organização de Conhecimento, OC, and
Aplicação do Conhecimento, AC)

On the level of curriculum planning, in the phase termed the Organization of Knowledge, teachers working on the interdisciplinary curriculum via the generative theme use the data and information from the Study of the Reality to draw out the generative questions for each of their subject areas from which are determined the specific concepts and content to be taught at each grade level. In other words, teachers from different disciplines organized the content areas in their subjects around the generative theme. For each subject area, a list of different generative questions were developed. The answers to these questions would be found in the content areas of the disciplines. Working with the students to develop responses to these generative questions would encourage their exploration of the subject area as well as train them in skills used in the particular discipline.

This moment in the curriculum planning process serves to organize the links between the universe of systematized knowledge and the themes, problems, and significant situations that emerged in the analysis of data carried out in the previous ER stage. Also, important intervening factors at this point are the theories and notions of the construction of knowledge and cognitive development informing the educators involved in the planning process, as well as their individual and collective notions as to what constitutes important knowledge and what the academic needs of their students are at a given grade level. At this stage teachers select the materials and resources to be employed as part of planned activities for each subject area. In the Inter Project, educators are encouraged to use a wide variety of resources including newspapers, field trips, guest speakers, journal articles, literature, and audio/visual aides.

To assist in this OC phase, the PT-MSE articulated the notion of unifying concepts, which were developed for each subject area. Project consultant, and a science educator herself, Marta Pernambuco, characterizes the teaching of the natural sciences at the elementary level as inherently interdisciplinary involving physics, chemistry, biology, astronomy and geo-sciences. Responding to the misperception that the *interdisciplinary curriculum via the generative theme* was an inappropriate model for the teaching of subjects other than the Social Sciences and Language Arts (i.e., Math and Science), Pernambuco argues for a Science education that provides access to the comprehension of modern technology, as much as it works for the construction of knowledge in the area. She writes, "The key is therefore to return to the production of the scientific knowledge we share, searching out its structured principles, its more generalized procedures which are valid in all the disciplines of the natural sciences: its unifying concepts."[14]

Figure 5.2 provides a graphic representation of the central role of the *unifying concepts*—as identified by the Subject Area Team for Science—in the construction of an interdisciplinary curriculum appropriate to the cognitive developmental level of students throughout the three cycles of elementary schooling. Table 5.2 outlines the significance and application of

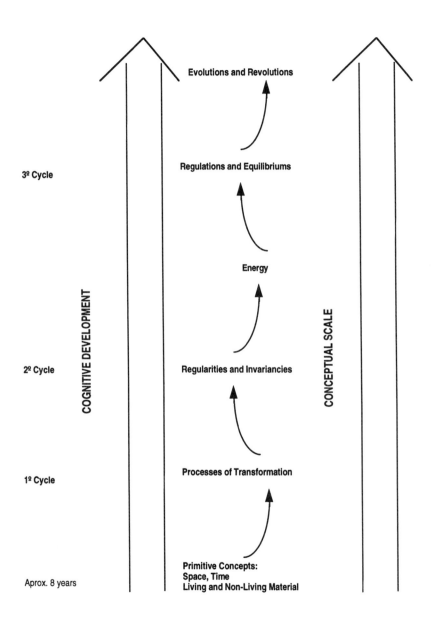

FIGURE 5.2 Unifying Concepts in the Elementary Curriculum. *Source: SME-SP. Documento 5—Visão da Area: Ciencias,* February, 1992, p. 17

TABLE 5.2 Significance and Application of Unifying Concepts

Unifying Concepts	Significance	Application
Primitive concepts: space, time, living material,, and non-living material	•Structuring of eternal reality in permanent relation with the individual •They should be qualified and serve as relevance for the different topics approached •Activities should involve skills such as classification, observation description, relations and differences within reality	•The construction of "things and their relationship with "me" and the "world"
Transformations	•Phenomena or situation that alters the conditions of the object in space and in time. •Agents of trasformation with respect to all the elements of the universe	•Changes in position, temperature, aspect, size, form, etc.
Regularities (cycles)	•It is the search for invariencies within natural phenomena (conservations) •The transformations occur linked to certain regularities, in other words there are aspects that remain despite changes occurred •Open and closed cycles •Regularities are present in theoretical models as much as in experimental work.	•Cycles of matter (water, oxygen, carbon, etc. •Systems of water, sewage, electricity, etc. •Food chains and webs •Consumption of combustibles and food •Movements in the celestial bodies •Static equilibriums
Energy	•The transformative agent •Conservation of an abstract agent that can be quantified and characterized in different forms	•Conservation of the different forms of energy in movements, reactions, organisms, ecosystems, etc.

(table continues)

Table 5.2 (continued)

Unifying Concepts	Significance	Application
Regularity and dynamic of equilibriums	•Previous concepts (principles of energy) readdressed from a higher cognitive level •Study of the controls, the schemes of dynamic equilibriums and the losses •Efficiency and inefficiency of static and dynamic equilibriums •Interaction between different cycles (flow of energy between cycles)	•Catalysts, productivity, biological regulators (hormones, DNA, Nervous system, pedatory/prey, natural adaptation), Ecological relations between living beings •Mechanisms of feed-back
Revolution and evolutions	•Reflection on scientific production •Evolution and Interation of scientific concepts and their historical transformation according to necessity and social relations	•History and philosophy of scientific models •Current topics emphasizing social relations in the production of sci-scientific knowledge (AIDS, Colera, etc.)
Scales	•They are the grand order under which all the other concepts occur, and therefore should be present simultaneous to all other concepts •Allows for extrapolations from micro to macro •Makes explicit the limits and and validity of the scientific models	•Scales of length, time, mass, energy, etc., associated with other scientific models

Source: NAE-6 Interdisciplinary Team, 1991

the unifying concepts presented in Figure 5.2. Figure 5.3 illustrates the relationship between the unifying concepts and generative questions for each subject area that evolves out of a single generative theme. The unifying concepts were intended to serve as a thread of reference woven into the curriculum plan, guiding educators in their selection of content and materials for the educational activities of the OC stage of the curriculum planning process.

The third and final stage, Application of Knowledge, represents the implementation and assessment of the academic program, i.e., planning of activities to demonstrate students' own constructions of knowledge. Central to this approach is the idea that subject area content matter is not an end in and of itself but a means by which to better comprehend a given aspect of reality, all the while rejecting the fragmentation and disassociation of knowledge from the life conditions of the students.[15] With this enhanced comprehension comes the ability and agency to act on that reality and transform it.

As a first step in the AC phase, teachers decide how they will evaluate the students' grasp of the concepts being taught. Group or individual projects are assigned that allow for the student to engage in the application of knowledge they have attained or constructed. Activities selected during the AC phase of curriculum planning aim at the assessment of student learning and comprehension. In it the PT-MSE envisioned a much more authentic and action-oriented assessment strategy than was traditionally used in the school system. The AC strayed from convention by encouraging assessment techniques that required students to apply and use their knowledge, allowed them to do so in cooperative groups, and suggested that this occur over a lengthened period of time using a variety of media. Though teachers and students alike had to get used to the idea that timed tests might not be the only way to assess student knowledge, with guidance from the NAE staff, school staff demonstrated tremendous creativity in this arena. Observations revealed a range of interesting AC activities including the design of posters and murals about particular political events (e.g., the threatened impeachment of President Collor), the development of a recycling program at one school that even included the kitchen staff, writing letters to factory owners, and creating voting guides to local elections. In addition to these meaningful projects, it is important to note that most AC activities were developed by the collective and, later, evaluated by all teachers as well—providing an additional significant space for dialogue and reflection on pedagogic practice.

The overall construction of the program, therefore, involves a dynamic process that merely signifies the initiation of the teacher's educational action and requires a continual process of action and reflection (i.e., ER-OC-AC). The reflective and dialogic character of the Project in all its stages

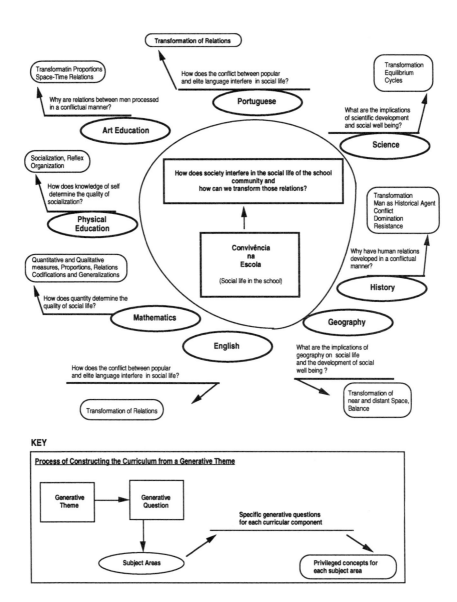

FIGURE 5.3 Interdisciplinary Curriculum Based on a Generative Theme: Generative Questions X Unifying Concepts. *Source:* Derived from curriculum presented at the first Municipal Educational Congress, Laerte School (NAE-6), 1991.

(from planning to implementation to assessment) is emphasized by the following guidelines offered to teachers:

1. The program under construction expresses the initiation of an educational action, and is in constant revision;
2. That educational action will be made substantially more concrete in the day to day life of the school, of the classroom, of the pedagogic work, of the curricular action;
3. Because it is process based, the construction of this program should allow for frequent moments of reflection on practice, which presupposes the permanent evaluation of the action which can point towards continuities;
4. Based on the presupposition of dialogue, these "dialogical negotiations" require that the educators engage in constant exchanges, in effect, realizing the notion that one educator can also learn from another educator.[16]

This theoretically sophisticated and methodologically complex process of curriculum planning is graphically illustrated in Figures 5.4 and 5.5.

Three Phases of Knowledge Production (ER; OC; AC) in the Classroom

Central to the development of the Interdisciplinary Project is the notion that curriculum planning and classroom practice have a dynamic relationship in which each informs the other. Ideally, then, classroom practice by teachers in the Inter Project would mirror the process described above by beginning with its own ER and proceeding with the OC and AC phases.

Beyond the initial investigation of the local reality, the Study of the Reality also represents a methodological point of reference for teachers in their implementation of the interdisciplinary curriculum. Pernambuco stresses the significance of this initial pedagogical moment in the overall educational process of the Project:

> It is the moment of comprehending the other and the significance that the proposal [any given set of themes or subject matter] has within his universe and at the same time it allows for the other to think, with a certain distancing, about the reality in which he is immersed. *It is the moment of the discourse of the other*, of the initial decodification proposed by Paulo Freire, in which it is the duty of the teacher, or organizer of the activity, to listen and question, understand and shake up the other participants, provoking them to immerse themselves in the moment to follow.[17]

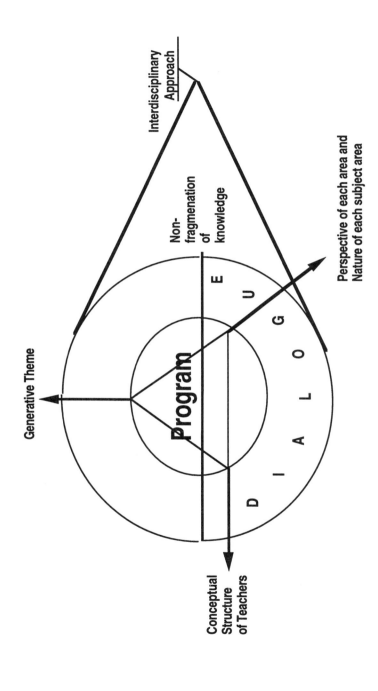

FIGURE 5.4 The Principal Elements in the Construction of the Program. *Source:* "Cadernos de Formação No. 1—um Primero Olhar Sobre o Projecto," *3ª Série—Ação Pedagógica da Escola pela via da interdisciplinaridade,* February, 1992, p. 40.

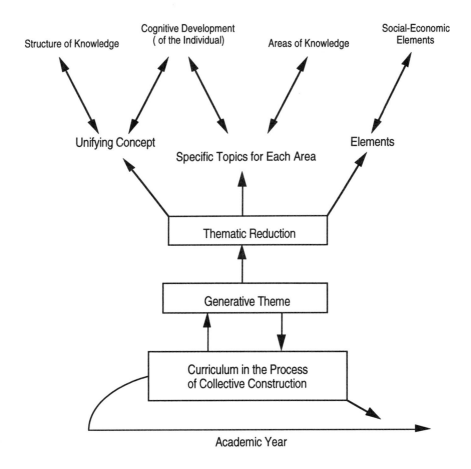

FIGURE 5.5 The Organization of Knowledge in the Collective Construction of the Curriculum Via the Generative Process. *Source: Nucleo de Ação Educative,* 6/1991.

Consequently, it is at the ER moment in the classroom that the discourse or *fala* of the student takes precedence over that of the teacher. The teacher's role is to present questions and topics for discussion with students for the purpose of introducing a specific content in the given subject area.

Yet the typical *teacher question/student response* pattern gained a new dynamic in the context of the Inter Project. As opposed to a mere introduction of content matter, the ER moment in the classroom corresponded to the "problematization" of the reality to be studied via the generative questions posed by the teacher. The written responses of students to these generative questions served as a basis for the teacher to initiate a dialogue in the classroom around the relevant socio-economic elements vis-à-vis the generative theme. These elements are necessarily: (1) generic in character; (2) require a degree of distance or abstraction; (3) relate to the broader context (e.g., the city of São Paulo). Moreover, the generative theme has significance to the local community; is the "effect" of a deeper cause (i.e., the complex of social, economic and political relations); and, is already present in the discourse of the community/student.[18] It is at the pedagogical ER moment that the limits of the common sense notions of the community are revealed and reference to the universe of systematized knowledge sought via the conceptual tools of the specific subject areas: the intention is to relate the generative theme to the social and personal spheres of reality of the student.

Hence, students were presented with a series of questions intended to prompt them to begin to analyze their reality or a given topic, as it relates to them. A common practice in this initial "Study of the Reality" witnessed in the Inter Project classrooms was seemingly a traditional question/answer approach. In the example provided below, a fourth-grade Social Studies student at Habib School answers a set of questions the teacher has written on the board for the class to copy into their notebooks. The purpose is to register student's initial perceptions of the surrounding region of Santo Amaro prior to a further exploration into the region's history of industrialization and the quality of life of the workers who reside there.

Example: "Study of the Reality" Questions in the Classroom
(Fourth Grade/ Habib School)

1. Have you ever been to the Santo Amaro Plaza or do you know about it?
   Res: *Yes already went to the Largo of Santo Amaro.*

2. Describe what it is like? If you do not know, describe how you imagine it to be.

   Res: *It is very busy full of houses, buildings, shopping, (street vendors) cars, thieves, drug dealing, bus stops and lots of people and prostitutes.*

3. In your opinion what is the major problem of Santo Amaro?

   Res: *The street vendors, a lot of people crammed together, few police and lots of drug dealers and prostitutes.*

4. Do you think that the problems of Santo Amaro have to do with our neighborhood? Explain your answer?

   Res: *No, because here in our neighborhood street vendors do not crowd the streets nor are there prostitutes.*

5. Do you think that it has always been as you imagine or have seen? Why?

   Res: *No, because before, Santo Amaro was a very nice locale surrounded by trees.*

Ideally, the intention with this first methodological step was to encourage students to express their opinions and experiences. Either individually or in groups they were to study materials provided by the teacher or collected by students from sources outside the classroom, reorganize the knowledge at hand and raise new questions pertinent to the topic of investigation. In this way the ER stage in the classroom offers students the opportunity to revisit knowledge previously learned in and outside the school and to express intuitive or common sense knowledge (both of which may or may not correspond to the theories and facts of so called scientific knowledge). Through the problematization of that knowledge via dialogic classroom interaction students are then motivated to investigate further and acquire new information thus building new knowledge. To facilitate this, it is recommended that the teacher maintain more a role of questioning students and guiding the problematization process than of providing answers and explanations.

It is through the investigation of questions raised by the classroom level ER that students and teachers proceed to the second and third moments, the Organization of Knowledge and Application of Knowledge, respectively. With the second stage of the Organization of Knowledge (OC), the discourse of the individual or persons organizing the learning activity takes precedence. In accordance with Vygotsky's concept of the zone of proximal development, the educator guides the learner(s) in taking a cognitive jump towards a greater level of comprehension of the subject matter at hand. At this stage in the pedagogical process the educator attempts to introduce new concepts and ways of viewing a given reality or set of problems. As such, the knowledge that the educator brings into the learning situation is essential for the educational act to take place. The reality of the learner is not the beginning and end point of this pedagogical approach.

Educator and learners collectively exchange and reorganize knowledge, ultimately resulting in the third moment of the "application of knowledge" (AC) which represents the synthesis of both the discourse of the other [learner] and the organizer [teacher] without one taking precedence over the other, allowing each to perceive and recognize their differences and respective limitations.[19] In this way, knowledge is socially constructed as the group works to reorganize what they have learned into a collective text or group project. Hence, during the final AC stage an effort is made to apply the concepts and knowledge constructed during the previous moment. The idea is to refer back to the generative questions presented in the initial ER in order to verify if the students have advanced in their critical ability to comprehend the relationship between the generative theme, the social economic elements identified and the curricular content being presented. The goal is to overcome the dichotomy between process and product, action and reflection and to arrive at a critical participant citizenship.

Students and the Inter Project

The radical changes in curriculum and teachers' practice necessarily implied new ways of being a student in the Popular Public School. True to Freire's vision of the learner as subject and object of the knowledge production process, the PT-MSE envisioned a more active and critical role for students at all levels in the system. This concern was strengthened after analyzing student opinions collected in a survey conducted by the Secretariat to understand the "vision of the students" with regard to the reality of the schools. Students throughout the municipal school system offered a negative assessment of the physical facilities of most schools, reporting that they were "poorly maintained," "ugly," "dirty," "marked with graffiti," "infested with rats," "with out light," "with out water," "with broken windows and chairs," "with bathrooms in the worse of conditions and in insufficient numbers."[20]

The Secretariat's report summarizing the students' assessment of their schools points out that the students' comments seemed to distance themselves from the negative reality they described, as though they did not take responsibility for the physical conditions of the schools. This attitude is attributed to the manner in which the institutional culture of the public school in Brazil perpetuates a "crystallized" view of the role and functions of the individuals who make up the school community: "the student dirties, the servant cleans and the teacher lectures, the students attends, etc."[21] One of the objectives of the Secretariat through the Movement for the Reorientation of the Curriculum was to break down the rigid roles played out by students, teachers and administrators and to lessen the separateness of the school and the community outside its walls. Through such an initial problematization of the reality of the school, the Secretariat intended that new approaches to their solution be envisioned and more collaborative efforts to improve the physical and curricular structure of the school carried out. In the words of the administration: "it is breaking the 'culture of silence', and hearing out the students, discussing with them their visions and remaining open to the reflection and action that can effectively create a perspective that leads to the construction of a public democratic school."[22]

This was precisely the intent of the Inter Project: to change the culture of the classroom from primarily teacher-centered and driven by a pre-established curriculum, to one in which the teacher and student engage in a mutual exchange of knowledge and experiences around situations and topics derived from their socio-cultural reality. In this way learning becomes a dialogic and dynamic enterprise aimed at the construction of new knowledge, at building bridges between common sense notions and popular knowledge that children bring with them into the classroom and the academic content areas to be taught. In this regard the Inter Project introduces the generative theme as the mediating factor in this process of knowledge exchange. It provides a kind of unifying focus in the struggle for the educator to find nexuses with specific areas of knowledge and an equilibrium between the general and the specific in an otherwise free-flowing dialogue. In effect, through each of the elements discussed above, students gained new opportunities to develop and exercise this voice in a manner that reflected greater comprehension of their own realities and greater command over the tools needed to transform those realities.

Teacher Practice, Curriculum Innovation, and Reform Challenge

Under Freire's leadership, the MSE offered several innovations that departed radically from the centralized and bureaucratized traditions of educational policy in São Paulo. Clearly, the explicit orientation towards a Popular Public School of quality was the cornerstone of their innovative and radical efforts. But it was in the implementation of this vision that breaks with the heretofore authoritarian policy tradition were most marked. First, as no formula or precise model was handed down from the Secretariat to the schools, the final curricular plan produced at each school was shaped by the different interpretations of the process to be undertaken and the local site realities. This variation was a far cry from the more conventional "teacher-proof" red notebooks that had historically programmed in detail what teachers would teach, when and how. Second, the whole notion of knowledge was reconstructed from a sterile, elitist concept of academic knowledge to one that integrated this universalized knowledge with common sense, lived knowledge from the popular classes. In doing so, knowledge also ceased to be an entity that could be fragmented into discrete subject areas and became a fluid interdisciplinary body that drew from a range of disciplines, was called into action around a particular *problematique* or generative theme, and emerged from significant situations in the community. Third, all relationships within the school (e.g., teachers and students, teachers and teachers, teachers and administrators, etc.) and relationships between the school and its local community were transformed according to democratic ideals.

These were lofty and ambitious goals and they were presented to an educative body that had suffered tremendous depletion in prior years—teachers' salaries were abysmally low, requirements for entering the profession were watered down, teaching conditions and other physical aspects of schools were almost unsafe. Even without these poor material conditions, the theoretical tenets of the PT-MSE's reforms provided significant challenges to the more accepted and conventional theories regarding education, teaching and learning and would have raised hackles even among well-paid teachers! Not surprisingly, then, the implementation of the Inter Project surfaced a range of reactions in school staffs that are discussed generally as the primary challenges facing the Project. These reactions came in many forms, stemmed from diverse causes, and expressed themselves in several ways. Though many educators viewed the Project as both an innovation and a challenge, they often struggled immensely with the practical application of its complex methodological approach to curriculum building and the Project's pedagogical orientation in the classroom. As a summary to this chapter, we discuss the obstacles related to changing classroom practice and in so doing provide foreshadowing of Chapter VI which examines in depth the specific problems teachers faced in fully implementing the Inter Project.

Despite concerted effort (both on the part of the NAE Inter Team members and the teachers most devoted to the Project) to organize learning around the three pedagogic moments of the Inter Project, the spillover to classroom practice was often barely perceptible. Quite often the actual activities being carried out did not necessarily reflect any innovation in the way teachers taught and students were expected to learn. Yet, what did stand out as one of the most distinctive features of an Inter Project classroom was the content with which teachers worked. The math problems presented below exemplify the manner in which teachers often superimposed content they perceived as relevant to a particular generative theme, in this case "Workers," onto traditional ways of presenting facts and assigning academic exercises to students.

Example: Texts Related to Generative Theme, "Workers"
(Fourth Grade/Habib)

"Severino Creates Surplus Value"
Severino has been a worker for Volkswagen of São Bernardo do Campo for the last four years. In this company, which is a multinational, he works eight hours a day, when he does not do overtime.

What is interesting is that for each eight hours of work, Severino remains with one hour of pay. In other words, one hour of work goes to pay his salary and seven hours go towards the profits of the boss.

Therefore, the seven hours that go to Volkswagen is called surplus value. The exploitation of the wage worker follows this law or general norm.

"May First"
It was May 1886.

The life of the workers was too hard. Much hunger, fatigue and many hours of work per day.

But the brave workers dreamed of a better life, with time to rest and better working conditions. So they fought to make these gains.

In the city of Chicago, in the United States, they could not stand such exploitation any longer and the workers went on strike demanding an eight hour work day.

The repression on the part of the police sent by the bosses was terrible. The eight leaders of the strike were imprisoned. Three were condemned to life imprisonment. One of them committed suicide. Four of them, Spies, Fisker, Engel and Parson, were tried and condemned to death by hanging.

It is because of this fact that the May 1st is the day of all the workers and their struggles and achievements.

Long live the 1st of May.

Example: Math Problems Related to Generative Theme "Workers"
(Fourth Grade/Habib)

1. In a steel plant there were 200 workers in the production line and three dozen in the offices.
    *   How many workers were on the production line?
    *   How many workers were located in the offices?
    *   How many workers were there in total?

2. In a auto factory there were 300 workers. With the current crisis, nine dozen were laid off.
    *   How many workers were laid off?
    *   How many were left?

3. In a small industrial plant there were nine dozen workers, eight dozen went on strike to improve their wages.
    *   How many workers are there in the industry?
    *   How many workers went on strike?
    *   How many workers did not strike?

Although the practice of the teacher handing over a pre-established text or a set of word problems for students to consume and complete is indistinguishable from any traditional teaching approach, in this case the specific content of each assignment marks a departure from conventional subject matter content and points to this teacher's underlying objective: to "raise consciousness" among her students about the exploitative relationship between labor and capital, given the generative theme of "Workers." Moreover, what is remarkable about the above examples is not so much the content (though this is a departure from conventional curriculum) but the fact that in each case teachers themselves created the activities and wrote the texts or problems. Throughout our observations of classrooms we saw many instances where teachers introduced texts that either they individually or collectively with other teachers in their subject area researched and wrote, or that they collected from other sources (e.g., poems, popular songs, books of renowned authors, etc.) as the starting point for carrying out the initial ER in their classrooms. This heightened creativity among teachers marks an important developing point in the reflective practice that the PT-MSE sought to foster.

Thus, though significant and widespread changes in teachers' classroom practice were not achieved, it is still important to highlight some noteworthy ways in which, despite their doubts, insecurities and objections, teachers' actions did change. The introduction of new and different content, as seen in the examples above, represented a significant break with conventional practice for many teachers. More importantly, however, was the fact that so many teachers—whether on their own or in collaboration with colleagues—discovered their own creative talents as a result of the Inter Project. Prior to the PT-MSE, both the form and content of curriculum was carefully monitored by forces outside the classroom and local school. With the Inter Project, teachers gained the right to create their own texts and bring in their own materials. This signified a major liberating experience for many teachers, even those who resisted the Project's more political purposes.

In summary, this chapter has detailed the process of curriculum construction following the three pedagogic moments proposed by the Inter Project and offers practical examples of the theoretical elements of the Popular Public School as discussed in the previous chapter. Through this overview, we can see that the PT-MSE developed a number of innovative reforms which targeted the authoritarian nature of Brazilian education as expressed in curriculum content, teaching strategies, student assessment and the role of the school in its local community. These reforms, even when poorly or incompletely implemented, gave educators, students, and families alike an opportunity to reflect on and transform the nature of their individual and collective reality. In the chapter that follows, four case studies are presented that elaborate on the ways in which these transformations occurred in the schools and how teachers perceived these changes.

Notes

1. Cf.Moacir Gadotti, *Pensamento Pedagógico Brasileiro* (São Paulo: Ática, 1987).

2. Ibid. p. 11.

3. SME- SP, "Tema Gerador e a Construção do Programa: uma nova relação entre currículo e realidade," *Cadernos de Formação* N° 3, *3° Série:—Ação Pedagógica da Escola pela via da Interdisciplinaridade*, March 1991, p. 18.

4. SME-SP, *Cadernos de Formação: Um primeiro olhar sobre o projeto* (São Paulo, February, 1990, p. 46).

5. Pernambuco, 1993, p. 33.

6. "By every day life world is to be understood that the province of reality which the wide-awake and normal adult simply takes for granted is the attitude of common sense. By this taken-for-grantedness, we designate everything which we experience as unquestionable; every state of affairs is for us unproblematic until further notice." (A. Shultz, 1957) "It is the unquestioned ground of everything given in my experience, and the unquestionable frame in which all problems I have to deal with are located." (Luhmann, 1977) Both cited in Jürgen Habermas, 1987, p. 130.

7. SME-SP, "Estudo da Realidade," *Caderno de Formação* Nª 2, *Series 3—Ação Pedagógica da Escola pela via da interdisciplinaridade* , October 1990, p. 21.

8. Authors and works cited include: Marli Eliza D. Afonso de André "Texto contexto e significado: algumas questões na análise de dados qualitativos," in *Cadernos de Pesquisa* São Paulo (45), pp. 66-71, Maio 1983; "A pesquisa do tipo etnológico no cotidiano escolar," in *Metodologia da Pesquisa Educacional*, Ivani C.A. Fazenda (org.) (São Paulo: Cortez, 1989). Carlos Rodrigues Brandão (org.), *Pesquisa*

Participante (São Paulo: Brasiliense, 1984). Karel Kosik, *Dialética do concreto* (São Paulo, Editora Paz e Terera, 5th ed., 1972). Eulina P. Lutfi, *Ensinando Portugues, vamos registrando a história* (São Paulo, Edições Loyola, 1984).

9. SME-SP, "Estudo da Realidade," *Caderno de Formação* N° 2, pp. 38-39.

10. Ibid., pp. 49-50.

11. Ibid., pp. 56-57.

12. As a reference for such a dialectic methodological approach, cf., Karel Kosik, *Dialética do concreto* (Rio de Janerio: Paz e Terra, 1967), cited often in SME-SP docouments, SME-SP, "Estudo da Realidade," *Caderno de Formação* N° 2, pp. 38-39.

13. Ibid., 52-53.

14. Marta Pernambuco, "Significações e Realidade: Conhecimento (a construção coletiva do programa)," in Nidia Nacib Pontuschka org., *Osadia no Dialógo: Interdisciplinaridade na escola pública* (São Paulo, Loyola, 1993, p. 91).

15. SME- SP, "Tema Gerador e a Construção do Programa," *Caderno de Formação*, Nª 3, p. 19.

16. Ibid., p. 30.

17. Ibid., p. 33 [italics in text].

18. NAE-6, "Projeto Interdisciplinar: Principios Norteadores" (mimeograph), February 1990.

19. Ibid. p. 34.

20. *Movimento de Reorientação Curricular: Problematização da escola: a visão dos educandos.* Documento 3. Secretaria Municpal de Educação de São Paulo. February 1991, p. 9.

21. Ibid. p. 10.

22. Ibid. p. 25.

VI

Pedagogy of Hope and
School Realities

This chapter presents the pedagogical hopefulness that flourished, and at times floundered, at four schools that implemented the Interdisciplinary Project during the Workers' Party administration. These school site realities are intended to illustrate the variations with which schools experienced the Inter Project. This variation was to be expected from a reform that focused much more on process than product and where the unique site realities were paramount in the orientation of the school transformation. In addition, each case illuminates the particular factors at each school that created conditions either conducive or unfavorable to the Project's development there. School culture, faculty characteristics, orientation of the NAE personnel and their relationship with the school, and the significant situations of the local community all shaped the manner in which the Project found expression in a particular school. Thus, the case studies included here contextualize in a more specific social milieu the theoretical elements of the Interdisciplinary Project's curriculum reform presented in the previous two chapters.

Though each case study tells a distinct story, several common themes run throughout and, upon further analysis, reveal some of the accomplishments and shortcomings of the Inter Project. Regardless of the extent to which the Project was implemented and developed at a school, one of the most prevalent accomplishments cited was the Project's facilitation and promotion of collective work by teachers and students. If anything can be said to have been achieved during the PT administration, it is that teachers entered into dialogue with one another about the fundamental issues of educating in an urban context such as that of São Paulo's municipal schools

and in a country undergoing a period of political democratization and economic stabilization. Teachers, alongside their colleagues and their students,
were faced with the task of problematizing in their daily work this complex reality in terms of these constant Freirean queries: What are we teaching? Why and for whom are we educating? In effect, this reform project
had as its objective the transformation not only of the way knowledge was
organized in the curriculum and what knowledge was considered valid
for the content and objectives of a collectively constructed interdisciplinary curriculum, but also worked at transforming how teachers related to
each other, to their students and the community around the school.

The Project's principles, generally speaking, were aligned with a non-
traditional approach to education. In speaking about the Project, teachers
often made reference to the fact that it meant a move away from the traditional practices of teaching from a text book and following a static curriculum plan formulated from outside the context of the school, "which is, in
reality, a-historical, conformist and unrelated to daily life . . . not taking
into account the 'primary culture,' and therefore unable to transmit a transformative 'elaborated culture.'"[1] Moreover, the proposed alternative would
be an integrated curriculum developed through a dynamic participatory
process which "sought to make less rigid the boundaries among the diverse areas of knowledge."[2] Thus, in each of the case studies, the Project
gave educators an opportunity to see their students' realities—often for
the first time—and gave them a vehicle (i.e., interdisciplinary curriculum
via the generative theme) to connect this reality with the various content
areas to be taught in the classroom.

In addition, the PT curriculum reform not only took as problematic the
role of teachers in the classroom but also questioned their role in society in
general, thus projecting, a vision of teachers as active agents of both educational and social change. In the words of a Secretariat team member charged
with coordinating the Project, "past administrations imposed their program. They told teachers, 'the program will be like this . . .' The proposal of
this administration cannot be imposed, but instead depends on the adher-
ence of the teacher. The teacher is presented with its theoretical principles,
understands the approach and chooses to adhere or not to the Project. If
the teacher does not willingly take an active role then the Project will not
work" (CONAE Team Member, interviewed October 1992). In this regard,
the PT administration intended to make the educational process an act of
continual questioning and reinventing on the part of teachers. One teacher,
whose thoughts were echoed by many other informants, pointed out the
intensity of this preoccupation as particular to the PT administration, when
she made the following observation: "Never in my 16 years of teaching

have I seen an administration so concerned with education" (Maribel, interview, September 1992).

Thus, it seems that from an analytical standpoint, the extent to which individual teachers or whole faculties were actually able to transform their pedagogy and recreate their classrooms into democratic spaces where universalized knowledge interacted on equal footing with popular knowledge was less important than the fact that the great majority of the teachers involved in the Project could identify and critique elements of a traditional, authoritarian pedagogy and articulate a viable and more democratic alternative. In this way, the Project succeeded in taking an essential first step with many veteran teachers—and newcomers to the profession as well—helping them to think differently and more critically. The "crystallization" of teachers' practice was beginning to crack.

Each of the case studies presents a brief history of the Project at each of the school sites, illustrating in detail how the Project impacted the lives of educators who struggled to bring its elevated ideals of curriculum transformation into practice. Hence, interjected in these school portraits are the voices of the teachers and Secretariat personnel who dedicated themselves to the Inter Projects' realization during the four years of the PT administration and in some cases beyond the PT's tenure. Together the voices of these Brazilian educators reflect the difficulties, failings and accomplishments of the Inter Project experience.

The fieldwork for the case studies presented below was carried out by Pilar O'Cadiz and Pia Lindquist Wong primarily during 1991 and 1992, in addition to follow up field work conducted during brief visits by O'Cadiz in 1994 and 1995. In 1991, both O'Cadiz and Wong conducted pilot studies pursuant to more extensive field research and observations conducted during an eight month period in 1992. During this pilot visit interviews were conducted with Secretariat level staff including Project director, Dr. Ana Maria Saúl, who provided a general orientation to the Inter Project and its organization and implementation. Dr. Saúl and her staff assisted both researchers in gaining access to several schools and in meeting with personnel from several different regional administrations (NAE-6, NAE-1, and NAE-4). These schools represented a range in terms of Project implementation and allowed for initial observations at schools where Project implementation was meeting Secretariat expectations as well as schools that were facing serious challenges. These initial visits provided both researchers with an opportunity to meet with Project personnel at various levels, introduce their respective research projects, and gain access to individual school sites as well as to teachers' meetings, regional meetings of the Secretariat, and other types of planning and organizational sessions. Both O'Cadiz' and Wong's pilot studies confirmed the feasibility of their research design and they returned in July 1992 to conduct more extensive field research.

Naturalistic observations of a variety of curricular and extracurricular activities at each of the school sites were carried out by both researchers together and independently. In general these observations took place during regular school hours (any time between 7:30 a.m. and 7 p.m.) and included: classroom observation; school assemblies; teacher curricular planning meetings; Inter Team meetings with teachers; Formation Group meetings; and teacher training workshops and seminars. At the NAEs various types of meetings between Inter Team members (at times with the participation of the Pedagogic Coordinators from the individual schools) were observed. We were also able to attend the First Municipal Conference on Education (1991) which had the participation of thousands of educators of São Paulo's municipal school system.

Extensive interviews were conducted with teachers and several Inter-Team and Secretariat personnel, including Secretaries Paulo Freire and Mario Sergio Cortela; individuals who coordinated the Project at the Secretariat level (e.g., the Project's director, Ana Maria Saúl; Meire Olveira; Maria do Carmo D. Mendonça) as well as with other university specialists involved in its development (e.g., Marta Pernambuco of the University of Recife and Marcio D'Olne of the State University at Campinas). Ongoing informal interviews with more than sixty teachers, students and other participants in the reform further enhanced the research. Virtually all formal interviews were audio recorded and transcribed, although some less formal interviews were recorded in varying degrees of detail into handwritten field notes. Wong also administered a teacher questionnaire to a total of 65 teachers at seven school sites.

In addition, analysis of a vast collection of theoretical, practical and conceptual materials published by the Secretariat informed this research. Finally, we collected samples of teacher- and student-produced curricular materials and various types of documents pertaining to the Project produced by the NAE Teams. Data organization and analysis procedures followed the conventions of qualitative research methodology which entails engaging in continual systematic coding of field notes and application of both descriptive and interpretative analysis techniques during and after the period spent in the field.[3]

As became apparent during our fieldwork, the Inter Project was not a clear cut curriculum reform program, nor was its implementation carried out in a cohesive fashion even within a given school. What was clear was that the Project made a definitive impact on the reality of the schools, the nature of knowledge exchange in the classroom and the professional development and identity of teachers. The four schools represent particular approaches to the Project that emerged out the distinct direction taken by the different Inter Teams at three of the ten NAEs charged with its coordination: specifically they include, NAE-6 (Sussumu School, Habib School); NAE-5 (Pracinhas da FEB); NAE-1(Manoel de Paiva).

The case studies presented include the following details about the Inter Project experience at each school site: (1) an initial description of the school site and community characteristics; (2) description and analysis of the school's involvement with the Project, focusing on meetings, curriculum development and instructional practices; (3) a summary of the Project's impact at the site as provided by teacher assessment of the Project experience (including effects on teacher professional identity; educational philosophy and classroom practice; and changes in the institutional culture of the school and the organization of the curriculum). It should be noted once more that these case studies draw from two distinct studies, conducted by O'Cadiz and Wong, respectively. To the extent possible attempts have been made to bring uniformity to the data presented, without distorting the original intention of participants' comments or the integrity of the separate research agendas being pursued. As a result, in some instances the case studies diverge from each other in both form and content.

CASE 1
The Inter Project at Sussumu School:
The Experience of a Pilot Site

João Sussumu Hirata School (Sussumu School) is located in the southern peripheral urban area of Pedreira at the edge of São Paulo's municipal jurisdiction. The school was selected as one of the ten pilot sites for the Inter Project. Sussumu School may not have been selected as a pilot site during a less radical and politically oriented administration. But given its location directly in front of a large *favela* (squatter camp), Sussumu School offered a desirable challenge to the Inter team at NAE-6. What better opportunity to test the effectiveness of their Project for radical curricular reorientation than to work directly with the populations most spurned by the inherently irrelevant and discriminatory content of traditional curricular programs?

The experience of Sussumu School highlights several important questions related to the Freire administration's ambitious plans for curricular reorientation, and the concurrent creation of a social movement with local schools as the focal point. In particular, Sussumu School faced some challenges with an important one being the institutionalization and sustenance of the Project. Though this would certainly be a concern for all schools involved in the Project, Sussumu School had a special set of characteristics because it was a pilot site—meaning that it received relatively high levels of initial support from the regional administration, had the longest tenure with the Project, and was to be held up as a model for other interested or participating sites. A related issue was the changing nature of the school's relationship with the NAE-6 Inter team that helped to facilitate the process of pursuing an interdisciplinary curriculum via the generative theme at the school. Initially, both the school staff and the NAE team viewed this relationship as very effective, a product of frequent opportunities for shared dialogue and exploration; eventually, however, NAE staff had to turn their attention to new schools in the Project, leaving the school staff at Sussumu with a feeling of abandonment and the NAE staff with worries as to how to build the school's capacity for self-sustenance. As an outgrowth of these situations, staff at the school struggled to understand the basic tenets of the Project and strained to initiate and sustain practical applications of them. As this case study unfolds, we can see the ways in which these issues surfaced and were addressed.

Sussumu School: A Description

The school building, a two story rectangle, resembling more an industrial warehouse than a school, sits on a lonely bend of the main avenue that winds through the remote bairro of Pedreira, at the southernmost end of the city. Entering through the front steel doors, one faces a large open hall where children gather at breaks for snacks, lunch and play, their collective voices amplified to a sharp shrill that bounces against the cold gray surface of the windowless and bare concrete walls, floor and ceiling. Built on a slope, one enters on the second floor which consists of a corridor that runs around the open indoor courtyard like a balcony. On the south side of the building's first floor is a concrete wall against which children bounce balls during recess. The principal's office or *direitoria* is on the second floor and on this same side of the building are two teacher meeting rooms and a room designated for science and art workshops. Posters with various messages promoting cultural and political campaigns produced by the PT Municipal Government hang on the walls adjacent to the school's administrative offices.

The classrooms are located on both the first and second floors on the north side of the building, just opposite the administrative offices. From inside any classroom you can look through small rectangular glass panes (many of them broken) encased in iron over a stark concrete playground that faces the busy highway with two large billboards looming overhead. In the foggy distance, a tall water tower stands erect over the modest homes that spread out over the rolling hills. The favela across the avenue is conveniently out of sight as none of the classroom windows faces in its direction.

On any given day, one could seek refuge from the cold gray walls of this concrete rectangle called a school in the warm white tile kitchen tucked away in the back end of the building. Teachers would make a point to pass through the kitchen on their break time to buy the cook's homemade *salgadinhos* (warm meat and cheese pastries) that she brought to sell to the staff to supplement her meager income. The school lunches were prepared and dished out to the children through a large window facing the inner courtyard. They lined up at this window to eagerly grab what was usually a warm chicken broth with crackers and maybe a hard boiled egg or hot dog.

The classrooms were cold and dank during the winter months. The paint was peeling off the walls and the windows were so filthy one could barely see through them, except for the broken ones. And although the desks looked relatively new, they too could have used some cleaning. A pile of broken discarded desks were stored in the yard behind the school building. With its limited resources, the school administration is often forced to allow such deplorable conditions to continue given the high level of use of the classrooms (three to four shifts a day) and few maintenance personnel to keep a minimal level of cleanliness.

But the repair and maintenance of existing structures would only take care of part of the problem. In 1992, the Secretariat reported that in the region comprised by both NAEs 6 and 5, as many as 122 schools would have to be constructed in order to truly democratize access for the population of that region alone (other NAEs ranged in need of four to 40 schools to be constructed).[4] This region of the city suffers in particular from many infrastructure deficits—from lack of street lighting, to limited bus lines to communicate the maze of paved and unpaved roads that crisscross the hills stretching southward from the city's central region. It is populated mostly by industrial and domestic workers, in addition to the thousands of people that participate in the marginal spaces of the city's complex and varied economic life (i.e., street vendors, panhandlers (*favela* dwellers), etc.).

If the picture painted above does not induce visions of a physical environment conducive to the creation of a joyful place of learning then it is an accurate depiction. Yet despite these cold and unfriendly facilities, teachers at Sussumu School and the children there managed to create within these concrete walls an atmosphere full of life, imagination—and even political passion—at a cultural fair organized mid way through the academic year of 1992 to exhibit the students' work. The gray walls of the interior hall were adorned with surprisingly captivating student-made posters vehemently denouncing the President of the Republic as a traitor and thief.

That semester's Inter Project curriculum for upper grades had taken as its focus the impeachment movement against former President Fernando Collor de Mello (resulting in the production of several "collective posters" referring to this most significant current event.)[5]

History of the Inter Project at Sussumu

When the Secretariat made its first request for proposals from schools that wanted to be considered as pilot sites for the Inter Project in 1989, the teachers at Sussumu School with the support of the principal and pedagogic coordinator decided to submit a proposal. At the time, over 70 percent of the school staff agreed with the prospect of being a pilot site for the PT-MSE's educational project. Being a pilot school gave Sussumu School several advantages, the most marked of which was the undivided attention of the NAE-6 multidisciplinary team for the first two semesters of Project development and implementation. By all accounts, the initial launching of the Project at Sussumu School found all members of the NAE-6 team spending long hours at the school site, thus establishing an intense pace of work and close collaboration with the school staff.

According to the teachers at Sussumu School who participated in the pilot experience, the Inter Project did not signify the mere acquisition of yet another new educational program but instead marked the beginning of a transformative process in terms of their professional identity and educational practice. A NAE team member recalls, "Our goal was to implement the process to the greatest extent possible. We stayed at Sussumu School more than at the NAE office, to the point that during the night session we often substituted for teachers due to the high rate of absenteeism on that shift . . . we were there (at the school) every day, in that way we could follow the process of the Project closely" (Antonio, 1991). A teacher who had worked at Sussumu School during these initial stages of Project implementation confirmed that the "NAE team practically lived at the school" (Francisca, 1994).

However, by June 1990 the Project had been presented to 20 more schools and 14 of them accepted. The NAE team members had to decide how to proceed with the induction of the new schools into the Project. At this point, Project implementation reached a higher level of comprehension and operationalization system-wide. Clearly the NAE-6 team no longer could provide the same intensive support they had been giving Sussumu School. They decided to conduct joint meetings (seven in total) at the fourteen schools, with the participation of 450 teachers during September through December of 1990. The first four meetings were organized by subject area, with teachers in Science, Math, and Social Studies, Portuguese,

etc., meeting separately. The remaining three meetings took place at each school bringing together all the teachers interested in participating in the Project at the individual school sites under the leadership of the NAE personnel assigned to that school. In January of 1991, the NAE personnel began to focus on training the Pedagogic Coordinators at each school to take on a more central role in the process of Project implementation. Starting in February of that year the NAE team members were divided up into pairs and assigned three schools each. From this point on, guidance provided to teachers was organized by subject area and grade level. That is, the subject area specialists in the NAE multidisciplinary team would meet with the teachers of each area from the different schools participating in the Inter Project at the same time. Also, each grade level was coordinated by one of the pair of NAE personnel assigned to the school.

This strategy had uneven results at each school. It was especially difficult to get teachers from each of the subject areas to meet regularly. Difficulties also arose with the coordination by grade level: while the primary grade levels had better conditions for collective work (i.e., teachers were consistently present at the school during the early periods of the school day), the upper level grade levels taught by subject area suffered in coordination due to the disparate schedules of teachers.[6] By October of 1991, the NAE-6 team was initiating this training process with an additional 10 schools making the logistics of organizing such meetings even more challenging.

Teachers at Sussumu School, accustomed to intensive NAE support, eventually felt abandoned by the NAE team. This sense of abandonment was a common theme of teachers interviewed at Sussumu School who were committed to the Project but felt frustrated at not having had sufficient technical support to carry it out more thoroughly for the long term. In addition they were placed in the compromising position of being the "pilot site" to serve as a model for the other schools, while in reality, they too had just been initiated into the Project's challenging process of interdisciplinary curriculum planning and collective pedagogical work.

Finally, the high rate of teacher turnover further exacerbated the efforts of the Project supporters at the school to move forward with full implementation. Several of the teachers who arrived after the staff had opted into the Project and received their initial orientation often lacked the same level of commitment to the Project than those who had already invested their time and energy to making it happen at their school. And with increasingly less technical support from the NAE team, the task of orienting these teachers to the Projects' principles and procedures fell upon the Pedagogical Coordinator (CP) and school director who had to retell the story of the Project's initiation at the school every time a new teacher joined the staff in an effort to win them over.

As a result of these factors, the Project moved forward in fits and starts, its implementation was uneven, with classrooms reflecting a range of democratic and traditional pedagogy, and many long-term teachers expressing a certain bittersweet nostalgia for the attentive support that had been provided initially.

Meetings

Despite the difficulties of this pilot site, Sussumu School did have a core group of teachers and administrative staff who were dedicated to developing a sense of purpose and direction in the school community along the lines of the Inter Project. This ongoing effort was witnessed on several occasions at School Council meetings and Teacher Formation groups. Significant in their regularity and attendance, these meetings also stood out because of the pedagogic nature in which they were facilitated. Thus, the very process of meeting constituted an important moment in this effort to change the institutional culture of the school. An excerpt from a School Council meeting provides a vivid example. The meeting was in fact conducted by the Pedagogic Coordinator who led parents, teachers and students present in a dialogue on the theme of "participation."

Narrative of School Council Meeting: Building a Collective Critical Consciousness through Dialogue. The CP initiated the meeting with a generative question—"What do we mean by participation?"—meant to problematize the community-school relations. She then instructed the 26 people at the meeting to break into groups and come up with one word definitions. The groups' definitions for "participation" included "help; cooperate; act; be present." To her follow-up question, "how do we participate?" the group called out the responses: "overcoming difficulties; communicating; not conforming; uniting; through conscientization; having the same objectives; acting creatively." The group was then asked to identify the obstacles to participation which they listed as including "lack of experience or interest; lack of information; lack of unity; too many commitments; fear of being exposed; pessimism and disbelief."

Following this animated discussion on the theme of participation, a video was shown depicting how ecological groups organize for the preservation of the Amazon forests. After viewing the videos, the group concluded with the synthesis that "participation" is synonymous with "conquest, interest and hope." Concerns about the lack of unity and difficulties in organizing around the issues of education were expressed by different individuals in the group. A teacher implored that they unite around common goals to achieve their objectives. The NAE team member added: "Its no use just having two or three parents here; the fire is too great, we need the presence of everyone [to help put it out]."

What is noteworthy of this particular meeting—in contrast with a more conventional meeting style where the agenda might have been pre-determined by the organizer—was the dialogical approach employed following the same methods suggested in the Inter Project curriculum development meetings, teacher formation groups and classrooms. That is, the steps of the study of reality, organization and application of knowledge (ER-OC-AC) are replicated in the presentation of the theme of participation, its problematization and further investigation (i.e., video) by the group and the group's synthesis of the main points covered in their dialogue.

After the meeting, the NAE team member who had previously worked as a teacher at the school made the following points about what she felt were the long term effects of the Inter Project experience at Sussumu School: "It is a form of pedagogic action. We are just beginning to crawl with this experience, although it will take a great deal of effort, it can work. Before we were not accustomed to speaking up, or we would complain without doing anything about it. This administration has facilitated the conquest of that space to speak and act. We cannot let that change" (Francisca, 1992). This meeting, therefore exemplifies the kind of opening of spaces for reflective and critical dialogic practice that the PT-MSE sought to instigate in schools and with the communities around them via the activation of the School Councils. Most significant, in this case, was the participation of members of the community from outside of the school. Hence, we have here a glimpse of the real possibilities of the PT's utopian paradigm of the Popular public school: in Freire's words, "a school with another "face," more joyful, fraternal and democratic."[7] What follows is another example of the possibilities that abound from such a bold and challenging pedagogic-political perspective of schools and teaching.

Narrative of Pedagogic Meeting (1994): Persistence of a Reflective Dialogic Approach. Indeed, opportunities for intense and participatory dialogue were a hallmark of the Inter Project and persisted at Sussumu School a year after the end of the PT administration. An example of the continued application of the method of collective dialogue was observed in a "pedagogic meeting" (a kind of teacher in-service) in 1994. The school's Pedagogic Coordinator facilitated this meeting which she initiated recalling that four months ago, at the beginning of the academic year, they had proposed to follow a curriculum along the lines of the Inter-Project. She went on to point out to the teachers gathered there that they now seemed somewhat lost and disoriented with regard to the objectives of the school's mission. In effect the mission statement of the school, posted in the teachers' lounge, reflected a persistence of principles advanced during the Inter Project experience: namely the pedagogic principles of building an inter-disciplinary curriculum based on the reality of the students and aimed at creating critical citizens and at opening up the public space of the school to the community:

Mission of the School

To contribute to the integral development of our students, through the realization of a serious [educational] work aimed at creating the conditions which—parting from their lived experience, their reality— leads to their attaining a level of dominion of universal knowledge. [The goal is] that they continually engage in a new reading of reality, realizing themselves as individuals and citizens. Therefore, we are working toward making the school a space for the constructive co-existence of the whole community, with the objective that they have access to knowledge in an inter-disciplinary and critical fashion.

In the context of bringing to light the contradictions between the school's stated mission and the pedagogic practice of the collective, the CP used an allegorical text to direct the group in a reflection of their position as educators with relation to the mission statement of the school. The text, entitled *A Síndrome do Sapo Fervido* (The Syndrome of the Boiled Toad), related the story of a toad leaping out of a boiling kettle into the fire while another stays put, preferring to boil to death rather than be scorched. The text was meant to present the analogy of teachers who, rather than risk any attempts at change, remain unmoved despite the crisis conditions that exist in the school. The text read as follows.

The Syndrome of the Boiled Toad
(A Text)
author: Luis Carlos Q. Cabrer

Various biological studies have proven that a toad placed in a receptacle with the same water of his lagoon will remain still the entire time during which we heat the water until it boils. The toad does not react to the gradual increase in temperature (changes in the environment) and dies when the water boils. Bloated and happy. On the other hand, another toad that is thrown into the same receptacle with the water already boiling, immediately jumps out, somewhat singed but still alive!
We have various boiled toads running about. They do not perceive changes, they believe everything is just fine, that all will pass, it's just a matter of

time. They are on the verge of death, but nonetheless remain floating, stable and passive in the water that gets hotter every minute. They end up "dying" bloated and happy without ever having perceived the changes. Boiled toads do not perceive that beyond being efficient (doing things the right way), they need to be effective (do the right thing).

And for that to occur, there must be professional growth, with the space for dialogue, for clear communication, to exchange, plan and develop a relationship of adults. The challenge is even greater in the humility of acting in a collective fashion.

For several years we have had a cult of the individual, but the current turbulence demands a collective space, which is the essence of effectiveness as a response. To take collective action requires, fundamentally, much inter-personal competence for the development of team spirit and requires an ability to share power, delegate and believe in the potential of people and to know how to listen.

There are boiled toads that still believe that what is fundamental is obedience and not competence, that whom ever is the most capable is the one [naturally] in charge and whom ever is prudent obeys.

The "Boiled Toad" text served as a point of departure for an insightful and at times impassioned dialogue among the 20 teachers participating in this meeting as they offered their own interpretations and assessments of its relevance to their daily lives as teachers. This reflective dialogue evolved as follows:

Teacher 1:   Here at Sussumu School we are hard working . . . for the past 10 years the water has been heating up and has started to boil. Meanwhile the world is everyday more dynamic and complex.

Teacher 2:   I think that the metaphor [represented in the text] is that when the water gets too hot, it's time to jump out of the kettle and do something to change the routine.

Teacher 3:   What is worse? He who sticks around and gets used to it or he who jumps out and never adapts?

Teacher 2:   Yes, but the one who jumps out isn't escaping!

Teacher 3:   Well ,when the Inter Project arrived, I thought "this isn't going to work" and I jumped out.

CP: You [referring to Teacher 3] may say that you think that the Inter was not an ideal [educational approach], but you changed.

Teacher 4:   For the toad his primary goal is to stay alive, ours is educa-
             tion.

Teacher 5:   I have my doubts, I think the thing is to jump out of the profes-
             sion, I'm burnt out in here.

Teacher 6:   As teachers we are in an environment which hasn't changed
             over the years. We can't allow ourselves to be boiled [to death],
             this would be a terrible thing. It can be marvelous, it depends
             on how you achieve change. If all you do is wait to retire you
             are keeping the flames going to boil the next generation. We
             can't go on with this infinite boiling . . . what group are we a
             part of [the boiled toads or the scorched toads]?

Teacher 2:   What's so great about dying bloated and content, I'd rather
             die lucid and happy.

After this initial discussion, teachers were divided into groups of five
in order to analyze the text on the basis of three guiding questions and
come up with a synthesis of the group's response. One group wrote this
synthesis:

> The boiled toad demonstrates the traditional position (the traditional edu-
> cator) who is not aware of changes that occur. The scorched toad is the
> progressive educator that perceives change and tries to innovate despite
> the difficulties. We believe that there are certain obstacles to the efficiency
> of such efforts at educational change: difficulties in the collective hour,
> lack of resources and didactic materials, lack of teacher development
> courses; and limited exchange of ideas among teachers.

Each group presented its synthesis to the larger group. One group argued against the dichotomy being drawn between traditional and progressive teachers. The idea being that by making such divisive judgments they
were essentially "throwing the water out with the frog." To this effect, one
teacher commented that change in and of itself was not good and added,
"we all have our cultural baggage, we can't simply view the traditional as
garbage." Still another group concluded that the boiled toad in effect is an
efficient means of reproducing the status quo. The results of each group's
synthesis of the meaning of the "boiled toad" text was posted in the teachers' work room for others to read. The chart is reproduced here in Figure
6.1.

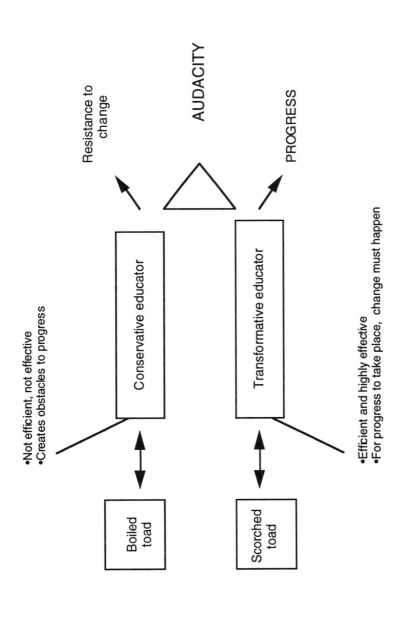

FIGURE 6.1 Synthesis of Pedagogic Meeting: Teacher Identity. *Source:* Derived from a handwritten chart posted on wall of Teachers' Meeting Room at Sussumu School, 1994.

These meetings are representative of both the pedagogical nature and political content of gatherings and dialogue at Sussumu School during the development of the Inter Project. The fact that the pedagogic meeting occurred in June 1994, a year and a half after the PT administration ended, speaks to the lasting impact of the reform efforts on the institutional culture of the school, specifically because most meetings used a process that mirrored the ER-OC-AC moments of the Inter Project and, notably, included a wide range of representative voices from the school and local community.

Curriculum Development

The outcome of Sussumu School's initial Study of the Reality (ER) was the generative theme of Lixo, which translates literally as trash, but connotes general conditions of sanitation and various forms of waste that contaminate the living space of the community. The principle socio-economic element of study became "basic sanitation" and the generative question guiding the educators' problematization of that reality was as follows: "How can we interfere (participate) in the decision-making process related to the location of dumping grounds?" The following comments registered from the population during the initial ER are representative of the "significant situations" facing the community that pointed towards the generative theme of "trash."

Example A: The Interdisciplinary Curriculum
Community Discourse Used in the Definition of Significant Situations
(Sussumu/1990)

"When they constructed the buildings they connected the sewage system with a channel that dumped out into the river of the favela."

"If people didn't throw their trash in that passageway there wouldn't be so many rats and flies about."

"The garbage truck passes up above and every one has to take the trash up there. It's far and people prefer to throw it in the passageways or in the middle of the favela."

"The children play in the little lake of the reservoir. The sewage contaminates the reservoir. The rats attack the small children at night."

"The students bath in the water box of the school."

In an effort to better inform themselves of that reality, the NAE team collected statistical data that further detailed the poor sanitation conditions of the community (e.g., the fact that as late as 1985 only 93 percent of the *favelas* in the southern zone of the city had running water and that 70 percent of the school's student body are favela residents). This latter fact made it all the more pertinent for the educators to address this situation considering that the serious health and social consequences related to the poor conditions of basic sanitation formed part of the daily life struggle for most of their students. From the universe of data collected the educational team inferred specific elements and conditions about the community, with relation to sanitation, that served and it oriented the subsequent steps in the organization of knowledge.

Example B: The Interdisciplinary Curriculum:
<u>*Specific Socio-Economic Elements that Characterize the Community*</u>

- Lack of infrastructure and planning (a complete sewage system does not exist in the area).
- Disorganization in the occupation of land.
- Lack of consciousness of the use of public and private resources.
- Lack of consciousness of the consequences of the deterioration of the environment: Environment pollution.
- Lack of rules in the organization and occupation of areas of recreation.

Prior to reaching the stage of designing the curriculum program, the qualitative and quantitative "Socio-Economic Aspects of the Theme" were identified and organized in a process called "thematic reduction," which serves as a guiding framework in the selection of content for the curriculum. In the case of Sussumu School, this analytical reduction around the theme of *lixo*, or waste, was completed in the following manner.

Example C: The Interdisciplinary Curriculum
Thematic Reduction of the Socio Economic Aspects of the Theme
(Sussumu, 1990)

Types/ Forms	Benefit/ Cost	Supply/ Demand	Local/ Time	Origin
•organic	•contamination	•great quantity	•gather periods	•urbanization
•cultural	•financial cost of	•habits	•garbage dump	•stoppages
•inorganic	production of	•quantity	•quality	locations
•recyclable	trash		•public locals	(channels, rivers)
•non-recyclable	•organization		relation of time	•unorganized
•solid	and treatment		to collection	occupation of
•liquid	•pollution		and treatment	land
•gaseous	•recycling			
•junk (*sucata*)				
•industrial				
(residues)				
•technological				
•food wastes				
•does not decompose				
•decomposes				

Human Relations	Other Aspects	Relation to other elements
•affects human relations	•Garbage workers strike	•health
•lack of prestige of	(contact of population	•leisure
professions associated	with trash)	•housing
with waste	•increase in trash on	•work
•consequences of	vacant lots (people	
strike by garbage collectors	living among trash)	
	•consciousness of where	
	trash ends up and its effects	
	on that location	

Based on these identified aspects of theme, generative questions were developed for each subject area and the ensuing curriculum developed. Figure 6.2 reproduces the actual curriculum guides developed by the NAE-6 Inter Team in conjunction with Sussumu School staff in the pilot stage of the Inter Project's implementation. This particular curriculum was used as a model in the training sessions that the NAE-6 personnel carried out subsequent to the pilot experience, as the Project expanded to other schools.

Interdisciplinary Curriculum Program
Generative Theme: *LIXO* [Trash or Waste]
(Sussumu, 1990)

E.R.
1. What does the trash in your home contain?
2. How does your community get rid of its waste?
3. What is trash to you is the same for others? Why?
4. What human activities produce trash?
6. The manner in which your community is free of trash causes problems? What are they?
7. Is the quantity of trash related to the problems that have been brought up? Why?
8. How can these problems be resolved?
9. How does the solution of the problem of trash relate to the improvement of the quality of life in São Paulo?

O.C.
•Table:
(i.e., Shopping News 8/25/90)
•Text:
"The destiny of trash in the
Greater São Paulo."

A.C.
1. How is the region of Sussumu represented in the table regarding waste (types and destiny)
2. Do other neighborhoods get rid of trash the same way?
3. Discarding waste is a problem for the city of São Paulo?
Why?

•Text:
"The problem of trash"
•Table:
"Trash" (Folha de S. Paulo 9/11/90)

1. Is the construction of more land fills the solution to the the problem of trash in São Paulo?
2. Why are there no dumps in the center of the city?
3. What explains the presence of a large number of people living near waste deposits?

[What follows are examples of the resulting curriculum program by subject area].

Subject Area: History
Generative Question:
How can society organize to seek solutions to problems that determine the quality of life in urban centers?

O.C.
•history of the barrio, emphasis on time and people
•letters, reports, photographs, interviews with the first residents
(documents: written and oral)
•internal migrations
•process of acceleration of urban occupation

A.C.
•Film: "The Gods Must be Crazy"
•Discussion: what can trash do to man and what can man do with trash?

Subject Area: Geography
Generative Question:
How should urban territory be occupied so as not to result in the degradation of the environment and quality of life?

O.C.
•pollution in general
•contamination of land and water by waste
•waste as a fertilizer
•the use of fertilizers in agriculture
•environmental contamination and interference in the quality of life

A.C.
•reuse of waste as fertilizer
•visit to a compost site
•registration of the interferences caused by inappropriate deposits of waste in the region

Subject Area: Science
Generative Question:
If humanity was producing waste for millions of years why isn't the surface of the earth covered in trash?

O.C.
•classification of waste in biodegradable and non biodegradable
•cycle of material in nature (bio-geo-chemical cycles), ecological balance

A.C.
•what can be reused

Curricular component: History
Concepts: time and space; transformation; subject of history

E.R.
1. What religion corresponds to your family?
2. What church do you frequent?
3. Do you believe in the existence of God?
4. When you heard talk about PC what did you understand? (footnote explaining political context)
5. Have you heard the word "Impeachment"?
6. Do you know what type of government we have?
7. When I speak of the President of the Republic do you know who I am talking about?

O.C.
•informal conversations
•Statute of the child
•Informative texts
•Graphic designs
•Photos related to the topic

A.C.
•questionnaire
•student talk (*fala*)
•group posters
•teacher observations

Curricular Component: Science
Concepts: transformation; cycles; equilibrium

E.R.
1. "Health is Life." What do you understand from this phrase?
2. Are there different types of beings?
3. Are all beings the same?
4. Plants belong to what family?
5. How can we improve the quality of life?
6. When should we take care of our health and why?

O.C.
•informal conversations
•informative texts
•essays
•reading of newspapers
•expository posters
•commentaries on TV

A.C.
•elaboration of group posters on
the topics
•responses to questioning
•information in essays

Curricular Component: Mathematics
Concepts: Relations; classification; proportionality

E.R.
1. Do we belong to different social classes?
2. What social class do you belong to?
3. Can money modify the personality of an individual?
4. What corrupts a person?
5. Can money buy everything?

O.C.
•various exercises
•systematization of problems
•reading of texts covering
content involved

A.C.
•resolution of exercises
•systematization of problems

Curricular Component: Portuguese
Concepts: Relations; transformation; time and space

E.R.
1. What media do you use to expand your knowledge?
2. Where do you usually find new information?
3   This year there will be elections, do you when and what we are electing?
4. Do you think it important to vote?
5. Should the voter be obligated to vote?

O.C.
•Readings of texts
newspapers, books
magazines
•comic strips, books
•poetry
•vocabulary

A.C.
•production of texts
•interpretation of texts
•questionnaire
•informal dialogue
•critiques and commentaries

Curricular Component: Geography
Concepts: Time/ Space; Transformation

E.R.
1. What neighborhood do you live in?
2. What is the trajectory that you make to your house?
3. What kinds of geographic accidents do you find in your neighborhood?
4. Does your neighborhood have clubs?
5. What is the purpose of these clubs?
6. What is the *Sociedade Amigos do Barrio* (Society of friends of the Neighborhood)
7. What churches exist in the neighborhood?
8. The church contributes to your education?
9. Have you heard of the Statute of the Child?

O.C.
•informal conversations
•Statute of the Child
•texts, maps, graphics
plans (trajectory home-school)

A.C.
•questionnaires
•posters
•group projects

Curricular Component: Art Education
Concepts: Space; Equilibrium; temporality; transformation

E.R.
1. What do you like most on TV? Why?
2. Of the Soap Operas on TV. which do you watch?
3. Have you ever watched the TV. news.
4. Have you ever been to circus, theater? If you have did you like it?
5. When watching TV. do you find a message that is to you liking? What type of message is it?
6. Do you usually read billboards and signs on the street?

O.C.
•informal dialogues
•collages
•colored pencil drawings
•free and directed drawing

A.C.
•dramatizations
•posters
•drawings
•paintings

Based on these general guidelines, teachers developed activities and lessons for students who, through various organized classroom activities, diligently sought to answer the generative questions posed for each subject area. What is compelling in this example is both the focus of the questions and the methods for addressing them. Clearly, the focus on environmental issues can be directly related to the unhealthy conditions in which many of the students at Sussumu School lived. Simultaneously, it helped them understand the root causes and possible alternatives to those conditions. Similarly, the process of achieving this clarity involved groupwork, research, analysis and the development of action steps.

Teachers' Assessments of the Inter Project

Many teachers at Sussumu School and elsewhere confessed to having initial doubts about the feasibility of the Inter Project and some even revealed that they had initially opposed it in their minds, but agreed to cooperate with the Project in order to go along with the rest of the school. However once they had the opportunity to study its theoretical tenets (i.e., Freireian strategies of dialogic interchange and thematic investigation coupled with Emilia Ferreiro's constructivist approach to literacy acquisition and learning), they were gradually won over and began to believe it to be the right path to follow. At the same time, there were others who felt an almost immediate affinity with the political goals and objectives of the Project and relished the opportunity to find a theoretical home to an instructional practice that they had always used. The following portraits provide a glimpse into the thoughts of teachers at Sussumu School as they reflect on their experience with the Inter Project.

SELMA: Selma was among the educators who at first were reluctant to join the Inter Project but eventually were among its most enthusiastic advocates. An African-Brazilian of working class origin, Selma, immigrated to São Paulo in 1974 as a young teacher from the northeastern city of Recife. She worked in MOBRAL [the military government's literacy program for adults] for two years, until 1976 when she began working as a pre-school teacher. She arrived at Sussumu School in 1985, teaching pre-school and first grade. In recent years, given her husband's persistent unemployment, she has needed to supplement her income by working during another shift as an administrative assistant to the principal. Selma recalled how for her the Inter Project carried with it the tag of the PT Party and therefore at first signified a negative and definitively partisan imposition on the school and teachers. This initial reaction on her part was mostly due to the fact that the PT had previously governed in her previous city of residence, Diadema, and she was displeased with their educational efforts making her "absolutely against the PT." Her experience with the Inter Project and the PT administration in São Paulo changed her view of the Party. For Selma, interaction with personnel from NAE-6 changed her views and allowed her to appreciate the PT administration's ongoing respect for the professional integrity of teachers. Once she decided to give the Inter Project a chance, she felt comfortable working within its principles and in 1992 declared that she planned to continue developing her teaching practice within the framework of an interdisciplinary curriculum via the generative theme regardless of the political party in power.

Selma believed that her experience in the Inter Project positively affected her educational thinking and practice. Prior to her involvement with the Inter Project she revealed that curriculum content was her principal focus; with the Inter Project her notion of what was important had changed. She elaborated, "now the essence [of my teaching practice] is the formation [of the student], I no longer have the preoccupation with finishing the book . . . [rather] I am concerned with forming a critical creative person." Selma considered the interdisciplinary curriculum via the generative theme as a more comprehensive educational approach than a traditional curriculum which limits the educational role of the teacher and school to the transmission of specific content matter. She asserted, "[that role should be] the integral formation of the citizen, departing from the daily life experience of the student and not what I [as the teacher] determine that the student needs. [The Inter Project] is a proposal that gives the student the opportunity to locate himself in their reality." She expressed her newfound professional identity in the following words: "[the teacher] is an agent that contributes to the formation of citizens, It is not just me who is doing the teaching, it is the student who is discovering [new knowledge] by means of my mediation."

Even though Selma perceived Paulo Freire as "very philosophical" and somewhat distant for the concrete reality of teaching in an urban school such as Sussumu School, although she recognized the importance of his theoretical contribution to the Inter Project, namely the idea of the generative theme. She explained, "it is impossible to disassociate Inter from the generative theme, one is intimately connected to the other." In general, Selma's assessment of the implementation of the Inter Project at Sussumu School was that it was carried out in an uneven fashion largely because of teachers' lack of comprehension of its theoretical basis. Despite the fact many teachers believed in the proposal and most teachers claimed to be working within the Project, in her opinion, the reality was that they were not and that it was very much up to the individual teacher as to whether or not their classroom was functioning under the Project's principles. Nonetheless, in 1994, she still reflected on the Inter Project experience as a positive one and in this statement reveals a very Freireian conceptualization of education: "It was a valid and enriching experience, I learned a lot, principally I learned how to learn. It showed us educators that education is not something closed: you take a course, you know, you teach. No, you must learn with your students. In this way the Inter showed us that teaching and learning is an exchange [. . . and that] there is no subject that is prohibited from being talked about [in the classroom]."

CLAUDIO. Claudio was one of the more vocal teachers in his support of the Inter Project although he was not without his criticisms of the PT administration. Like other teachers at the school, his principal complaint was that the NAE-6 personnel "abandoned" the school once the Project expanded to other sites. He had been teaching since 1976 and working at Sussumu School since 1986. He had taught fifth through eighth grade, high school, and teachers' college (Magisterio) and had some experience in school administration.

Theoretically he identified the Inter Project as constructivist and therefore expressed his support for the curriculum reform proposal on that basis. To this effect Claudio made the following statement: "The Project seeks to do away with the fragmentation of knowledge following the presuppositions of constructivism in which I believe." In as much as the Freireian contribution to the Project is concerned, however, Claudio did not think that the generative theme was such an essential element to the overall process of constructing an interdisciplinary curriculum; he stated, "the generative theme is one of the means by which the process of "interdisciplinariness" can occur, but it is not the only one. Personally I believe that "interdisciplinariness" through language would be more successful. [For example,] my participation in the Inter Project changed my educational practice. As a Portuguese teacher I seek to make it possible that my students acquire linguistic competence through the use of language."

Though he recognized the administration's effort to establish channels for communicating its proposal through publications (i.e., *Cadernos de Formação*), he had some reservations about how well the Project was actually communicated to and internalized by teachers. Despite the fact that these principles may have had enormous relevance for classroom practice, Claudio believes that the Secretariat presented them in a manner too theoretical for the majority of teachers to grasp, speaking to the limited professional formation that most teachers receive and to the fact that many of the designers of the Project were university specialists accustomed to thinking in sophisticated theoretical terms.

Claudio's general assessment of the Project is that it did impact the practice and thinking of teachers at Sussumu School. He maintained that as a consequence teachers became more willing to work collectively and demonstrated a willingness to break from the routine: "Teachers have become more active, participatory, creative and critical," he added. Claudio pointed to a visible transformation in inter-personnel relations in the school, emphasizing a reduction in authoritarianism, a greater integration of the technical team and teaching staff, and the appreciation of the pedagogic coordination. "The school became more concerned with the community and gave greater attention to individual differences among its members." Also, Claudio recalled, like many teachers, that his students initially reacted negatively to the Project because they felt uncertain about such innovations in the way the classroom was organized. Once they became more accustomed to working in groups and learning without the use of single subject text books, they began to enjoy their new educational program. He did not consider the changes that have occurred to be necessarily permanent ones, but in fact quite precarious throughout the municipal system. Nonetheless, in 1992, immediately following the PT defeat in the municipal elections, Claudio still held fast to the conviction that certain pockets of resistance would fight to keep the Project alive at the school site level, despite a political change in administration. In fact, at a follow-up visit to the school, one year and a half later, he was part of precisely such a group at Sussumu School as was Selma.

Although they did not perceive the Inter Project necessarily in a negative light, other teachers at Sussumu School were less ardent in their support of the Project or not quite ideologically or pedagogically coherent with its original conceptualization in their adaptation of its principles. This was the case of Adriana and Vera who are each representative of two such middle ground positions.

ADRIANA. Adriana was a relatively new teacher at the school and hence represents the previously identified problem of newcomers who did not feel as committed as they might to a Project which was initiated prior to their arrival at the school [She had only been at Sussumu School for six months at the time that she was interviewed.] A young middle-class woman, Adriana had finished her teacher training in 1983, and had been working on her Master's degree in Education since 1989. Adriana initiated her teaching career working at different private high schools where she taught various subjects. At Sussumu School she taught history for fifth through eighth grade classes. She identified her students as generally poor or of lower middle-class origin, without culture and with difficulties in learning due to their limited vocabulary and inability to understand what the teacher attempts to convey.

Philosophically, Adriana characterized herself as a humanist but did not claim to adhere to any particular educational theories, while admitting to being somewhat "rigid" at times in her classroom approach due to her experience working in traditional schools. As a teacher, she believed her role was to provide students with basic standard academic skills and to assist them in gaining a more critical perspective of reality.

With regard to the Inter Project, she agreed with its overall purpose, which in her words was intended "to create a movement that rethinks schooling." Although Adriana aligned herself "within the Inter ideologically," she described her experience with the Project at Sussumu School as at times giving her the feeling of being "in the middle of chaos." Since she was a relatively new member of the school faculty she had not accompanied the initial stages of development of the Inter Project at the Sussumu School and felt limited in her ability to comment on its effectiveness. Still Adriana was able to say, in corroboration with many of her colleagues, that what was most positive about the Inter Project experience was that teachers have been pushed to rethink the process of curriculum construction taking into account all the subject areas at once. She agreed with the basic notion of interdisciplinariness in that subjects should not be divided up into discrete areas of knowledge. Although Adriana insisted that she only had a limited knowledge of Freirean educational principles, she felt that such principles had served their purpose with the Inter Project, in as much as a Freirean dialogical and reflective approach facilitated the process for teachers to rethink their pedagogical practices and guide their work in the classroom. Still, she felt that teachers should not be tied to the interdisciplinary method of curriculum organization based on generative themes, reflecting a resistance to this central feature of the Project shared by many teachers encountered at Sussumu School and other schools. In fact she overtly admitted that she does not strictly follow the Inter Project in her daily classroom practice and pointed out that making the connection to other subject areas (i.e., an interdisciplinary approach) is not always easily achieved.

She further alluded to student resistance to the new more demanding approaches to teaching and learning brought on by the Project, stating that "the students have the need to copy, the fifth graders made posters, working in groups and doing research but the students did not like it because they had to work harder." The greatest contention she had with the Project was related to the various programmatic innovations made (i.e., the institution of cycles and evaluation by concepts) that were part of the PT's broader educational reform policies. According to Adriana, these policies were associated with what she perceived as an increased lack of control and authority on the part of teachers with respect to their students. She concludes: "[As a result of these changes in grading and grade promotion policies,] there is doubt as to whether or not students understand what the teacher is passing on to them. The student feels a need for the traditional teacher."

Adriana herself felt somewhat uneasy about her ability to fully implement the Inter Project because of its complex nature, although she did align herself ideologically with one of its fundamental educational principles, in as much as she believed that the reality of students should necessarily be respected within the curriculum. Her assessment was that the Inter Project stopped short by failing to teach children about realities beyond their own.

VERA. Vera was an older teacher who taught fourth grade at Sussumu School. Though she claimed to be working with the Inter Project, she demonstrated a limited understanding of its methods and objectives in both her articulation of her interpretation of the Project and its application in her teaching. Like many educators in São Paulo that failed to fully grasp the project's theoretical underpinnings or refused to embrace its political purpose, Vera adapted some superficial characteristics of the Project to her own pedagogical-ideological framework, thus affecting in a limited way her approach to lesson planning and delivery. In general, she associated the Inter Project with vague ideas of constructivism which she defined as giving validity to the knowledge that the student brings from home. According to Vera, "before [the Inter Project], the teacher was not concerned with the student. Now [within the Project] the objective is to work with the critical sense of students and to guide the student in reflecting on what they say and think." The most salient characteristic of the Inter Project in Vera's perception was that the programming of content was not predetermined but remained open ended: she maintained that with the Inter Project, "the content matter has become more broad, we are no longer stuck in that traditional content of 'turning the page in the book.'" In accordance with a generally held perception about the greater feasibility of associating a given generative theme with certain subject areas (over others), Vera determined the Inter Project most effective in the area of the Social Sciences, concluding that as a result of the Inter, "students are more interested in subjects such as history." She added that the Inter Project requires a great deal of consciousness on the part of the teacher, but was not explicit as to what kind of consciousness, i.e., political versus pedagogical awareness. Vera reflected this oversimplification of the Inter Project curriculum model with statements to the effect of, "Fiz Inter da Folklore." (I made an Inter out of Folklore.) In other words, in her perception, any attempt to introduce a discussion of popular culture or contemporary issues into the classroom is considered "doing the Inter Project."

Summary: Project Impact

The profiles of the selected teachers offer a subjective assessment of the ways in which the Inter Project had an impact on Sussumu School. In addition to their impressions and opinions of the ways in which the Inter Project transformed this working class school, a brief stay in 1994 by O'Cadiz allowed for a series of follow-up visits to Sussumu School. By this time, the PT administration had been out of office for over one year, replaced by a right-wing, traditional administration that had retained much of the no-menclature created by the PT (e.g., teacher formation groups and interdis-ciplinary curriculum) while summarily eliminating the political content and ending all technical support for Project development. Despite these conditions, the follow up visits to Sussumu School (after the PT adminis-tration) offered some hope.

In spite of the change in administration, it appeared that there was still a group committed to addressing community issues and working on com-munity development in the school. One example of this effort to raise the consciousness of the school community occurred during a School Council meeting focusing on taking preventive measures prior to the undertaking of an improvement of the school's facilities. A video was shown that de-picted vandalism of public schools. After viewing the video, more than 30 teachers, parents and students at the meeting engaged in a discussion around the causes of vandalism and the need for the community to come together and take ownership of the school, and at the same time demand adequate maintenance and timely repairs from the responsible public offi-cials. The group came to the conclusion that students would not respect the school if they were unhappy there. Parents cited the lack of supervi-sion and orientation at home as contributing to the problem. The principal proposed that the Council work with the student and parent associations at the school in devising a campaign to make the school more sensitive to these issues.

Also, as evidenced in the narrative of the pedagogic meeting in 1994 presented above, a debate around the validity of the Inter Project persisted one year after the PT administration. At that time, about 30 percent of the staff at Sussumu School made a serious effort to continue to work with the Project. Francisca, a teacher who had previously worked as part of the In-ter Team at NAE-6 and returned to Sussumu School after the PT's demise, related in a follow-up interview in 1994, the difficulties they were facing in keeping the Project alive at Sussumu School:

> Last year we didn't even undergo a Preliminary Study of the Reality. The
> teachers just came up with a generative theme. I thought it was a con-

tradiction to say we were doing the Inter Project in the plan submitted to the Delegacia [formerly what would have been the NAE] when we hadn't even done a preliminary study. The next year, some 22 of us went into the favela one morning in groups of three and four, to engage in conversations with the residents. .. When we returned to do the evaluation of the data, it became apparent that many had never entered a favela before, the experience made them question some of their prejudices . . . In the end the group thought that the theme of sewage or trash would come up yet again. I questioned the analysis, how can it be the same significant problem, after five years? For many this meant that the model did not work and that the Project failed to progress. Still, the experience of going into the favela was beneficial in that it ended the perception on the part of many teachers that the favelados are the source of problems in the community. . . . This year, the presidential elections opened up the community discourse to include many commentaries of the political process, consequently the generative theme of "citizenship" emerged.

In reference to this continued effort among teachers in the municipal system to keep the ideal of the Inter Project alive in a context unfavorable to its survival, one former NAE team member (who was active in such a group at the school to which she returned after the PT administration) offered the following metaphor:

It is like in that movie "Quest for Fire" where the prehistoric tribal people, having discovered fire but unsure of how to ignite the flame, guard a burning torch diligently, day and night, obsessed with the fear that somehow it will suddenly be extinguished by a gust of wind, downpour of rain or even flicker out by itself. We [in the group pursuing the Inter approach to the curriculum] are like the tribal people in the movie, desperately trying to keep the flame of the Inter light, killing ourselves against all odds so that it doesn't go out.

The continual evolution of the interdisciplinary curriculum model at Sussumu School—during the PT administration and after—demonstrates the far-reaching impact of the Inter Project experience on the conceptualization of the curriculum and its practice at that school. While the program detailed above was among the first to evolve from the Inter Project effort, it is significant that a group of teachers at Sussumu School were still struggling to develop a curriculum following the model of the interdisciplinary approach via the generative theme one year after the PT administration's demise. In May of 1994, on the wall of the teachers' meeting room and under a sign which read "Interdisciplinaridade," four large charts were posted that outlined the interdisciplinary curriculum plan for the semester by cycles: (ciclo basico 1,2,3) (ciclo intermediario 4) (ciclo intermediario 5,6) (ciclo final 7, 8). As an example, the curricular plan for fourth grade (the first year of the intermediate cycle) is presented below.

Example: Interdisciplinary Curriculum—Outline of Program
(Intermediate Cycle/Sussumu, 1994)

Significant Situations:
- Lack of perspective in life
- No political and religious conscience
- Disillusionment with governmental institutions (corruption and dishonesty)

Generative Theme: Constructing Citizenship
Unifying Concepts:
Relations X Transformation X Time Space X Subject of History X Cycles X Equilibrium
Generative Question: How does education contribute to the exercise of citizenship?

Again the "elements" and "socio-economic aspects" are identified and listed with the intention of intersecting the theme of education and citizenship into the curriculum design. These serve as reference points in devising "specific topics" or content matter and learning activities which will specifically address these aspects of the generative theme from the perspective of the various areas of knowledge. Examples of these two curriculum design elements follow.

Example: The Interdisciplinary Curriculum—
Thematic Reduction of the Socio-Economic Aspects of the Theme
(Sussumu, 1994, Post-PT)

Types/Forms	Benefit/Cost	Local/Time	Origin
•family	•education	•home	•poor income
•school	•health	•school	•family dysfunction
•professional	•financial resources	•streets	•migration
•political	•space	•reservoir	•occupation of space
•social	•purchasing power	•work	•family dysfunction
•recreational		•market	
•affective		•church	
•sports		•businesses	
		•bars	
		•shopping malls	

Human Relations	Other Aspects	Relation to other elements	
•Human rights	•cultural habits	•leisure	•education
•family dysfunction	•legislation	•housing	•work
•social discrimination	•media	•health	•communication

Example: The Interdisciplinary Curriculum— Specific Topics for Subject Areas (Sussumu/Intermediate Cycle, 1994 Post PT)

Portuguese:
- •Texts for reading and interpretation: dialogues, poetry, comic strips
- •Production of texts: individual and collective
- •Collective correction of texts and rewrites
- •Linguistic analysis: grammar, punctuation, spelling, structure of text
- •Use of the dictionary
- •Formation, order and expansion of phrases

Math:
- •Natural numbers
- •Operations with natural numbers (+,-,X, ÷)
- •Percentages
- •Monetary system
- •System of measurement
- •Introduction to geometry: angles and polygons (perimeter)

Science:
- •Hygiene of the body and mind
- •Nutrition and food hygiene
- •Functions of human body: digestive system, circulatory system, reproductive system (cycle of life)
- •Animals and plants (food chain)
- •Utilization of natural resources

History:
- •Human rights (citizenship and constitution)
- •Status of the child and adolescent
- •History: family, neighborhood, municipality, state of São Paulo
- •The greater São Paulo: settlement, indigenous population, migration and immigration
- •Time line: work and industrialization

Geography:
- •Geographic location and orientation
- •Scale
- •State of São Paulo, rivers, principle cities, relief, climate, reservations
- •Brazil: state boarders, five regions

Art Education:
- •Work in groups: collages, drawings, paintings
- •Folklore
- •Theater, mime, dramatic play
- •Music

Physical Education:
- •Know and respect rules of the game
- •Notion of space and time
- •Cooperative games, collective and individual
- •Registration of popular culture

With the above curriculum as evidence, we believe that the continued enthusiasm and commitment to some form of the Inter Project is a tribute to the profound ways in which the teachers' involvement with the Project initiated a transformation in their professional identities and values. Nevertheless, and particularly given cutbacks in support initiated by the succeeding regime, a primary challenge continued to be the creation of a popular public school that addressed the fundamental problems of the local community. What seemed to still pervade at Sussumu School was the conception, exemplified by Vera, that to engage in the construction of an interdisciplinary curriculum via the generative theme was to add frills onto the conventional curriculum. This perception seemed to relate to teachers' inability or unwillingness to fully understand the conceptual framework of the Project, and, in a related way, their difficulty putting its complex pedagogical ideals into practice.

CASE 2
Habib School: Creating a Curriculum for the Working Class

Dr. Habib Carlos Kyrillos School (Habib School) is easily accessible by taking one of the many buses that run along the corridor of Cupece Avenue, a principal arterial that connects the working class neighborhood of Americanopolis with the rest of the city of São Paulo, be it the more affluent areas to the North, the impoverished periphery to the South, or the industrial city of Diadema to the Southeast. Consequently, Cupece Avenue teams with a heavy flow of cars, buses and cargo trucks and is lined with shops and businesses selling all kinds of goods and services, ranging from bakeries to auto repair shops. The PT has a strong presence in the area, as evidenced by the location of a party headquarters office at a prominent site on Cupece Avenue. Also on the street corner that leads from Cupece Avenue to the school—next to a Shell gas station—is a large store front church, a testimony to the growing influence of the Pentecostal religious movement among the Brazilian urban poor. Hence, although Habib School was in the southern peripheral part of the city, it was well connected by transit to employment, commercial and cultural centers, and therefore was not as marginalized or isolated as other schools in NAE-6.

The intense commercial activity, dense population and strategic location of the region between two cities (Diadema and São Paulo) contributed to the high level of criminal activity, namely drug trafficking, that flourished in the area. The school was built halfway up a very steep hill that rose above Cupece Avenue. Walking away from the commercial strip, one quickly entered into the more dangerous part of the neighborhood, "the nest of thieves" according to residents. Locals told harrowing stories about the violence that permeates the reality of the indigent and working class community that surrounds the school: a body shot dead in the school courtyard was discovered a year previous to the research; students related that sometimes bodies would be left lying in the streets for days before the police came to pick them up, no one daring to go near for fear of being associated with the crime by the police or with the victim. Students were protective of both researchers, refusing to let them walk unaccompanied to the bus stop two blocks away after dusk. And, tragically one of the teachers who lived in the area and was very active in the school and community, was murdered in 1994. She was very much loved by her students and her violent death cast a deep sadness over the school.

Clearly, the chaos of the surrounding neighborhood, which infected the daily lives of the students at the school, deeply affected the school site, and the teachers and other staff who worked there. At the same time, this dire situation almost demanded a reform movement like the Inter Project which might offer the opportunity to understand and overcome aspects of this violent enviornment and the daily fear it caused. The community of Habib School faced several prominent issues in its quest to develop the Inter Project. Of these, the primary task was to find ways of building consensus among a very strong-willed, articulate and experienced staff. Similarly, this staff, while needing to negotiate some shared ideas and meanings within itself, also needed to find ways of expanding its boundaries to include students, particularly upper grade students, in the development of the Inter Project. With this task of redefining the school culture into one that was inclusive and based on shared goals and objectives, the community faced a third challenge: the reality of resistance to the Project from many different sectors.

Habib School: A Description

Like Sussumu School and many others schools in municipal system, Habib School was constructed mainly out of concrete and possessed few windows—many of which were broken—to interrupt the monotony of its stark walls and bland architecture. Apparently the building design came from a French architect who had won a competition, the reward for which was the construction of this school and its design was absolutely unsuited for a school in a tropical country. On strange vaulted portions of the ceiling were vertical glass windows that remained half open all the time because there was no mechanism for closing them. When it rained, as it often does in São Paulo, water built up on the roof, periodically overflowing into the classrooms. The outdoor court yard was surrounded by a high wall, topped by a chain link fence giving it a prison-like appearance and the iron door at the entrance was kept locked while school was in session. The eight classrooms were located on the second floor to which the only access was a curved stairway enclosed by two walls making the ascent and descent of students a very noisy event. The hall at the top of the stairs was brightened by floral murals painted on the walls some time ago, but the classrooms were badly in need of painting and repair. Classrooms were cold and damp, with leaks in the ceiling and windows, the desks wobbly and the chalkboards marred by worn out patches. In short, Habib School was physically falling apart.

On the lower level, where the administrative offices were located, the school boasted a relatively well-kept library and spacious reading room, both recently renovated. The reading room was truly multipurpose, and hosted everything from staff pedagogic meetings to a theatrical performance to a student sexual orientation class. In addition, a much smaller room served as the teachersí lounge where staff convened during breaks and in-between shifts. A long table dominated the room and was usually crowded with papers as teachers sat preparing for their classes, while others ate and drank the constantly supplied tea and coffee and generally chatted amongst themselves. The walls too were crowded with closets where teachers stored their materials because no storage space was available inside the virtually barren classrooms.

History of the Project at Habib School

At Habib School, the Inter Project intially started out with only 11 teachers who were interested in adopting the Secretariat's proposal. Gradually, others joined in and by December 1990 the majority opted to join the Project. The principal at this school was a PT militant and therefore strongly supported the Project. However, she and several other teachers from the school were called out to work as part of the NAE-6 staff during the PT administration, consequently draining the school of staff that would have been key to the Project's success there. In fact, after the PT lost the elections in 1992, the principal and three of the NAE-6 personal returned to their teaching positions at Habib School. They were an important part of the effort to organize teachers interested in continuing working in an interdisciplinary fashion well after the Project's demise in 1994.

Fortunately, in the absence of the regular principal, Luciana, the Pedagogic Coordinator at Habib School and a strong supporter of the Inter Project, persuaded the teachers under her supervision to participate. She recalls the moment of the preliminary investigation that took place in the first semester of 1991 as "a great festival" generating both enthusiasm and anxiety in that teachers were initially apprehensive about the radically different approach to curriculum called for by the Project. But at the same time, many looked forward to effecting positive change in the school's program. The first semester's generative theme at Habib School was determined to be "Precarious Transportation." The theme arose out of interviews with neighborhood residents in which the problems and issues around public transportation took precedence.

As in other schools, organizing the intermediate level teachers with their disparate schedules proved a logistical nightmare. Yet, despite these obstacles, the Pedagogic Coordinators at Habib School remained committed to the Project and organized meetings at different time blocs throughout the day in order to accommodate the conflicts in schedule. The CP, Luciana, recalls the early stage of training meetings: "[During these initial meetings] words like 'dialectics' and 'epistemology' began to appear. There was a lot of theory. We began with theory and a month of meetings, it was exhaustive but animated." After the initial training, the CP related that teachers remained confused by the complexity of the theory behind the pedagogic moments they were expected to put into practice (i.e., ER;OC;AC). She observed that it was difficult for teachers to organize their lessons using all three pedagogical moments, and they gradually perceived that the Project required much more professional preparation than they had imagined. Other problems arose in relation to the selection of content matter: Luciana recalls, "at first we almost killed our students with so much content matter." As a result of the broad categories suggested by the generative theme, a curriculum quandary was created as teachers disputed what such an approach stipulated as the relevant content to be taught. Yet, according to Luciana, this conflict also led to the initiation of a constructive dialogue with teachers across disciplines, and the exchange of ideas on a sophisticated pedagogical level. In her assessment, by May of 1991, "the collective began to truly function" (Luciana, interview, 1992).

Yet, the Project did not remain without its opponents at Habib School. A major point of contention was the break down in pupil discipline pointed out by those who opposed the Project. As teachers increasingly began to organize their students to work in groups, many also felt that they were giving up classroom control a because students were allowed to move about more freely and to talk among themselves. Consequently the school was divided: "a escola se dividiu," Luciana points out, emphasizing that the division was very marked. As one teacher put it, there were those who preferred the comfort of teaching a class of students who are expected to keep quiet and those who were willing to take on the challenge of attempting to make their classrooms more participatory.

During the second semester of 1991, the school engaged in its second Study of the School Reality, this time taking into account the perspective of the students. Students were given a questionnaire of thirty questions including "What is it that you would like to build in place of the school?" At this point student discourse gained greater importance in the curriculum planning process and teachers moved away from the single textbook by bringing in content from various sources. In particular, History, Geography and Science teachers were able to employ para-didactic books and they sought alternative resources for their classroom instruction, namely newspaper articles, teacher-prepared texts based on outside research, and data collected by students through surveys and the like. "It was a good moment, very gratifying, our practice was good . . . the most beautiful part was the final planning and elaboration of the AC . . . we put together books, it was a great deal of work. [The main concern of the group was] how were we to continue to advance?" Luciana, the school's CP, reflected. By 1992 the primary grade teachers were completely outside the Project: this stemmed from a problem of lack of pedagogic coordination on the one hand; and on the other , there was the persitant problem related to the fact that a large number of new teachers had arrived who were reluctant to join a process that was already underway. Some felt forced into the Project and at one point exclaimed, "I hate this and I don't want to continue," the CP recalled. Furthermore, the new teachers demanded to see practical applications of the theories presented to them. One teacher related that the staff began to accept the Project on the basis of teachers who demonstrated how it might work in practice gradually "forcing others to reflect and come out of their conformist position."

Still the CP and several teachers interviewed concurred that many had agreed to join the Project because they were motivated merely by the prospect of making extra money with the JTI, and they believed that they could continue to teach as they pleased in the privacy of the classroom. This seemed to be a common strategy among teachers who dissented from the Project's methods and philosophy or merely felt incapable of carrying them out. One teacher pointed to the fact that many felt a sense of guilt as though they had sinned for not closely following the Project's guidelines and therefore had to cover up. In her view, working with the Inter Project did not consist of a particular methodology but required a certain attitude, "a belief in what you are doing." Many teachers who dissented simply did not agree or believe in the Inter Project. In contrast to the Secretariat's claims, some even felt that they had been left out of the development process of the Project.

Meetings

At Habib School, the CP's active interest in a more profound comprehension of the Project and a more coherent application of its principles resulted in a concerted effort to organize regular pedagogic meetings for teachers. Meetings organized to this end —during and after the PT tenure —were very dynamic and at times even somewhat ideologocally confrontational in their nature. These meetings were mostly run by the pedagogic coordinator with a high level of participation by the teachers present. Occasionally NAE-6 team members would attend such meetings and contribute to the discussion. Teachers were typically assigned a reading for the week which they read prior to the meetings and then discussed as a group, often very heatedly. Teachers were observed—more so than at other schools—engaging in very serious debates about the theoretical underpinnings of the Project and its educational outcomes. In this regard, the group of teachers at Habib School could be characterized as among the most efficacious and collegial of any of the schools visited. They were respectful of each other, worked well and often together, and were capable of being very focused as they struggled together to understand the new concepts introduced to them through the Inter Project.

Teachers at Habib School were often observed going to great lengths to prepare activities for and with their students, with whom the majority appeared to have exceptionally good rapport and hold in high esteem. This was made especially evident in a sex education meeting with the school's upper grade students where they spoke seriously and candidly in front of their teachers of their most intimate concerns as adolescents. It was a very large faculty and diverse in terms of age and experience. This diversity, in addition to the exceptional commitment of the staff, contributed to making otherwise dull and routine meetings interesting and lively; it also allowed for a great deal of supportive mentoring between faculty members. [This was especially the case during the post-PT period observed when former NAE members played a key role in maintaining interested staff involved in the continued development of an interdisciplinary curriculum based on a generative theme.]

Curriculum Development and Classroom Practice

Habib School was distinctive in that teachers truly took to heart the dual and interactive goals of the Project related to curricular reorientation and democratization of the classroom. Evidence of this could be seen in classroom practice as well as in the content of lessons and activities. Relative to other sites included in this research, classroom practice at Habib School was very student-centered with learning activities revolving around issues of immediate concern and importance for the daily lives of its students and aimed at fostering a more critical reading of their world. For example, in one class observed while the 1992 Olympics were taking place (the generative theme for the semester was "the Olympic Games"), students engaged in a heated debate using political economy to explain why some countries such as the U.S., win so many medals while others, such a Brazil, win so few. In all the classes, group work was the norm, discussions seemed engaging to most students and teachers seemed to truly work in a coaching role rather than a lecturing one.

As an example of how the curriculum was genuinely transformed by the Inter Project, in the second semester of 1992—with the generative theme of "Human Relations"—a teacher of a fifth grade Geography class presented her students with a text for discussion: "Urban contrasts and the distribution of poverty." The text briefly summarized that inequities in the distribution of goods, services and opportunities create the differences between the rich and poor neighborhoods that develop in urban settings such as São Paulo. The same teacher had her sixth grade students discussing the eminent impeachment of then President Collor. Students worked in groups and wrote up opinion posters with titles such as "The problems of Brazil"; "Do you know what impeachment is?"; "Brazilians deserve justice." Such manifestations of a more politicized curriculum and the creation of opportunities for students to critically reflect on their current reality led many teachers (especially those ideologically opposed to the Workers' Party) to discern a politically dogmatic and educationally unsound tone in the Inter Projects' classroom curricular outcomes. Still, many other teachers held the conviction that it was precisely that aspect of the PT reform they most embraced.

The Collective Construction of Knowledge in a Dialogic Classroom. In her mid 20s, the teacher's young face simultaneously expresses both enthusiasm and a certain degree of anxiety about her immense responsibility teaching the thirty fourth graders that sit facing her in uneven rows. The majority of the 29 students seated in five rows are girls, ten students are boys, representing a broad spectrum of mixed European and African racial heritages which is typical of the working class neighborhoods of São Paulo. The blackboard is in a deplorable state with a huge white area where the board's green surface has completely worn off; this is also typical of the schools in such neighborhoods.

Before class, the teacher, Elena, is speaking with a parent resolving a problem of suspension of a child from school. This prolonged encounter in the middle of her class is an indication of the limited time teachers have to deal with such administrative and discipline problems because they are constantly interrupting instruction time with duties such as parent conferences and teacher meetings.

Without needing to call her class to order, Elena's presence at the front of the room commands the children's attention. They sit patiently and listen while she explains what they are to do today for Social Studies. She indicates that due to the brief time they have—as a result of the teacher meeting that was just held in the morning period during class time—they are only to copy some questions off the board. She refers to a text that they have already copied off the board during a previous lesson and tells them: "I will now write questions about the text that will be your homework." The class faithfully copies the homework off the board, but shortly thereafter, a different, more inquisitive energy takes hold as the teacher turns and faces the class between writing sentences.

It is customary for students to have a notebook for each subject where all lessons are copied off the board because of the lack of materials and logistical support, i.e., few books or texts, no photocopy machines and short supply of copy paper available to teachers. Hence teachers often write out selected texts for reading and study on the black board for students to copy, into their notebooks as well as any academic exercises related to such texts. Again, what is remarkable about this particular lesson is how an otherwise traditional pedagogic practice—the copying of text and questions to be answered for homework—is converted into a dynamic dialogic moment between teacher and students around themes of enormous relevance to the reality and daily lives of the students. The generative theme in Elena's classroom is "Workers."

<u>Script of a Dialogic Classroom</u>

The teacher writes on the board:

a) Para você o problema de falta de moradia e de emprego tem relação com a alta taxa de natalidade?
[a) In your view do the problems of housing shortage and unemployment have any relation to the high rate of birth?]

She finishes writing the sentence and initiates a brief dialogue with the children posing the question to them orally. A student immediately responds:

Com emprego você pode pagar coisas, sem emprego você não pode.
[If you have work you can pay for things, without work you can't.]

Other students join in the discussion, enthusiastically responding to the question posed by the teacher. The discussion becomes animated as the teacher continues posing new questions related to the text the students are currently studying. Students begin to tell their own personal stories of poverty and struggle, and one particularly expressive student goes on about a family she knows with 20 children. The teacher brings the impromptu discussion to a close by emphatically stating [in response to the idea of the 20 kids]:

Que locura !
[What madness . . .]

She turns and continues writing questions on the board pausing to check on her students' comprehension of each question before going on to the next. Three female students, in particular, are able to articulate the relationship between economy and family, relating personal experiences with employment and family and stating that once you have children you need to work more to support them. This leads to a discussion of the differences between urban and rural families. The teacher asks:

Porque no campo tem mais filhos?
[Why do people in the countryside have more children?]

The students respond:

Porque as crianças ajudam no coleta.
[Because the children help in the harvest]

A male student remarks:

Os grandes poderão ajudar se arrumam trabalho mas já é dificil prá adulto.
[The older ones might be able to help if they got a job, but it's already hard for adults to get work.]

A female student further argues:

Mais aí o dinheiro vai acabando com os filhos, com os remedios, as escola . . .
[But then the money is spent on the children, medicine, school . . .]

The teacher reinforces her examples:

É, com o costo da medicina, a escola . . .
[Yes, with the cost of medicines, school . . .]

The discussion subdues and the students resume writing for a few seconds, but soon discussion is initiated again by a student. This time, the student, after having further contemplated the contradictions between urban and rural life, muses:

Aqui não se planta e chove . . . la eles plantam mas não chove . . .
[Here there is no planting and it rains, there they plant but there is no rain.]

This comment reflects the fact that many students' families are immigrants from the poverty-stricken and drought-ridden Northeast. Another student makes reference to the discrepancy between the price of lettuce in the countryside and the city where it is three times more expensive. He explains:

No campo vendeu pra alguem e depois soubem muito o preço por que não esta dando lucro com o preço da condução.
[In the countryside they sell it to someone who then raises the price very high because with the cost of transportation there's no profit.]

One student adds:

Na cidade é mais dificil prá familia numerosa por que não . . .
[In the city it's much harder for a large family because . . .]

Another student finishes the statement:

Não tem trabalho e tudos querem lucro.
[There's no work and every one wants to make a profit . . .]

She continues relating her family's own story.

As the students engage in this dialogic exchange regarding the issues, elicited by the questions the teacher has written on the board, Elena pauses again to check her students comprehension of a particular word:

O que é boia fria?
[What is a boia fria?]

Among several answers that are yelled out, one student offers:

Trabalhador rural!
[Rural worker!]

The teacher continues questioning.

Ele ganha . . .
[He makes . . .]

Students [in unison]:

Pouco!
[Little]

Teacher:

Trabalha muito, ganha pouco.
[Works a lot, makes a little.]

Student:

Por isso se chama boia fria porque trabalho muito, ganha pouco e só pode levar a comida fria ao trabalho.
[Because they work hard and make little and so they can only take a cold lunch to work.]

The discussion continues intermittently as the teacher pauses to ask questions while some respond and others continue copying. The teacher

then turns to the students and solicits answers to the last question she has
written on the board:

Porque atualmente as mulheres trabalham fora?
[Why do women work more today?]

The students offer responses explaining that women have to work to
complement household income, or because their husbands have died. About
one third of the students in the class participate while others remain outside of discussion preferring to take on passive role of copying questions.
With the exception of one boy, the girls seem more willing to communicate
their thoughts to the class.

One girl continues:

Muitas contas, a luz, agua, aluguel, as vezes não da!
[Lots of bills, electricity, water, rent, sometimes there's just not
enough!]

The teacher asks:

Diminiu a quantidade de criança por que a mulher foi trabalhar fora?
[Did the quantity of children fall because women began to work
outside the home?]

A heated debate ensues with this one leading the teacher to rephrase
the question she had written on the board based on the points brought up
by the students in the discussion. The students help rewrite the question
dictating while the teacher writes it on the board for the rest of the class:

*Na sua opinião o numero de criança diminuo na cidade porque as mulheres
estão trabalhando fora de casa ou por causa da dificuldade finaceira?*
[In your opinion, did the number of children in the city drop because of the fact that women are working outside the home or because of the financial difficulties?]

The teacher stops to clarify:

O que é dificuldade financeira ?
[What is financial difficulty?]

One student announces to the class:

Eu ja respondi tudo.
[I already answered all the questions.]

The teacher admonishes her:

Não quero resposta boba.
[I don't want any silly answers.]

Another student responds to her initial question:

Quer dizer que uns ganham mais do que outros.
[It means that some make more than others.]

The teacher probes her student for deeper analysis:

Porque uns ganham mais do que outros?
 [Why do some make more than others?]

Student:

Uns trablaham em melhor emprego.
[Some work in better jobs.]

Teacher:

Então isso é distribuição de renda, uns ganham muito, outros pouco.
[O.K., then that's income distribution, some make a lot, others little.]

A student adds:

Os trabalhadores têm direito de ser registrados.
[Workers have the right to be registered.]

The teacher writes and asks the question:

Para você a situação precária de vida está relacionado com uma mal distribuíção da renda?
[Do you think that the precarious life situation is related to the poor distribution of income?]

Student:

Achou que sim, não é que tudos devem ser iguais mais cada um tem seu valor.
[I think so, not everyone should be the same, but everyone is worth something.]
Student:

Um quer comprar uma roupa e não pode porque não tem dinheiro, deveria ser igual.
[You want to buy clothes but you can't because you have no money, it should be the same.]

Teacher:

O justo . . .
[What is just . . .]

Exasperated by the topic of discussion, one student finally blurts out:

Tabalhar, trabalhar, sacrificar sua vida para ganhar uma miséria, não da!
[Work, work, make sacrifices all your life to make a miserable living, it can't be!]

This classroom dialogue demonstrates a problematizing approach to teaching that the Inter Project sought to promote and that indeed persisted at Habib School after the end of the PT tenure. In this particular script of a dialogic classroom, the teacher allows students to consistently voice their opinions about the subject matter and to reflect on its relevance to their own experience. Even when a child relates a personal story, the teacher validates that student's participation.

This kind of dialogic exchange is exemplary of many similar student-teacher discussions encountered in classrooms participating in the Inter Project. North American critical pedagogue Ira Shor aptly defines such pedagogic practice as a form of desocialization in as much as such "critical democratic dialogue questions traditional classroom relations, teacher-talk, unilateral authority, and the official syllabus [. . .]" He further elaborates on what should happen in a desocializing classroom in order to promote critical dialogue as the basis of the development of an educational counter-culture. Shor writes:

> The thoughts of students on the subject are the point at which critical dialogue begins. Those thoughts are social outcomes learned in mass culture and the traditional curriculum. two socializing agencies. In a desocializing class, existing knowledge is examined with the goal of gain-

ing critical distance on what has been absorbed uncritically in school and
every day life.[8]

Vivid examples of such learning abounded at Habib School.

Teachers' Assessments of the Inter Project

As with those in other schools, the teachers at Habib School held a
range of opinions about the Inter Project and implemented it with varying
levels of success and fidelity in their classrooms. Interestingly, a distinctive
feature at this school was less whether to engage with the Project than how
to understand it and utilize its principles. Though the teachers had several
outlets where they could negotiate a shared understanding—most notably
the formation group meetings—dissension and competing points of view
still remained, as the following profiles illustrate.

JENNY: An articulate and motivated educator in her early forties, Jenny
worked two jobs: as a principal at a school in the state system and as a
Portuguese language teacher in the municipal system. Educated throughout her life in private elite institutions, she studied under Franciscan nuns
during her secondary and teacher training. Despite her high level of education [two college degrees, one in Language Interpretation and another in
Pedagogy], she claimed that the combined salaries she recieved from her
two jobs as a teacher and a principal were not enough to keep her in the
profession. It was her sense of responsibility to serving her country which
motivated Jenny to remain commited to working as an educator.

Jenny purported to hold "progressive educational beliefs." In fact, she
was observed employing up-to-date teaching methods in her classroom
reminiscent of the cool efficiency of North American models (e.g., mastery
learning). Her students sat in a very orderly manner at tidy desks and followed her well organized lessons faithfully. Still, she cited Freire as essential to understanding the role of education in contemporary Brazilian society, and although she did not position herself completely in line with the
PT's political or educational philosophy, she had this to say about the Inter
Project in the municipal schools:

> I believe that the authors that deal with education by means of transfor-
> mation are the ones that have more to offer in terms of solutions to our
> social problems, because education is very close to that social aspect. I
> believe that education is the very basis of things, of the comprehension, of
> the consciousness of the individual, in the formation of his/her citizen-
> ship so that he/she acts within the society, fighting for his/her rights,
> complying with his/her duties, demanding his/her rights . . . I believe
> that it is one of the three points of the infrastructural tripod of a country—

education—if not the most important aspect of the country's infrastructure. This project gave us an outlet, a change in what was going on in terms of education in the city, I believe it was even a somewhat radical change for many of us who were still working with a different methodology, another line of thinking. But in the process of its implementation it demonstrated results, changes in the behavior of our children, a greater degree of conscientization that the project was bringing about on an individual basis. I feel this to be extremely important, a conscientization of oneself and of the society, because the children did modify themselves. They stopped destroying things in the school and began to perceive the school as a space to which they have a right and which is theirs. It is not a public space to be anarchalized and vandalized but a space of the people, for the people's development.

For the most part, Jenny viewed the Inter Project in a positive light, but not without expressing her reservations about its feasibility and recognizing the limitations entailed in its implementation on a large scale. In this regard she argued:

The public school implies something very large. That thing that is so large is difficult to reach. It can be accomplished at the level of obligatory implementation [of a given reform], in other words, all should follow specific educational guidelines established by the administration. But this does not guarantee by any stretch of the imagination that all will be affected by the internal changes [brought on by the reform]. People can be changing merely externally and continue not to work out the school's [curriculum] within the Inter [Project] and not authentically engage in the change process. Therefore we need not measure how much this administration affected schools in terms of the system as a whole. The system is very large. Yes, there was wide-spread implementation of the Project but with many effectively continuing without having a real consciousness about it.

Jenny's observations synthesize well what both the NAE personnel and teachers who enthusiastically supported the projected came to recognize: the Project's implementation was uneven within schools and across the system due to the inability or unwillingness of teachers to fully comprehend its design. To a large extent, teachers agreed to work with the Project without really understanding what it was about. This lack of consciousness on the part of some teachers speaks again to their limited training and high degree of professional burnout that can be associated with the broader conditions of the Brazilian economy and society. For instance, many teachers are forced to work at more that one school to make a living wage [as was the case with Jenny], rendering them with little time and energy for the intensive work and analytical processes required for planning and carring out an interdisciplinary curriculum via a generative theme.

MAGDA: Magda spoke candidly of how much she had enjoyed working in the municipal system for the past 17 years as an art teacher. Well-educated in her field, she received training in design, plastic arts, art education, and pedagogy at four different post-secondary Institutions, including the Faculdade de Bellas Artes, São Paulo. For the past six years she had to work in both the municipal and state system, as have many of her colleagues in the face of dwindling teachers' salaries and skyrocketing inflation. In the past, she worked in private schools and in art schools teaching design. Her experience in the municipal school system is extensive and includes early involvement in the organization of the municipal system's *supletivo* [adult night school].

Despite her extensive professional experience, Magda, true to her artistic self, offered the following simple answer when asked to identify the theoretical influences in her pedagogy: "I am very much me [. . .] I have a broad formation in the arts, I also do theater, cinema, television, advertising-media. I understand a little of each area. So each year I go along according to the interests of my students, I'm used to not having a static plan."

Given her flexible approach to curriculum planning, Magda was very open to the idea of creating a curriculum according to a generative theme selected each semester. She recognized, however, that the initial change in curriculum structure did not sit as well with her students. She recalled that the first reaction of her students when the system [of the Inter Project] was implanted was one of resistance. According to her Magda, her students "did not know what was going on, they asked to be taught subjects, they thought they were not receiving any lessons in any subject matter. They would say 'Everything is great, but when are classes starting?'" But with the passage of time, Magda pointed out, her students became consciencitized to the purpose of working in this new manner. They began to understand the Project and eventually, in her estimation, came to fully accept the proposal. She elaborated on her students' change in attitude:

> The fact that they perceived that all that was formulaic and neatly presented to them before gave them a false sense of security since they had something concrete to memorize and to answer. Now [with the Inter Project] they had to research, look for things, investigate, they had to develop their own opinions about things. This made them feel insecure. Then they felt they were being challenged, called upon to respond. They had to react. It was no longer something comfortable, a finished product that

was passed on to them, they had to look for [their own answers]. They came to like the Project very much.

For Magda, in addition to the students' eventual acceptance and enjoyment of the challenges that the Inter Project presented for them, its relative success at Habib School had to do with the fact that there already existed a firm sense of teacher camaraderie which matched up well with the Projects' principle of collective work. "At this school we have a very strong bond of friendship among the teachers. Specifically at level II [intermediate grades] we have a community of teachers, and the Inter came to reinforce that spirit that already existed among us."

Teacher-student relations improved significantly as well. Traditional distances between teachers and students diminished as a result of the methodologies of dialogue and continuous problematization of students' reality which were introduced into the classroom with the onset of the Inter Project. Magda commented on related changes in teacher practice, specifically in teachers' perception of their students, that occured with the Project's onset:

> From the traditional approach the teacher says to the student 'you are over there, I am over here. I am the supreme authority you need to respect and obey me. But there are some teachers that understood that concept [suggested by the Project], that we need to give a space for the student to open up because you are going to work with the discourse of your students. It is not just the preliminary investigation that you do. The investigation needs to take place on a daily basis, you have to always analyze what the student says in order to work with that material, to modify [your classes] along the way. There are still teachers that resist, but that isn't the majority, at least in this school.

Finally, she identified the role of the Pedagogic Coordinator as key in the successful development of the Project at any given site. Although she felt that Habib School was fortunate to have an excellent CP who was able to understand the Project theoretically and guide the staff in its implementation, "because if she [the CP] does not have the ability to comprehend the process, nothing comes of it, the teachers are going to feel lost. Here at this school we have that."

Interestingly, she cited lack of support from school's administrative staff [i.e., the school secretaries and support personnel] as the source of greatest resistance toward the Project at Habib School. They failed to see the validity if the educational work teachers were carrying out within the Inter Project. Magda attributes their rejection to a bureaucratic mindset :

"They do not understand the flexibility we have in the classes and the liberty that the students have to have [in this Project]. They tell us that 'you're just having a good time while we have to work' . . . that we are making money without doing anything." As a result of this disapproval, Magda reported that the administrative staff would use the few punitive controls they had on teachers. For instance, "if we arrived one minute late they would discount us a point." The situation deteriorated to the point that the school principal had to intervene to ensure that teachers were being paid for the hours they put into the Project.

Similar to many other teachers who agreed with the Project in principle and made an effort to implement the new curriculum, Magda bemoaned the limited technical support that the NAE personnel were able to provide as a result of the Project's rapid expansion through out the municipal system. To address this problem Magda suggested that NAE should have created a central unit where teachers could go access resources, such as teaching materials and videos, and receive direct technical assistance.

In light of these and other perceived shortcomings of the PT's administration of the municipal schools, she had this to say:

> They had all the good intentions, they were qualified with great capabilities, but they were too few to be able to attend to the needs of all the schools. This is a process that is merely being initiated, if there were time to continue . . . We hope to have that opportunity to continue, now that we are facing a change in government . . . I have an enormous fear. If the candidate from the PT wins he will surely continue the Project, but if the other wins, he is of the authoritarian party, connected to the former military regime, so he has another position, he doesn't accept this openness. They are of that system that believes the teacher needs to remain in the classroom and teach that which is programmed for them to teach. [According to such a position] the people don't need to be critical, they need to obey.

Despite the threat of a change of administration in late 1992, Magda held firm to the belief that the Project had fundamentally changed the way she and other teachers perceived their role as educators. She offered the following optimistic view of the perseverance of the Project's essential elements into the future:

> I don't believe it will disappear because the teachers who are in the Project have a different outlook. They were transformed, we've had a certain liberty and whoever has had a taste of that liberty will never accept returning to that old pattern. It may be that from above, the Secretariat, there is a change in policy. But in the classroom we will never have the same

mindset. The type of class we teach will never be the same, so I think in that way a little seed will remain: [from which will continue to evolve] a new kind of class, a new way of treating the students, and living out their problems.

FRANCISCO: Among the teachers most enthusiastic about the Inter Project at Habib school was a fourth grade teacher, Francisco. He exemplified what could be called a "militant educator" in contemporary Brazil. Born and raised in the impoverished neighborhood where he still teaches, he took his role as an educator as part and parcel of his political work in defense of the rights of his community. Illustrative of his educational militancy was the fact that in addition to his day time shift at Habib School, he was an active participant in a night-time adult literacy training group that formed part of MOVA, the literacy movement initiated by Freire's administration.

A 24-year-old husband and father of two, Francisco lives and works in the southern periphery of São Paulo. His tired, but otherwise young face reflects the hardships of his daily life and his battle to become a school teacher despite having been born in the heart of slums. He spoke candidly of his harsh up-bringing: "As for myself, I never had a mother, she left when I was three. I had many stepmothers. I lived in a little shack that was falling apart. I would get food to eat from the floor of the street market . . . [Growing up in poverty] I have learned above all to love people for who they are not for what they bring, without concern for their social position. We all have value, through education you need to discover your own value in order to learn to grow."

Consequently, Francisco's students respected him because he fully respected them as equals in the larger struggle to build a better school, city and life together. His own struggle to become educated despite adverse conditions had a marked effect on his political-pedagogical vision:

> I live the same reality as my students, I live here in the periphery. I didn't attend college because in this country it is exorbitantly expensive which make university access prohibitive for many. I completed magisterio [normal school training] two years ago and I intend to study Law or even Pedagogy, but it will be difficult for me to attend the university. You work all day . . . even when I was in high school . . . I went to classes in the morning, worked at the bank all afternoon . . . I would come home to no running water and would barely have a cup to drink and still have to do my homework for the next day. This has made me understand my students better. That experience also made me search out the reason behind the school failure of most children. School failure is related to the life conditions of the student . . . no food, no one to watch over them, no mother,

no father. To make matters worse [at school] the child remains on the outside, receiving information that is not relevant to him . . .

When Francisco arrived at Habib School, the Inter Project had already been initiated. Still he witnessed the early stages of its development at another school where he had previously worked as a substitute teacher. He immediately found that the Inter Project matched well with his own convictions of the transformative role of education in Brazilian society: "I am a son of the periphery, a child of the public school, so how could I not embrace something that spoke of my own life."

Not surprisingly, Francisco agreed with the Inter Project's premise of departing from the students' local reality, especially when teaching children of poor working class neighborhoods in a city like São Paulo. Accordingly, he argued, "there is no point in talking about Paris if the student lives in *Missionaria* or *Jardim Miriam* [two low income districts near Habib School] and doesn't even know about Santo Amaro [a neighboring commercial district]." Also in accordance with the Project's pedagogical perspective, he viewed his students as "active subjects" in this learning process and conceived the role of the teacher as a catalyst for the conscientization of his students. To this end, he believed that "the teacher has to use his or her creativity to take advantage of what exists concretely in the classroom. You have to speak the language of the student, the popular language."

Francisco's remarks reflected a particular stance regarding the nature and purpose of dialogical interaction that the Inter Project intended to cultivate in the classroom. At the same time, he argued that the role of a liberatory educator is not to make excuses for why their underprivileged students can't learn; instead, Francisco insisted, teachers should help their students understand their life conditions in order to awaken their desire to change those conditions. He elaborated on this point in a forthright manner: "You shouldn't say to her, 'look you don't have this and that, therefore you are incapable. It's to the contrary, because you don't have those [material] things you need to demonstrate your capabilities. You have to reverse the process.'"

In Francisco's eyes, the Inter Project's goal of educating for conscientization is realized by employing the Freireian principle of the generative theme. For him the generative theme is a problem that stands out for the community, but it does not stop there. The educator's role is to problematize the significant situation for the community that is embodied in the generative theme. He explained for example, that if the generative theme is "violence" [which was the case at Habib during the Projects' implementation there in 1992], then the teacher must construct his or her curriculum around a series of "significant questions" such as: "What types of violence am I talking about?"; "How do I commit violence?"; "What factors make that violence intimidating for the community, for individuals?"; "What other values are hiding behind the problem of violence?" He asserts: "Its not enough for you to just look at the problem. You have to look at the causes and what can be done to transform the process. So the generative theme is a challenge for revision." Apparently, Francisco directly associated the pedagogic use of a generative theme [as the axis of an interdisciplinary curriculum] with what he held as a political imperative to address social problems through a process of collective conscientization and transformative action. From such a position the school becomes an essential element in the struggle for social justice and a critical citizenry. In his own words:

> That is why I say the work of school cannot be limited within four walls, because from the moment that you are within four walls, you are alienating the student. There is no point in handing children books to read if they are not understanding what is happening on their own street. So, only [by] departing from her [the child's] daily life experience can we form a critical citizen and [instill] the idea of the right to citizenship.

When asked how his experience in the Inter Project affected his educational practice, Francisco again demonstrated a decisively critical stance. Within the Inter Project, Francisco insisted "you don't approach history the way society wants, the way society determines that it happened. You become a teacher-researcher. You work at searching for means and artifices to demonstrate to the student that the history that is there is an alienating history, and that there is another history of people who contributed but were simply erased from our history." Hence, he questioned [as did the PT-MSE] conventional notions of what constitutes valid knowledge and recognized the presence of a history and knowledge outside the "official" discourse that needs to be taken into account within the transformative classroom.

In addition, like many of his colleagues at Habib School, Francisco reported enhanced professional interaction among teachers as a result of the Inter Project's implementation; but at the same time, he pointed out that the Project failed to achieve the objective of promoting community involvement in the school's educational program. Francisco attributed this increased unity within the teaching staff at the school to the collective hour, introduced with the Inter Project: "because teachers now have a specific time to sit and discuss, analyze and review things together. Suddenly the concerns that before were yours alone, became the concerns of everybody."

Although the greater task of galvanizing the community around a movement to build a popular public school was yet to be undertaken, Francisco
believed that the Inter Project provided the necessary ground work for that
process to begin: "We are taking steps. We cannot say that we have effectively achieved unity [with the community] because we haven't. Its a
gradual process . . . because we have had years and years of traditional-
ism." The Inter Project therefore signified a first step to changing not only
the frame of mind that teachers have of their work and of the school's role,
but also entailed a shaking up of the traditional perceptions of the school
held by the community.

Francisco was one of the few teachers interviewed who positioned himself as strongly sympathetic to the Workers' Party and its over all project to
build a popular public school aimed at the education of a critical and participatory citizenry. Unlike many of his colleagues for whom the Project's
association with a PT administration made them suspicious of its intentions which they perceived as intrinsically partisan and ultimately unde-
sirable, for Francisco the PT association gave the curriculum reform program immediate validity. He passionately articulated his position with the
following words: "The PT is a government of the workers, which is precisely how it differentiates itself from previous municipal governments.
The PT is a party with a very beautiful history. There were years of struggle
and conquests. This is why I wear the PT star on my shirt , because I believe that when something is good we must announce it." [He refers to the
Party's insignia—a red star with the initials PT in white—commonly worn
during the mayoral election campaign in progress in October of 1992]. Like
other PT supporters in the municipal schools, Francisco was very conscious
of the fact that if the party lost the elections, it would most surely mean the
end of the Inter Project.

Summary: Project Impact

Students in a seventh grade class who, by 1992, had experienced two
years of schooling under the Inter Project at Habib School, reflected on the
Project's relative success in achieving its goal of enhancing students' critical consciousness. These students were very articulate in expressing their
comprehension of Brazil's social and economic conditions and how the
Inter Project had helped them to relate school knowledge to their current
situation. They understood the Project's principles of collective work and
dialogic exchange well and were quite satisfied with its effect on how and
what they were learning. Accordingly, they made statements such as, "We
learn more with the Inter Project"; "What we learn stays more in your head";
"It has to do with our lives." Students were able to give specific examples

of how their classroom had changed; for example, one student related that in her English class they had translated rap songs and discussed the strong cultural ties between Brazil and the United States and the effects of "cultural imperialism." "Look at us!" she exclaimed, "we all wear jeans and 'tennis,' we all want to look like Americans." Although such revelations were certainly not novel, in the eyes of the students, they were born from their experience of critical dialogue carried out in their classrooms under the pedagogic-political umbrella of the Inter Project. More importantly, when the question as to what was their ideal school was posed to students their answers resonated with the PT-MSE's broader objectives of creating a popular public school through the promotion of a critical consciousness and commitment to community: in general they projected the utopia of a school where all are united, working and learning together, not in competition, but in solidarity to build a better future.

Habib School was one of the sites at which follow up fieldwork was conducted in 1994. As a result, the impact of the Inter Project can be discussed in concrete terms, analyzing the elements of the Project that remained despite the change in administration. It should be noted once more that several of the NAE-6 personnel were on staff at Habib School prior to 1989 and returned following the 1992 elections, certainly bringing with them their expertise and enthusiasm for the reforms of the previous administration. The vignette that follows describes a meeting among a group of teachers as they develop a generative theme, two years after the PT electoral defeat.

Collective Analysis of the School Reality. The small group of nine teachers (seven women and two men) discussed, often heatedly, the data they had collected through a series of interviews with residents in the neighborhood. Reading aloud from notebooks, the participants shared the various statements of the residents and codified them as they went along. For example, a streetwise statement recorded from a youth in the neighborhood was, "the trick is not to get mixed up with the drug dealers and criminals," which was categorized as "security." Other categories included "health," "hygiene," "housing," "leisure," "transportation," "schooling," and "social relations." Once the data was categorized, the team constructed an extensive table of the different categories with corresponding fragments of the community's discourse.

At a second meeting the group worked collectively to determine the significant situations revealed in the data. At one point during this meeting teachers discussed the contradictory nature of the statements made by the community. For example, one teacher pointed out how the same person who observed that "the neighborhood is calm" later stated that he is "afraid of the neighborhood." Others present at the meeting questioned the categorization of particular items; for example, one teacher in the group questioned whether the statement "the people on the hill ruin everything" [referring to residents of a poorer section of the neighborhood] should be considered as falling under the category of security or of social relations? In other words, did the statement represent a discriminatory position against the poorer people who live on the hill or did it express a legitimate concern for the criminal activity that emanates from that part of the neighborhood?

With regard to another epigrammatic expression from a community member, "peace with god and the devil," a teacher [and former NAE Inter Team member] remarked emphatically, "that one is very significant" drawing attention to how it represents a survival strategy for those community members who are law abiding but at the same time revere the criminals with whom they are forced to coexist. As a result of this interactive and dynamic process of collective analysis, a set of significant situations were identified and a consensus reached as to the generative theme around which to construct the curriculum.

This level of commitment to the Inter Project—represented in these teachers' willingness to continue to carry out a Study of Reality to derive a generative theme and design an interdisciplinary curriculum despite the new administration's efforts to discredit and discontinue the PT curriculum reform—is significant. Nevertheless, these observations should be tempered by the impressions of other teachers who also remained.

For instance, in a follow-up interview in 1994, Francisco was more critical in his reflections of the successes and limitations of the PT reform experience. Like others, he cited the institution of the JTI[9] and cycles as two factors that worked against the Project's development in the final months of the PT tenure. Also, he saw the theoretical murkiness of the proposal as ultimately casting a cloud on its future. He explains: "The proposal was not clearly defined. Things often remained at the level of theory, I didn't always feel that they were being practiced, the teachers often didn't know how that theory was useful in the classroom. [In this sense], the NAE committed a sin, they should have done it in a different way. Instead of sitting us down to discuss theories they should have given us more concrete methods." Still he recognizes the positive impact of the Inter Project in as much as "it turned teachers into researchers . . . if they were willing they could become active participants in the process of educational planning. The Secretariat saw teachers as professionals and as professionals they had their rights as well as their obligations. [Consequently,] teachers discovered they were professionals, not baby-sitters."

Despite these negative assessments, Francisco concluded with the following remarks: "the Inter Project offered the conditions to put into practice all my aspirations as an educator. I never perceived myself as only a teacher, I've always seen myself as someone who stood beside my students. I never merely passed knowledge to them but engaged in a reflection of lived practice, my own as much as theirs." Reflecting on the general experience of the Inter Project, Francisco remained steadfast in his belief in education as a transformative tool: "As an educator I do not like to maintain a partisan outlook. I am not of the PT, I have no formal ties to the party, but I believe in some of the proposals of the PT. I believe in the public school as a space for changing society."

It is clear, based on the work that Habib's staff did during the PT-MSE and their perseverance after the PT's defeat, that their commitment to the democratic transformation of society was very strong, at least among a core group of faculty. Though each of the teachers profiled in this case expressed their solidarity with the popular public school in different ways, they each reflect the type of "responsible" educator that Freire describes[10] who works with clarity about their political values and in a manner that reflects coherence between these values and their educational practice.

CASE 3
**Pracinhas da Forças Expedicionarias Brasileiras:
Curricular Reorientation as a Community Project**

Pracinhas da Forças Expedicionarias Brasileiras (FEB) School (Pracinhas School), though not a pilot site for its regional area, NAE-5, was one of the first schools to participate in the Inter Project. In many respects, Pracinhas School undertook the Inter Project amidst ideal conditions. The school enrollment was relatively small—just under 300 students per shift with a full-time staff of 10 teachers and three administrators (including two CP); the local community, though working class and poor, was fairly stable; and the staff had experimented with a similar type of reform prior to its entry into the Inter Project. Nevertheless, the experience of this school community with the curriculum reorientation project highlights several challenges touched upon in the previous case studies. The most significant issue faced by Pracinhas School was the creation of a true community space. This meant addressing head-on parent resistance and student to the Inter Project, which, with tools provided by the Inter Project, was resolved in an exemplary manner at Pracinhas School.

Pracinhas da FEB: A Description

Pracinhas School is located in a neighborhood locally known as Jardim das Flores, within the larger southwest section of São Paulo known as Campo Limpo. Though official data are available for the larger Campo

Limpo area, they do not completely reflect the situation in Jardim das Flores. Fortunately, the comprehensive nature of the school's Study of the Reality allows for a fairly detailed profile of the school community and informs this overview. Historically, this neighborhood occupied an urban expansion area, peripheral to the city and inhabited initially by *favelas*. Gradually, more permanent structures and infrastructure have been added. Today, the neighborhood is a fairly well-established residential area. Residents generally live in modest homes which they own. Unlike Sussumu School, the neighborhood is completely serviced; most streets are paved, though sparsely lit and in need of repair, and all homes have sewer, water, and electrical services. Most of the men in the neighborhood are employed as semi-skilled laborers and work in the different factories located further south in the industrial area of the city. Most of the women work, though they do this by balancing domestic duties with participation in more informal labor activities such as providing manicures, cleaning homes, and making baked goods. Average household incomes in the area ranged between three and six minimum salaries in 1990. This places these families within the working class but towards the mid to upper ranges of the salary scale. Despite this relative financial stability, the adult residents are characterized by low levels of education (particularly among women).

The neighborhood is adjacent to a major regional park, formed primarily by the Guarapiranga Dam; though most residents and students report infrequent use of the park because of safety concerns. The neighborhood has both a health clinic and a police sub-station within a 10 kilometer radius. At the same time, the area is relatively isolated. There is only one major thoroughfare, Avenida Guarapiranga, that connects Jardim das Flores with other parts of São Paulo, and mass transit on this avenue is infrequent.

A visit to Jardim das Flores confirms the descriptive picture painted above. The bus stop for Jardim das Flores is the last one before the bus route begins to barrel through a largely invaded and precarious favela. Small auto mechanic shops line the Avenida, giving the Jardim das Flores (or "Flower Garden") neighborhood an ironically gritty feel. The walk from the bus stop to Pracinhas School is strenuous. The 10 blocks to the school wind up and down steep hills, made all the more treacherous by uneven and cracked pavement. Nevertheless, the slow pace one must take affords a pleasant opportunity to observe the houses. They are mostly very small. Some are decorated by pots of colorful flowers, others harbor dogs that bark menacingly, and still others advertise small businesses —freshly laid eggs at one house, *pão de queijo* (cheese bread) treats at another. Two partially constructed multiple-story buildings rise curiously out of the otherwise low-lying horizon, apparent victims of the most recent recession which halted the construction industry.

Pracinhas School sits nestled among the residential structures, its bright blue gate welcoming interested visitors. The school grounds include a main building, a smaller ante building connected by a walkway, and lush school grounds complete with a playing field. It is a new facility, constructed and dedicated during the previous administration in 1989. The main building houses the school office, an open area which doubles as cafeteria and auditorium, the kitchen, a small teachers' lounge and classrooms. All the classrooms and the media center are on the second floor. Each classroom is relatively well-lit, with natural light entering from windows that line the exterior walls of the school. The library is very well-used and unusually well-equipped. There appear to be ample books, science lab equipment, a television, and a VCR. Despite the general cheerfulness and relative opulence of the school (such extensive science lab equipment was not present in any other school), Pracinhas School still shares with other schools the drab concrete walls, the occasional leaky faucet, the splintered wooden floors, and the broken desks and chairs.

History of the Inter Project at Pracinhas School

Staff at Pracinhas School, somewhat self-servingly comment that they have always been a school open to new ideas. Of course, this school is relatively young (only four years old at the time of this research), so it is not possible to establish solid historical patterns. At the time of its founding, the school attracted an experienced, knowledgeable, and well-known principal, Silvia Tarraran, who had worked closely with Guiomar Namo de Mello,[11] a noted educator who was Secretary of Education during the Covas regime in the early 1980s. Teacher professionalization and collaboration had been a theme during the Mello administration and in building the new school staff, Ms. Tarraran made considerable efforts to attract a faculty that would be committed to a more collaborative and innovative professional environment. Though she was mostly successful in her recruiting, her staff acknowleged that their primary concern was initially "purely pedagogical"; that is, concerned with their own individual classrooms.

Tarraran's efforts to introduce more collaborative and integrated curriculum development occurred slowly and were greatly bolstered by the initiation of the Inter Project during the 1991-92 school year. The Project was first presented to the school staff by representatives from the regional administrative unit, NAE-5, and by staff accounts, their reaction to the administration's proposal was favorable. They viewed participation in the

Inter Project as a vehicle for continuing the collaborative work that they had experimented with in the past, while receiving much more in the way of administrative support, resources, and technical assistance. Furthermore, the political clarity of the Project provided additional motivation to participate in the Inter Project. As one teacher stated, ". . . [P]rior to the PT's [Inter Project] you received the red notebook from the state which told you what to teach, when and how. And that program (responded) directly to vestibular [comprehensive national exit exams]—but it was so vast and comprehensive that you could be certain you'd never get through everything. Education here in Brazil is a game of force with the objective being that the students leave school completely dominated, completely within the project of the dominant classes."

For many of the teachers at Pracinhas, participation in the Inter Project signified a way of obviating that dominant project. Thus, though their training and professional experience predisposed them to concentrate on "purely pedagogical" concerns, their ideas regarding a range of educational issues including collaboration, interdisciplinarity, the objectivity of knowledge, and the neutrality of the classroom teacher changed dramatically with the introduction of the Inter Project. Based on staff accounts, though the level of enthusiasm varied from teacher to teacher, all of the staff willingly opted to participate in the Project.

Given this overview, we can turn to a brief description of the ways in which the staff at Pracinhas School operationalized the Inter Project during their two year involvement with it. In the following section both the ER-OC-AC phases of the process will be described as well as the staff's continuing professional development meetings.

Meetings

At Pracinhas School, unlike other schools studied, the Inter Project and its accompanying Professional Development Group interfaced with an already collaborative school culture. The seeds of this culture were planted by the school director, and nurtured by the teachers themselves who gradually began to see their collaborative efforts as fruitful elements of their professional practice. Until the introduction of the Inter Project, the nature of the staff's collaborative efforts was piecemeal. All of the teachers (prior to the Project) worked in at least two schools; as a result, extra time for meetings after or before their shifts at Pracinhas was almost non-existent. As their curriculum was already prescribed by municipal and state guidelines on an almost daily basis, there was no real opening to discuss integrated lessons or to consider extending a particular lesson or activity. Instead, the collaboration focused more on discussing instructional ideas and such discussion happened in a sporadic way. For example, these ideas would come from an article distributed by Ms. Tararan or an idea brought in by one of the teachers (several were pursuing graduate studies and almost all of the teachers also taught in State schools where other reforms were underway). Teachers would arrive a little early one day (which was quite a sacrifice as their shift began at 7 a.m.) to discuss the article over morning coffee, or a Friday evening barbecue would begin with some time set aside to talk about new theories and practices in education.

However, despite serious intentions—initially on the part of the school director and gradually shared by the teaching staff—there were concrete structural impediments that prohibited the school from truly institutional-izing working norms around collaboration and innovation. For these teach-ers, the Inter Project represented, at the very least, a solid opportunity to have a remunerated structure for efforts they had previously undertaken on a volunteer and ad hoc basis.

With this history in mind, the highly productive quality of the Profes-sional Development Groups and Integrated Daily Meetings (i.e., JTI) at Pracinhas School is easier to explain. There were several features of this professional development time that distinguish the staff at Pracinhas School. First, the meetings were clearly valued as teachers' time for discussion, dialogue, and planning. The school director and the pedagogic coordina-tor occasionally attended but their participation was on equal footing with the teachers; all ideas were honored and the presence of the director did not change the nature of the discussion. In addition, meetings (held Mon-day through Thursday from 11:15 a.m. until 1 p.m.) tended to begin fairly punctually and the discussion became focused very quickly. One teacher reflected, "I think also that there are some teachers that don't really know what to do with the collective time. So they may have times set aside but they don't know how to use them, or what they are supposed to be doing. They don't have topics. They aren't interested in doing something produc-tive. This time is so important for us. We exchange so much information and [so many] ideas."

Second, meeting topics were almost always centered on key teaching and learning issues. Prior to developing units around the generative theme or creating activities for the application of knowledge phase, planning, de-veloping lessons, organizing activities, sorting out logistics and schedules, and finding appropriate materials and props constituted the main content of meetings. During periods when various units around the generative theme were in process, meeting dialogue was more apt to include such topics as obstacles to creating a more democratic classroom, the challenges of a constructivist pedagogy in science class versus geography class, or reflections on students' evolving understanding of the generative theme.

Third, this was a staff that was interested in ideas and had some capacity for engaging with the research literature. Discussions around more theoretical issues were driven primarily by two staff members, one who was completing graduate studies and another who was involved in an innovative reform at her state-run school. Nevertheless, the other members of the staff appeared to willing engage with the ideas brought forth by their colleagues. In addition, several meetings involved discussions of PT-MSE published documents regarding the nature of interdisciplinarity, the theoretical roots of constructivism, assessment issues, the notion of critical citizenship, and so forth.

Finally, the staff had found a comfort zone around which they discussed substantive issues, expressed their opinions, disagreed with each other and yet still found a working balance from which to develop a common understanding of the topic under scrutiny. As this teacher states, "The process has been interesting. In the beginning we made small advances and people would share little things here and there but basically people were still pretty closed. Then we had a little bit of a confrontation, a break down in our harmony and after that things really started to flow and all the protective devices were eliminated. I say whatever I want and I'm not careful at all. And I think this is the result of Inter."

Such a dialogical dynamic allowed for several developments. First, for each of the teachers, the educational and political ideas promoted by the Inter Project (and the PT administration, in general) represented a radical departure from the ideological underpinnings of their own education and training. Moreover, none of these teachers was a PT activist. Thus, understanding the underlying principles of the Inter Project forced each of the teachers to confront their own dearly held assumptions about education and their role in that process, as well as to lay bare the limitations of their professional knowledge. One teacher offered this critique of his training and experience in relation to the demands of the Inter Project:

> For me, studying math at college was very rigid. The problem with the way that math was taught was that you learned only to follow a certain sequence into which you plugged in different numbers. But you didn't learn the logic behind a certain operation, to reason mathematically. There was one right answer and one right way to get that answer—so really, my university studies brought me very little. And until today, I am trying to construct something for myself that is more meaningful and break away from this rigid mathematical tradition.

Similar experiences could have been described by all the teachers at Pracinhas School. Yet because the limitations of their training and knowledge were exposed in an environment where lack of knowledge was seen as an opportunity for learning, discovery was seen as a group endeavor and divergent opinions were respected, each participant felt encouraged to continue on in the group as an active member. In a related way, this dynamic allowed for each teacher to take risks appropriate to their own comfort level, while receiving the benefit of support and feedback from group members. In addition, each teacher felt that the discussions and debates, while sometimes difficult both conceptually as well as interpersonally, forced a reflection (and subsequent reaffirmation or rejection) of core professional and personal beliefs which ultimately strengthened their own understanding of their educational philosophy and practice. Finally, this on-going experience created a tremendous sense of group unity and cohesion around norms that were educationally positive and classroom-centered. As one teacher observed, ". . . [W]e are always learning quite a bit. Here we have our group and everyone helps each other make progress from one place to another. Even when certain people are not interested in doing a particular thing, for whatever reason, they continue to be included and those that are more interested push the others to eventually get involved."

Curriculum Development and Classroom Practice

Pracinhas School began its participation with the Inter Project in January of 1991. Though the staff had contemplated "thematic" planning, considering such themes as "the evolution of numbers" and "the Republic as a form of society," their efforts had not ever been implemented. The structural support and technical assistance offered by the Inter Project made their curriculum planning much more substantial. Moreover, the clearly political nature of the Project reoriented their efforts. Since initiating the Inter Project, their themes reflect the grounded and political nature of the Study of the Reality by focusing on such topics as "work/employment: does it improve people's lives?" and "humans and the planet: will they survive?"

The staff's Study of the Reality led them on an exhaustive survey of the surrounding community. Teachers interviewed parents and students, polled local merchants, catalogued neighborhood amenities and services (e.g., police substation, health clinic, etc.), visited churches and other private and state-run schools and day care centers, and collected archival information about their school. In collecting data, they considered such issues as: the history of the neighborhood, difficulties in improving it, various institutions that serve the area (churches, schools, political representatives, etc.), employment opportunities that exist in the neighborhood, and the general level of education among neighborhood families.

Having amassed these data, the teachers began the task of organizing them and trying to pull out significant situations. Such significant situations ranged from water resources to homelessness to the economic, social and geographic isolation experienced by neighborhood residents. The teachers created separate "mind-maps" for each of these significant situations. These mapping exercises helped the teachers visualize the ways in which each significant situation generated additional areas of inquiry and, ultimately, additional avenues for curriculum development. For example, the significant situation of "water resources" introduced a variety of additional topics: water treatment, the extent of sewer services in the neighborhood, the various uses of the Guarapiranga water reservoir, and the water cycle. Residents' feelings of isolation generated other topics for exploration including: the Brazilian model of economic development, distribution of services within the city, and the political process (e.g., an analysis of stakeholder and constituent groups in the city).

The process of identifying and mapping the various significant situations unfolded over many meetings and was recorded on reams of chart paper. Once the significant situations had been identified and discussed in detail, the teachers began the process of cross analyzing each of the significant situations in order to develop a main theme for the semester (or longer depending on their decision). During the research period, the generative theme under development was: "Human beings and the planet: will they survive?" Departing from this particular theme, each of the teachers developed curriculum that appropriately drew on their subject area to address the theme. Although Table 6.1 illustrates the various different concepts and skills that teachers from the different disciplines incorporated around this generative theme, it is helpful to look at the work of two teachers in detail (in fifth and sixth grades, respectively) in the distinct content areas of Science and History.

A major focus for the fifth grade science classes was on various aspects of pollution, particularly air and water degradation which were of primary concern in the neighborhood. Concentrating on pollution allowed for inquiry into a range of topics each of which related to the core content areas: the water cycle, basic sanitation, various causes of water quality degradation and air pollution, health effects of water and air pollution, and the process of biodegradation all related to science; the relationship between explosive urbanization and pollution was suitable for history, geography or math lessons; and the development of intervening actions that students and others (industry, automobile drivers, etc.) could take drew on several disciplines including the humanities and history.

Students carried out a number of different activities around these concepts. Classroom discussion focused on the harmful effects of water and air pollution with which the students were familiar because irritated eyes

TABLE 6.1 Generative Theme: Human Beings and the Planet—Will They Survive?

	Study of the Reality *(includes student activities)*	Organization of Knowledge *(identifies core content, concepts, and issues)*	Application of Knowledge *(projects and assignments)*
Art Education	• Visual arts: collages, painting, modeling • Musical activities • Understanding landscapes: natural and built	Week of modern art activities/ Folk music as a means of questioningreality	• Visual arts/Music/Poetry/ Dramatizations
History	• Questionnaires • Interviews • Debates	Industry/Class struggle/ Living standards/Pollution/ Discrimination/Colonization/ Human rights	Essays/Group projects
Language Arts	• Posters, billboards, ads • Newspapers	Lectures/ Writing projects/linguistic analysis/analysis of advertising campaigns and consumption patterns	Group projects
Sciences	• Debates • Interviews • Group discussions	Environment/Recycling/ Pollution/Basic sanitation/ Conservation/Human body and reproduction/Physical and mental health/nutrition	Group projects/Writing projects addressing a community issue

(table continues)

Table 6.1 (continued)

	Study of the Reality (includes student activities)	Organization of Knowledge (identifies core content, concepts, and issues)	Application of Knowledge (projects and assignments)
Math	•Questionnaires •Debates	Cost of living/Basic computation/Monetary systems/Percentages/Fractions	•Graphing cost of living, inflation, and income data/Written analyses
Geography	•Interviews •Debates •Reports •Maps	Social groups/Social classes/Unemployment/Violence/Social and physical space/Migration and population explosion	Drawing maps/Group projects about urbanization/of neighborhood
P.E.	•Questionnaires •Interviews •Debates	Body awareness/Leisure time	Demonstration of good health habits

Source: Pracinhas da FEB Primary School, 1992; Pia Lindquist Wong, 1994

and congestion were common health problems. Dysfunctional sewer systems were also cited as a water problem in the neighborhood and students complained vehemently about their discomfort with puddles and gutters full of stagnant water from unknown sources. From these discussions, students worked in groups and with the teacher's guidance to develop different projects that explored some of the issues noted above. In addition, the teacher structured his/her inquiry around the use of lectures, readings, and lab activities.

The culminating activity for this unit of study was the development of a school-wide recycling project. Students and the teacher developed a design for a compost container. Students also mounted a public information campaign, posting signs and talking with different classrooms and with other staff members (particularly kitchen staff) about recycling and separating out "wet" garbage for the compost container.

In the sixth grade History classes, students departed from the generative theme by exploring the evolution of social and political thought and organizing systems. They began the exploration by discussing the concepts related to and involved in the idea of "quality of life," such as material necessities, social support systems, family and community ties, professional relationships, environmental factors, and so on. From this discussion came a dialogue about the role of individual citizens in maintaining or struggling for a suitable "quality of life." Consulting journals, magazines, newspapers and other publications, the students tried to discern the ways in which different groups of citizens defined "quality of life" and how their gender and social class shaped their definitions. The class engaged in an extended and formal debate on this issue and also created a collage of the different images which represented aspects of "quality of life" to them.

The class then expanded on the "quality of life" metaphor by looking historically at the conception of citizenship, determining how citizens at various points in Brazilian history struggled or organized to gain improvements in their "quality of life." From this journey into the past, students generated observations about the concept of citizenship, the ways in which citizens had mobilized throughout history, and the lessons that past victories could offer to present situations encountered by students and their families. These observations were compiled by individual students into essays, which they ultimately exchanged with their peers, and then rewrote, using suggestions and comments from their classmates.

In general, classroom practice at Pracinhas School showed strong movement in the direction of the pedagogical ideals of the Project, though there were variations by classroom. Without exception, an observer would find students working in groups in every classroom on any given day. This was as true in Portuguese language class as it was in History or Geography. In courses such as History, Science and Portuguese, group work focused on long-term projects that were developed on an issue related in some manner to the generative theme. A quick review of student work would also reveal a wide range of resources including student-generated surveys and print media. Teacher creativity was also evident in these classrooms—teachers frequently conducted their own independent research and supplied students with data, summaries of relevant research, and journal articles.

These features of a student-centered classroom still seemed to sit somewhat uncomfortably with what tended to be a relatively strong teacher presence. A fair amount of lecturing continued to occur and teachers often dominated debates and discussions; though it seemed that they were sharing relevant information, their input was also disruptive and occasionally dampened student participation.

Even though relative to an "ideal" constructivist classroom, instructional practice at Pracinhas School still appeared to have elements of teacher domination, it is important to recognize, nevertheless, the significant nature of the changes in pedagogy that had occurred at Pracinhas School. Cooperative learning, the incorporation of a wide range of materials, project-based activities, and the incorporation of the generative theme were present in varying degrees in every teacher's practice at the school.

The teachers at Pracinhas School represented a range of ages and levels of teaching experience. For the most part, these teachers were in the earlier stages of their careers. The median number of years of teaching experience was six, though teachers ranged in age from late twenties to mid fifties. Half of the group held permanent tenured positions at the school. Only one of the teachers was actively pursuing graduate work in her area, though others had taken advantage of periodic refresher courses offered through local universities. For the majority of the teachers (with one exception), Pracinhas School represented their primary place of employment (a situation made possible in part by the extra compensation provided by the Inter Project). Two of the teachers did not work at all in any other school. The remaining teachers had part-time appointments at other schools, which meant that on certain days of the week (but fewer than three days a week) they also worked at another job after their shift at Pracinhas.

Discussions with teachers at Pracinhas School revealed both a philosophical predisposition towards the Project and a comprehensive understanding of its underlying meaning and concepts. During a meeting, a group definition of the Project emerged as follows:

> Inter is a process of arriving at a particular theme, based on the students'
> concerns [*a partir do aluno*] and working on this theme with your group of
> teachers. . . . This generative theme comes from the student and from the
> teacher . . . . Your subject area "finds" itself in this generative theme and

we all develop the theme together . . . . Not that we all work on exactly the same things—but the theme generates problems, topics that can be worked on in each subject area. Then you develop various so-called content-areas (*conteudos*) that follow along with these issues, showing a practical, visible way for the student to understand and participate in solving the issue or problem—but not in a static way like, "today we are going to study this concept, which is defined in such-and-such way and one day if you need this, you will understand it and can then use it." No, if the issue arises or some opportunity arises, then you teach about it. You teach about something that already exists for the students. That's why Inter is something that is very visible and clear for the students—we teach something that is often immediately understandable for our students because it is something that they live, a problem that they face in their lives.

Another teacher added:

In addition to the liberty to create that we have had in these last four years, the administration has also been concerned with the creation of critical and analytical students, with citizenship, and the creation of responsible citizens. This was quite an advance. Before, the students would come to school, listen, maybe agree, maybe disagree—but none of this was ever discussed. As a teacher you never knew the students' opinions about anything—and you didn't help them develop opinions about anything either. You didn't discuss things like [the idea that] popular culture also is valuable—that it's not only elite culture that is important. This has been a really important development—not only for the students and for the teachers but also for the parents and for their participation in school life. The students now have their own space within the school.

Through this discussion and others, it became clear that teachers at Pracinhas School had a solid understanding of the major tenets of the Inter Project. As a whole, their implementation of the Project emphasized specific components over others in a manner that might not have meshed completely with PT-MSE ideals. For example, the integrated nature of the curriculum around a generative theme was very clearly present in classrooms at Pracinhas School, and making linkages and connections among subject areas were a frequent concern in teacher meetings. Similarly, practical applications of lessons and projects, either through school-wide efforts (e.g., a composting/recycling campaign that even involved kitchen staff) or classroom by classroom efforts (e.g., one classroom's voting guide), involved a considerable amount of staff planning time. At the same time, instructional practice seemed the slowest to change, relative to the other developments in curriculum. Though dictation and standardized tests had been replaced by more Project-based assignments and most classes involved some aspect of student group work, teacher lectures still occupied a fair amount of class time and student attention. While the majority of student assignments were very grounded in genuine problem-solving, the creation of critical citizens tended to be a more implicit endeavor, in most classrooms, and the deliberate incorporation of popular knowledge was intermittent at best. In history classes and occasionally in science classes, the link between a particular lesson or Project and students' future lives as citizens in a democratic society appeared most commonly as an afterthought.

This differential emphasis of Project components offers interesting insights into the way in which the staff at this school embraced the Inter Project and ultimately put its components into practice. First, it appears that their theoretical understanding of the Project is fairly solid. As will be discussed below, this level of understanding came from diligent work during the school's JTI hours, where reading PT-MSE materials and discussing them were a matter of course. In addition, there is clearly a philosophical match between the underlying concepts of the Project and the opinions of the majority of the teaching staff. This philosophical congruence facilitates the staff as they try, through experimental practice and reflection on those experiences, to make the Project make sense for them. As a true outcome of their praxis, these teachers understand the Project first as a process for identifying critical community issues around which to develop integrated and interdisciplinary curriculum, second as means for creating avenues for students to understand better their daily realities, third as a Project for critical consciousness and citizenship, and fourth, as a transformation of instructional practice and classroom hierarchy.

More significantly, however, teachers framed their observations in terms of lasting changes to their professional practice, both in the classroom and in relation to other colleagues and the community. For the teachers at this school, the Project provided them with an opportunity to make real and meaningful connections with their students and the surrounding community. They valued the chance to use a curriculum that clearly had relevance in their students' lives. As mentioned earlier, integrating community issues and concerns into the curriculum made students more involved and engaged in school and consequently made the teaching more rewarding. As one teacher reflected, "Everything that we do and that they do has a practical application—or is something that they actually do and has results and implications that they can actually see. In this way, it's really worthwhile."

Similarly, the highly participatory process of developing the curriculum made teachers feel more efficacious. This increased efficacy came on many levels: more confidence about their own content knowledge, increased awareness and understanding of other content areas, discoveries of their own creativity and teaching ideas, and discoveries about their students' potential. One teacher described this enhanced efficacy as,

> The possibility for us to create. Before, we had a certain content to get through and this was mandated from above. We entered the classroom, shut the door, and taught away; if kids got it they, if not, they didn't. Then we gave a test, did reviews, etc. Now, we have the opportunity to create things with more spontaneity, in a way that is more enjoyable. Its pretty difficult to coordinate everything—for everyone to see the problem the same way, to agree on solutions, etc.—and to find the time and space to deal with the whole process. And we have learned as we have gone on— you get ideas, you become more creative, you see things in a different way so that what you may not have considered a viable option/idea at one time, becomes one during this process.

Another teacher provided her assessment in more concrete terms:

> There are three basic points to be mentioned in relation to what we had before Inter and what we have with Inter—a) the opportunity to study and earn money for these efforts; b) we learned how to use different re- sources for teaching—before we used to use lots of chalk, lots of chalk- board space, etc.—and now we are using a whole variety of different re- sources in our teaching and in our prep work; c) we have the opportunity in our collective meetings to learn about the different subject areas and what our fellow teachers are doing in their subject areas—what types of content they are covering and how they are doing it.

In addition to important changes in classroom practice, teachers high- lighted significant changes in the ways that they operated as a faculty. As discussed earlier, the Project, principally through the provision of the col- lective meeting times, gave teachers important time and space for dialogue, exchange of ideas, problem-solving and sharing of concerns. At Pracinhas School, this time was highly valued and productive, though not without its challenges at times. For these teachers, their conversations, planning efforts, discussions, and even disagreements made both individual and group contributions. One teacher summed up the individual benefits in the following statement: "One of the most important things that we have is the opportunity to present our own points of view. There are rules and schedules and all of this but you are also constantly out there stating your point of view and trying to make progress." For many teachers, not only in

Pracinhas School, who had grown up during Brazil's military dictatorship, such discursive democracy was unknown in any sphere of public life. Thus, their experience with this type of democratic exchange further prepared them for their role as educators of new citizens for a democratic society.

The group benefits have been highlighted previously and pertain primarily to the discovery of talents, moral support, and camaraderie. This has helped this group of teachers feel less isolated in their profession and more a part of a collective effort to make a positive impact and contribution to an entire community.

On the eve of municipal elections, the teachers at Pracinhas School were apprehensive but determined. They felt that they had finally been teaching in a manner that made sense to them, while they feared that a PT loss could strip away their newly honed skills. At the same time, their resolve seemed firm. As several teachers made declarations to this effect:

> I'm not a PT supporter, but this administration was really very good. They really supported us. Paulo Freire really had a vision that made sense. They were able to do something that will have lasting effects. For those schools that were really involved in the collective work and meetings, they will continue working in this way. They can't revert back to the more traditional way. And they really paid us a lot more—its' still not nearly enough but we have significant increases—at least twice the state salaries for teachers. There has been no other administration that gave so much to education as this one has. We are fairly worried about Maluf winning the election because it will make our work much more complicated. But even if he does win, he will not succeed in changing the way we do things here.

In addition to teachers' praise for the Project and their own growth as a result of it, they also highlighted some of the challenges that they faced in implementing the Project that resulted from district policy, student attitudes, and community responses. Like any significant transformational process, the Inter Project brought with it its share of obstacles and challenges. What is noteworthy at Pracinhas School is the manner in which the challenges (most of which were simply systemic and therefore faced by all schools involved in the Project) were resolved. Again, the approach to the challenges at this school was pragmatic and oriented towards problem-solving in a manner consistent with the overall philosophy of the Project; e.g., through democratic process and using a Freireian praxis model where reflection, refinement and action and reflection were key elements.

The types of challenges raised by the Pracinhas teachers fell into three categories: (1) student attitudes and adjustment; (2) parent attitudes and adjustment; (3) district policy. The first two categories required site level strategies for resolution, while the last category was seen more as part and parcel of a large education system, with very few alternatives for resolution.

Just as the teachers were aware of their own process of adjustment and understanding of the Project and its objectives, they observed a similar pattern in students. Often, a policy is designed and speaks strictly to the different types of activities and actions that a teacher will coordinate and execute. Rarely do policies predict student reactions or offer contingencies if students resist or do not respond to teacher actions. Even with a model built upon constructivist theories of learning and a liberatory pedagogical practice—both taking as a central concern the cognitive and cultural makeup of the student and its contribution as a starting point in the educational process—there was little discussion about potential student responses to such radical shifts in pedagogy and curriculum. The final outcomes—e.g., more engaged students, critical citizens, etc.—were identified, but in a manner that did not provide details on the unfolding process. What teachers at Pracinhas School found was that the student experience of the Inter Project clearly proceeded in several stages. They described student induction in the following manner:

> I think that part of their [the students'] disinterest comes from the very newness of the Project. Last year they were very enthusiastic because it was a totally new thing and very different—particularly because they were given so much liberty and consequently felt so much freer. But now that they've become quite used to this greater liberty, they are taking it for granted and have become more relaxed. Although I do believe that they will return to taking the whole idea more seriously too. It's just part of a process. Right now they are just learning how to use this liberty and testing the limits.

> Our students are also trying to get used to this idea of the *ciclos*—but they are slowly realizing that one of the main points is the idea that the grade is not the most important thing, that they may not feel compelled to learn about the subjunctive—principally because they don't have that threat of a failing text grade—but on the other hand, they will have to understand the subjunctive to be able to do some of the other stuff later on—and for that reason, they should apply themselves and learn the subjunctive. And also they are starting to understand that if they don't learn it, they are the ones that lose.

Thus, in addition to the stark adjustments that teachers had to make to be involved with the Project, students also had to reflect on and redefine

their own relationship to each other, to their teachers, and to their expectations about school and its importance. Because of the Inter Project, the daily
school experience for students changed in both content and form. Though
core subject areas such as math, science, history, geography and humanities were still covered, key concepts became more engaging because they
were explored in relation to personal and community issues. In addition,
because the scope and sequencing of the curriculum was determined by
the three phases of the Inter Project rather than more traditionally academic
formulas, the learning process for students became one of more authentic
comprehension and mastery rather than mere exposure. The interdisciplinary nature of the curriculum allowed them to approach similar issues
using strategies and concepts found in each of the disciplines, thus deep-
ening their understanding of the issues and broadening their problem-solving skills.

Moreover, the transitions to a more student-centered classroom where
students worked with each other, discussed ideas and developed group
projects departed starkly from the traditional classroom where students
historically have sat quietly and absorbed information presented by their
teacher and/or text. While many students relished the opportunity for what
seemed like a more social and liberated classroom, not all students initially
embraced such a dynamic. The transition to a student-centered classroom,
though ultimately more engaging for students, also required them to take
a much less passive role than they historically had. For some students, this
new and more active role made school a much more challenging place. As
one teacher remembered,

> The students also posed a difficulty in the beginning—they were reserved
> in their acceptance of the Project initially and weren't really enthusiastic
> about the change— although that is not the case now. Some of the difficul-
> ties included their own fears of exposing their weaknesses, things that
> they did not know, the unknown or new.

Such assessments of student reactions to the Project corroborated with those
offered by teachers in the other schools studied.

Parents also expressed concern and reluctance about the Project. The
absence of traditional symbols of "learning"—spelling lists and math dit-
tos—made many parents fearful that whatever the new "Project" was, their
children were not learning in a proper fashion. Another concern that parents had revolved around the concept of interdisciplinary thematic curriculum and instruction. As a teacher explained, "the idea of a common
theme unifying all of the subject areas seemed to indicate to them that either all of the teachers were copying each other or none of them knew

anything." Finally, parents were hesitant about fully engaging in the new governance and decision-making opportunities available at the school through the Site Councils. This was clearly an unfamiliar role for them, and they were suspicious of the intentions behind these new invitations to participate in school life.

At Pracinhas School, the staff developed a unique strategy for forging a new relationship with families and other community members in the neighborhood. To a large extent, this strategy grew out of both the staff's genuine commitment to the transformation of Pracinhas School into a community school and their authentic excitement about the Inter Project. The staff invited parents and other community members to several evening and Saturday sessions at the school. During these sessions teachers explained the basic components and underlying philosophy of the Project to attendees and also showed them samples of student work. More importantly, however, the teachers designed mini-lessons that used a constructivist and interdisciplinary approach. In debriefing discussions, the teachers and participants identified differences between the interdisciplinary approach and the more familiar traditional approach. Through this type of reflection, parents deepened their understanding of this "new" instructional method and increased their level of comfort with it; in particular, parents were able to experience for themselves the power of learning in this manner. As a result of these sessions, teachers at Pracinhas School felt that parent support and interest in classroom activities increased significantly and more parents became interested in being involved in a variety of school functions including volunteering at the school and serving on the Site Council.

A final challenge that teachers discussed frequently related to district policy-making and educational policy-making in general. As the PT term entered its second year (out of four), the MSE initiated several new policies, which, in the teachers' opinions, reduced their time to engage with the Inter Project. While they applauded the educational value of the other projects, they felt that there was a lack of integration among them, which resulted in teachers feeling pulled in many directions. Among these new projects was the Projeto Genese (a Project to introduce computers into the school curriculum). While students clearly enjoyed it and teachers were in awe of the technology, schools working with Genese had to have Genese sessions and meetings on particular days and at particular times. The staff at Pracinhas viewed this mandated schedule as decreasing their autonomy and interfering with a schedule of Inter Project meetings that had met their needs well. In addition, due to budgetary constraints, the MSE had made some adjustments as to what types of teachers could receive full compensation for participating in the collective meeting for the Inter Project. As

mentioned previously, during the second year of the Project, compensation was only offered to tenured teachers.[12] This had negative consequences
for three of the teachers at Pracinhas School whose tenure was at a different school. Though they remained undaunted in their commitment to the
Inter meetings, their attendance came at a much higher cost than it had in
the previous year and raised questions about the long-term feasibility of
continued participation.

Summary

Clearly Pracinhas School represents somewhat unusual circumstances.
First, the school's newness meant that the physical plant was still in fairly
good condition which allowed administrators, teachers, students and parents to devote their energies to the school's educational program. Second,
the school was a relatively small; unlike most schools which have four shifts,
Pracinhas School had only three daily shifts of students, with each shift
enrolling less than 300 students. Third, the director of the school, Ms.
Tarrarran, tried to create a collaborative culture at the school even prior to
the introduction of the Inter Project. Fourth, most teachers felt some type
of philosophical disposition towards the Inter Project, so initial levels of
cooperation were relatively high.

Even with these unusual characteristics, Pracinhas School still stands
out as a compelling example of Project implementation. These ingredients
were in no way a guarantee that the teachers would be able to develop the
productive meeting sessions that they enjoyed or that each teacher would
be able to transform their teaching practice to reflect many of the
constructivist, dialogical and conscious-raising principles hailed by the
Project. That they were able to do so is a tribute to the Project as well as
their commitment to it. But probably the most striking feature of the school's
participation in the Project was the extent to which it was truly a community effort. This community presence was evident in numerous ways. First,
students' work in most classes tended to include a community application;
whether it was a recycling campaign, observing household conversations
to watch for foreign influences on language (a Portuguese assignment), or
monitoring the newspaper for reports on labor strife, students had many
opportunities to engage with the world around them in a thoughtful and
analytical manner. Second, there was a strong sense of community within
the school—teachers had a cohesive professional community and teachers
and students enjoyed constructive relationships. Rare among the schools
in this study, Pracinhas School had two school-wide events during the three
weeks of observations. Teachers and students often met during lunch or
after school to work on projects or get caught up on assignments. Third,

ties between the school and its surrounding community, including students' families, were strong. Parents understood and supported the curricular and pedagogical reorientation happening at Pracinhas School; teachers respected parents' wishes and made opportunities for them to participate in their children's educational experience. In these ways, the Inter Project at Pracinhas School was truly a community endeavor.

CASE 4

Manoel de Paiva School: Conflict and Controversy

Manoel de Paiva School was a school in transition, a process which made for several difficult contradictions which came in many forms. By and large, the teachers at the school were from solidly middle to upper middle class backgrounds; faithfully and enthusiastically implementing a reform to empower the working/popular classes challenged many of their most deeply-rooted beliefs and values. The school had historically been one of the academically superior schools in the municipal system and was a sought-after assignment for the mostly veteran teachers. Asking them to radically transform their teaching practice constituted a major challenge. Finally, the surrounding neighborhood and the students' families represented a slice of recent Brazilian economic history; many of the students had the appearance of a middle class homelife which was in actuality built on very shaky foundations that were slipping more and more into poverty each day.

Manoel de Paiva School: A Description

Manoel de Paiva School fell within the jurisdiction of NAE-1. This NAE covers the central region of the municipality and is therefore bordered by six of the nine other NAEs. It is one of the more densely populated regions of the city, with about two million people residing in neighborhoods that range from poor (zero to eight minimum salaries) to mostly middle class (eight to 30 minimum salaries) and a few enclaves of residents who enjoy a much higher income bracket than most in the city (more than 30 minimum salaries). Geographically, the school was in the neighborhood of Vila Mariana. In 1987, less than 20 percent of the residents of this neighborhood were classified as low income and all the residential units were serviced by water and sewer lines. Moreover, 100 percent of the neighborhood residents had completed primary school.[13] A walk through the residential areas around the school revealed mid- to large-sized homes with nicely manicured gardens. At the same time, Manoel de Paiva School sat at the outer edge of Vila Mariana, and while a tidy middle class residential area bordered one side of the school, other adjacent areas included a motel (in Brazil, motels are distinct from hotels because rooms are primarily leased by the hour), a large discount store, and a number of small textile factories and auto mechanic shop. One block from Manoel de Paiva School was a central arterial; on the other side of this arterial was a large favela.

In addition to this physical sensation of straddling two distinct realities, the school's student population and teacher population struggled with internal tension and contradictions. At one time, the school served primarily neighborhood residents and enjoyed a good reputation as a high-quality public school. Gradually, with the decline in public education in general, neighborhood families made an effort to send their children to private schools. With this overall pauperization of São Paulo public schools, Manoel de Paiva School eventually became a school primarily for working class and poor children. Within the seven to eight years prior to this research, however, the school population was again shifting, with increasing numbers of neighborhood children returning to the school, due to economic crises in Brazil that made it impossible for many of the middle class families to continue to pay private school fees. As a result, it was a school where social class was a dominant but confusing issue, for students and teachers alike. Many of the students had a middle class frame of reference, but were aware that their families' financial status was drastically declining. Other students were abjectly poor and mixed in among their wealthier counterparts. For the school staff, this duality in student population was a constant challenge.

Contributing to the confusion was a series of mixed messages that many teachers perceived. On one hand, district personnel policies bestowed upon these teachers relatively high status. First, the school's reputation as a quality school (though in decline for several years) contributed to teachers' self perception of superiority. Similarly, institutional memory was selective and many of the long-term teachers still conceived of Manoel de Paiva School as a place where middle class students excelled, even though more recent data showed otherwise. Second, the school's central location indicated status; one of the benefits of a large number of years of service was placement at centrally located (and thus better served) schools. These types of messages from the district were seeming contradictory to other messages that called for drastic reforms, of the type championed by the Inter Project. Many of the teachers at Manoel de Paiva School wrestled with these multiple messages and ended up fairly frustrated and stymied in their efforts to be effective in the classrooms.

It was against this backdrop of tension and contradiction that the implementation of the Inter Project at Manoel de Paiva School will be described.

History of the Inter Project at Manoel de Paiva School

The staff at Manoel de Paiva School knew about the Inter Project from its initial stages. Their long-time pedagogic coordinator took a leave from the school at the invitation of the district office to work on formulating and providing technical assistance for the Project. According to teachers, she kept them abreast of developments and encouraged them to participate in the Project, even during the pilot phase.

There was a split among the staff as to the exact manner in which their participation came about. Some staff felt that they had made the decision voluntarily and with adequate information. During our reconstruction of the decision-making process, the current pedagogic coordinator reminded the staff, "Remember that we did not accept the first proposal. Instead, we just observed other schools that were in the Inter." Others remembered that the Project was indeed imposed on them by the administration. Still others felt that a combination of factors contributed to their decision—both subtle pressure from the NAE-1 and district staff, who because of proximity were able to visit the school frequently [the DOT, Technical Orientation Directorate offices of the Secretariat was located in Vila Mariana], as well as interest and curiosity on the part of the staff.

Nevertheless, this staff was distinct from other school staffs in their forthrightness. Many staff members (but certainly not all) did admit during casual conversations that the most appealing aspect of Project participation was the additional salary. Echoing the earlier descriptions of contradictions in this school, the decision to participate in the Inter Project certainly exemplified another instance in which the school did not act under a unified vision, but rather responded to and remembered very different impulses and forces.

Meetings

This school followed a unique and fairly ineffective meeting schedule. Like many other aspects of the school's involvement in the Inter Project, the school's meetings and professional development work had a compliant flavor rather than something more indicative of genuine interest, enthusiasm, or commitment. Unlike other schools that had a more staggered meeting schedule, the teachers at Manoel de Paiva School met for six hours on Monday afternoons. To complete the required 10 hours of the JTI, teachers were encouraged to meet on their own for the remaining four hours; a small group of five teachers did meet independently. The Monday meetings were scheduled to begin at 1 p.m. and last until 7 p.m. The meetings were unevenly attended and teachers slipped in and out during the marathon event. The meetings were directed by the pedagogic coordinator, though she was often unable to arrive until 3 or 4 p.m. There did not seem to be a mechanism for determining or communicating the agenda in advance. Thus, during the time when the pedagogic coordinator was not yet at the meeting, teachers sat and socialized; their conversation most often focused on the terrible behavior and attitudes of the students.

There were only two occasions during the six month period of field-work at this school[14] that meeting activities focused on topics related to the Inter Project. During one occasion, two science teachers worked together to develop a common unit around animals. However, they worked together in a corner of the room, largely ignored by other teachers engrossed in casual talk. At another meeting, the group worked together on a request from the NAE to complete a self-evaluation on their involvement with the Inter Project. The pedagogic coordinator led the staff through a series of questions which initiated responses and some dialogue from the teachers. Though this meeting seemed more substantive than the previous ones, many of the same troubling process characteristics of past meetings were clearly evident.

The staff struggled to maintain dialogue, and often once discussions were actually initiated, they quickly deteriorated into emotional arguments. The struggle around initiating and sustaining a dialogue seemed to be based on two overriding factors. On the surface, teachers expressed exhaustion and disinterest. Teachers often lamented additional work focused on curriculum development or NAE requests, claiming that it was more than they could handle after a long day in the classroom. After observing many extremely contentious discussions (even during the more conversational portions of meetings), it appeared that some of the reluctance that the staff had towards engaging in discussions or group work stemmed from their own inability to engage in civil and productive discourse. In fact, just the opposite was true with whole faculty interactions, even around seemingly mundane issues, frequently breaking down into emotionally charged confrontations. Thus, opportunities for dialogue were avoided by this staff because of numerous discussions in the past which were emotionally draining and divisive.

Because of this history, the "teacher talk" during meetings tended to stay on very "safe" topics: weekend plans, stories about naughty students, a department store sale, and how tired people were feeling. Without leadership from the pedagogic coordinator, the NAE staff, or any teachers on staff, the level of dialogue at Manoel de Paiva School remained fairly stagnant and a sense of common purpose and collective action among the teachers was almost nonexistent. This had profound impacts on the development of the school's curriculum using the generative theme, the transformation of classroom practice, teachers relationships with students, and teachers relationships with each other.

Curriculum Development and Classroom Practice

Most teachers and the pedagogic coordinator characterized the school's Study of the Reality as a very worthwhile effort. Prior to conducting this study, teachers had assumed that because many students had the commodities of middle class life—Nike tennis shoes, braces, and the occasional Walkman—they indeed led a middle class life. That is, they assumed that most of their students lived with both parents, at least one parent held a well-paying professional job, students were supervised when at home, and education and its importance was stressed. In conducting the Study of the Reality, teachers were shocked to find these assumptions completely disproved. They found that many of their students lived in the nearby favela, and many others lived two or three families to a one-family dwelling unit in a poorly maintained *cortiço* (tenement house). And while some students did live in a more middle class setting, it was not the environment that they pictured. First, many of the school's more solidly middle class students' families were experiencing economic hardship due to the prevailing economic crisis in the country. Second, though the students might have enjoyed the material comforts of middle class existence, the other attributes that teachers thought accompanied such material comfort (supervision, reinforcement of school values, emphasis on education and enrichment, etc.) were often absent.

The Study of the Reality, then, gave the teachers at Manoel de Paiva School a sobering look into the realities of their students' lives. In truth, not only was this reality quite different from what they had expected to find, it was also a stark contrast to their own mostly middle and upper middle class lives. With this new awareness, the staff developed the generative theme of: Social Awareness. Included in this theme are issues related to citizenship and civic life as well as explorations of the community's social and physical environment.

However, it was clear in conversations and classroom observations that only the pedagogic coordinator and a few of the teachers that showed some active commitment to the Project were teaching and using curriculum in a manner that related to this theme. Consequently, there was no overall curriculum plan developed and in operation at this school.

Classroom practice at Manoel de Paiva ranged from traditional and authoritarian to interactive and student-centered, although the former was considerably more prevalent than the latter. In the traditional classrooms, teachers demanded silence while they either lectured or wrote on the board.

Students worked individually from textbooks and completed worksheets. In the more innovative classrooms, students conducted experiments in groups, they discussed with the teacher their ideas and explanations about concepts, and they used a variety of resources such as television programs, newspapers, and material procured by the teacher. In the traditional classrooms, teachers often admonished students with phrases such as, "This is information that you really need to know." In the more innovative classrooms, teachers were more apt to say,' It is important that you as an individual and a citizen understand this information and use it to make good decisions."

Several of the classrooms evidenced an active incorporation of the generative theme and elements of a democratic classroom. In one social studies class for sixth graders, students had been working on a long-term project to chart the ways in which power relations had been transformed through history. Focusing primarily on labor history, the students explored the changes in the relationships between labor and capital over time; this allowed the class to learn about feudalism, slavery, and the rise of modern capitalism. The teacher had helped them to develop portfolios of the different types and sources of information that they had consulted in creating their final projects. The teacher emphasized using sources that would provide students with the human dimension of these relationships. As a result, many students consulted diaries of slaves, read novels about factory conditions at the beginning of industrialization, and scoured daily newspapers for any news about current labor relations, strikes or negotiations. Students worked in groups, but fairly independently and without a great deal of direction from the teacher. Students also exhibited a good deal of interest in their projects and spent most of the classroom time actively engaged in their work.

In another fifth grade science class, the teacher was quite ambitious in her integration of the generative theme and science lab experiments. She worked with students on a series of labs related to natural cycles. Students did experiments with dirt and composting as well as with the water cycle and condensation. Though limited equipment forced students to work in unwieldy large groups, they cooperated nicely and made thoughtful observations. The teacher was creative in her use of a range of "everyday" situations to reinforce key concepts. Students kept a "Water Diary" where they recorded daily uses of water at school, in their homes, and in their neighborhoods. Students also visited a water treatment plant. This teacher very comfortably used Socratic questioning to help students to draw relationships between the lab experiments and the larger issues they were exploring related to the generative theme.

Those teachers whose classroom practice fully embraced the Project's principles numbered approximately three. There were two additional teachers who talked with ease about the Project's student-centered pedagogy and incorporated some aspects of it in their classroom, but also readily admitted their "authoritarian ways." While neither of these teachers used a curriculum that strongly reflected the school's generative theme, both teachers had made significant changes in that students worked in groups and on projects that they had independently designed. In addition, they did use a fair amount of non-textbook resources, such as literature and print media. In these teachers' classes, which were language arts and social studies, students were dealing with contemporary issues in their lives. At the same time, the teachers provided an apt description of their instructional practice. While students were more at liberty in these classes than in others to voice their opinions and to interact with one another, the teachers controlled the classroom dynamics and discussions in such a manner that students were not really able to fully explore different options and ideas. In the end, both teachers made sure that their opinions and ideas were the dominant ones. And although students could disagree, such dissension was not encouraged, nor were they given the tools or opportunities with which to develop strong counter-opinions. Thus, the authoritarianism came not so much in the teachers' affective manner, but in their ultimate control of the students' thought processes.

Another example of traditional instruction styles was particularly evident in Portuguese language classes and in mathematics. Course content was driven by the textbook and a stack of dittoes. Memorization of grammar rules and computation formulas were the main activities. No efforts were made to link this content with the generative theme or to make it in any other way relevant to or interesting for students. Students worked alone and in silence, and competition between students was implicitly and explicitly reinforced. Observations of these teachers' classes revealed that the same exact lesson plan was followed for each successive class, regardless of how many students submitted homework, what proportion of the class understood the assignment, and the questions students raised regarding the content.

In a few of the more disturbing cases, teachers actually acted with noticeable hostility towards their students. In one classroom, the "good" students sat on one side of the room, while the "poor" students sat on the other. The teacher informed observers of this seating arrangement while the students paid close attention. In another classroom, students who misbehaved were forced to stand at the front of the class near the trash can while the teacher stated that their behavior was so "trashy" that they really deserved to be in the trash can rather than just next to it. In a third classroom, an overweight boy was admonished for not volunteering to write an answer on the board. The teacher told him that perhaps he could lose a little weight if he participated more in class.

Though classroom practice is generally considered the most difficult of all aspects of teaching to transform classroom observations at Manoel de Paiva School revealed that the impact of the Inter Project was minimal, with only five of 15 classrooms using instructional strategies central to the Project. Similar to other tensions within this staff, those who ascribed to the Inter Project student-centered classroom stood in stark contrast with those who didn't. Each group tended to think that theirs was the most effective method of teaching (or at least "what the students needed") and both groups had long since abandoned any effort to truly engage the other in a dialogue about what they were doing in the classroom, what was working, and where the challenges were. In effect, the isolation characteristic of conventional schools continued at Manoel de Paiva School.

Teachers' Assessments of the Inter Project

Despite the broad range of Project implementation at Manoel de Paiva School and some clear Project opponents, teachers were fairly positive in their assessments of the Inter Project, though their accolades were directed more at the PT-MSE administration than at the Project itself. For the most part, teachers acknowledged that the administration had genuinely boosted the professional status of teachers and improved their working conditions. As one teacher stated, "This administration has really given value to what teachers know and what students know." Others concurred, adding: "This administration has given us ample space and this action has really proved to be productive. Even the NAE has been a place for us to have space to learn and develop things. We had the city-wide conference, courses, and other events." Another teacher offered this perspective on the staff's growth: "We have been able to create our own vision of our subject area. We have also learned."

In addition, teachers valued the new relationships that they had developed with the NAE and the MSE. They felt that it was different, in both substance and procedure, than relationships with previous administrations. As one teacher noted, "There were various moments in which different things were imposed and we didn't accept them. But this had its positive side because it helped us to develop our critical and reasoning abilities, to figure out what was important to us and to find our own options. We also benefited just from the opportunity to criticize and to protest." Ironically, though few of their students had the opportunity to develop their own critical citizenship skills, the teachers at Manoel de Paiva School recognized their own growth in this area as a result of their interactions with the PT-MSE.

In addition to identifying aspects of their own professional growth experienced as a result of PT-MSE reforms, the teachers also mentioned benefits directly stemming from the Inter Project itself. These benefits related to changes both in students and in student/teacher relations. Some teachers felt that student learning improved as a result of changes wrought by the Project. One teacher asserted that "the school has changed for the better . . . . I think that the students have been able to learn more, although each teacher is different. The different subject areas are always linked and you have knowledge forming upon knowledge." Several teachers also noted that students seemed more comfortable and engaged in school. As one teacher described, "We also have come to know our students better with this Project—the students have become more visible elements of the school."

Commenting on important changes in the student/teacher relationship, several teachers applauded the value of the Study of the Reality, noting its importance in helping them better understand their students' lives and concerns. One teacher summed up the moderate support for the Project felt by other teachers in saying, "[I]n fact, I agree with the idea that teachers should become more familiar with students' realities. I also like the general idea that the curriculum reflect these realities more." In a more persuasive manner, another moderately active Inter Project teacher offered this view of the improvements in student/teacher relationships that she had experienced:

> [T]his administration gave us the opportunity to know who our students are—to know how they feel and what they think, how they think, how they work, what is important to them—in a way that was more real and defined. It made for a more natural and enjoyable relationship. I don't remember—not even during the Covas regime—this kind of thing happening before.

Though these assessments do point to many positive aspects of the Inter Project, they were conveyed by a relatively small group of teachers and were overshadowed by the challenges and concerns that many teachers voiced regarding the Project. In addition, observation of classroom practice tended to contradict many of the positive student attributes that these teachers noted.

Moreover, despite the generally positive attitudes expressed towards the Project, there appeared to be tremendous unevenness in staff's understanding of the basic philosophical underpinnings of the Inter Project, its primary objectives, and its implications for classroom practice. Discussions

with the pedagogic coordinator revealed her very comprehensive understanding of the Project, at both the theoretical and practical levels. A small
fraction of the teachers (perhaps three out of 18) also shared this philosophical and theoretical understanding of the Project. One of these teachers had recently completed graduate studies at the Pontifical Catholic University in São Paulo where Freire and key leaders on his staff taught. But
the vast majority of the teachers exhibited serious and fundamental confusion about the main ideas undergirding the Project and the primary objectives for classroom practice and curriculum development.

During a group discussion, teachers were asked to describe the Inter
Project to someone who might be curious about its philosophical base and
how it was operationalized in a school. All of those present (including the
three identified above as having a good understanding of the Project) nomi-
nated the school's media specialist to provide an answer. They clearly held
her in high esteem based on her knowledge of and work with the Project;
in addition, she and some students from the school had represented the
school at the city-wide Inter conference earlier in the year. Despite their
strong endorsement, her description of the Project was disturbingly confused and distant from the most basic elements of the Secretariat's vision
of the nature and purpose of interdisciplinariness in the curriculum. She
said:

> Inter is based on a return to the past where the different subject areas were
> not separated or compartmentalized. All of the subject areas were given
> at the same time. As time passed, however, the subject areas became more
> and more separated, to the point where you have specialists in the most
> minute areas. This type of organization of knowledge has been passed on
> to the students, such that they learn the different subject areas as separate
> units. So what we are doing with Inter is returning to the past—like what
> they had in Greece—and integrating teaching. So if I talk about animals
> and habitats, I am dealing with sciences —but if I also talk about where
> they can be found, then I am introducing geography. If I measure the sizes
> of animals, then I am doing math. So it's in this form that we can really
> relate the various subject areas so that they all fit together in the student's
> head. That's basically Inter.

Quite characteristically, these teachers processed their understanding
of the Inter Project through their own very academically oriented perspectives, and in doing so, managed to render the Project politically neutral,
stripping it to its most basic curriculum function. Though some teachers
infrequently talked about efforts to be "less authoritarian" or to incorpo-
rate the students' reality into their work, most teachers' actions and dia-

logue seemed to confirm that for them, the Inter Project was really a matter of making connections among content areas. It was not a Project that had wider instructional implications or political meaning.

As previously noted, observations at Manoel de Paiva School revealed relatively minimal implementation of the curricular and instructional practices envisioned by the PT-MSE for schools participating in the Inter Project. This absence of genuine Project development stemmed from considerable dissatisfaction related to challenges that teachers encountered with the Inter Project. Such challenges included disagreements over the interpretation of the Study of the Reality results, difficulties in understanding new subject area guidelines, problems arising from new authority relations in the classroom, and conflicts with parents and students.

In teachers' comments above, it seems that many teachers viewed the Study of the Reality as a very valuable activity in which they gained tremendous insights about their students and their lives. A small but vocal portion of the teachers consistently disregarded the information in this Study and insistently continued to consider their students as solid members of the middle class. This was a particularly touchy issue for two teachers, who persistently complained of not wanting to indulge "spoiled" children. This exchange between two teachers is typical of those during most Monday meetings:

Teacher 1: If these kids are really slipping into poverty, why is there such a parade of fancy cars dropping them off at school every day? I mean, some of these students have imported tennis shoes and clothes that I can't even afford! And if you look around at the houses here—they're nice and big. I think these families have plenty of money—the parents just don't care about school.

Teacher 2: Look, a car is a sign of status—but it doesn't necessarily mean much more than that about the student's family life. We have a few students that are from upper middle class families—we do. But the majority are from the lower middle class. There may be students in your classrooms who wear imported tennis shoes and so on and so forth and you go to their house and you find that they live in the depths of a tenement house (*no fundo de um cortiço*). As a matter of fact, the living conditions are so bad that often the mothers don't want you to visit the house because they don't want you to see how they live. But the fact is that these living conditions are the reality for some of our students who came to this school from private schools—

and they had these living conditions when they were in private schools too.

Though there were only two teachers who consistently challenged students' social class status, the debate above (and others that were similar) seemed representative of a much larger issue brought to the fore for these teachers as a result of the Inter Project. In a small way, the school, with its student population whose families were slowly slipping from middle class status into the working or popular classes, was emblematic of the larger trends in society. Surprisingly insulated, the staff at Manoel de Paiva School had been able to enjoy the façade of teaching in a middle class school, with its accompanying good student behavior, parent support, and comparatively high status, long after economic crises had squeezed the Brazilian middle class. Facing the reality of this fact and all of the inevitable changes in status, attitude, and eventually curriculum and pedagogy was a tremendous difficulty for all of the teachers, and, clearly insurmountable for a few.

Still, most of the teachers at Manoel de Paiva School were able to make the attitudinal adjustments necessary in the face of the new information that they gained about their students' lives. Though this did not mean that most of the teachers changed their teaching practice to respond to these new realities, it did mean that they viewed their students in a different light, one which was frequently more compassionate and less judgmental.

More challenging, however, were the fundamental cognitive shifts necessary to embrace the visions of subject areas proposed by the PT-MSE. Several teachers, particularly those who taught mathematics, language arts, and visual arts, voiced serious concerns about this redefinition of their subject areas. One teacher criticized the changes in this manner: "My field [visual arts] is a classic field. I was trained in a very rigorous way. There are certain things that must be learned and in certain ways. There are standards to uphold. What Barbosa [Director of the São Paulo Museum of Modern Art and an advisor to the PT-MSE] thinks is the new direction for the visual arts is an atrocity. It popularizes something that is really classical and beautiful."

This teacher's critique reveals a deeply felt conflict that several teachers at Manoel de Paiva School experienced in relation to the Inter Project. They felt that the redefinition of their particular field threatened both their knowledge base with regard to their subject matter and the manner in which that knowledge had been acquired. They did not view the new subject area visions as an enhanced conceptual understanding of their subject area but rather as a negation of what they understood their subject area to be. This negation was further worsened by the PT-MSE's attempts to give value to non-academic, popular knowledge and skills. Though not all teachers bristled at this idea as did the teacher quoted above, this concern echoes earlier complaints voiced about students' socio-economic status. In addition, the interdisciplinary nature of the Project seemed to signal yet another reduction of the importance or singularity of their subject area. Thus, in varying degrees, these teachers experienced tremendous professional destabilization as a result of many of the components included in the Inter Project.

Compounding this sense of discomfort and instability was the PT–MSE's push for a student-centered classroom and democratization at all levels of school governance. For many of the teachers at this school, their authority and control in the classroom were symbols of their ability to command respect and obedience from the students, most often exhibited in sedentary, quiet behavior. Though the Inter Project did not propose a reduction in respect for teachers, it did advocate cooperative learning, discussion, debate and dialogue—activities which many teachers interpreted as threatening and diminishing to their classroom authority. Echoing the complaint of many other teachers throughout the municipal schools, one teacher at Manoel de Paiva lamented, "This administration allowed too much liberty to be given to students— they were allowed to talk more in class, they were allowed to suggest ideas. Students no longer respect the teachers or the teachers' control in the classroom."

Teachers also pointed out a related concern with what they viewed as rhetoric regarding the democratization of schools. On one hand, teachers appreciated an environment that afforded them more autonomy and decision-making power, as evidenced by their voluntary decision to participate in the Inter Project. On the other hand, teachers felt that anarchy rather than democracy was really the order of the day, a situation which also resulted in a disrespect of traditional roles and authority. Similarly, teachers felt that the democratization of school and district relations was oddly selective. One teacher sarcastically commented, "NAE supervisors waltz in here and say there is no more hierarchy—but still look where they are and where we are. And they've given too much to the students. Now, if the students want to speak to the supervisor all they have to do is call her up and have a chat?! This is too much democracy."

Concerns about teacher authority also extended to teacher/parent relationships, and it was in this arena that this staff demonstrated the highest levels of conflict, both internally and with the parents. Internally, teachers were both resentful of the increased opportunities for parents' participation (e.g., on the Site Council) and confused by the parameters guiding their participation. One teacher complained, "None of these parents is a teacher—yet they can come in and tell us how to teach." In another exchange, teachers debated different ideals of parent involvement. One group of teachers felt that only the more involved, professional and educated parents should participate in school governance. Parents without these qualifications would have a hard time understanding the issues and the full ramifications of different decisions. Many teachers opposed this view as elitist and felt that having a strong interest in their child's welfare was the best recommendation for parent involvement on the Site Council. Once again these teachers revealed their struggles with social class identity and the conflicts surfaced by the Project.

The external conflicts with parents were more intense and disturbing. Site Council meetings were frequently the site of heated debates that were emotionally draining and potentially devastating for school/community relations. Parents were often accusatory in their language and insensitive to teachers' sense of professional efficacy. During one meeting a father complained that he felt his children found school "boring" and wondered if there were ways in which the teachers could make their classes more engaging. Teachers responded angrily that parents left it to them to be everything to their children—nurse, psychologist, and counselor—with very little left over to teach. In their opinion, parents needed to do more to impress upon their children the value of education. Teachers felt that if parents monitored their children's homework, limited their television viewing, and stressed the importance of doing well in school, the problems would be solved.

Interestingly, the two sides were raising two distinct issues. On one hand, the parents were pointing out a weakness that they saw regarding the extent to which the curriculum provided at the school was able to engage students' interest. This clearly hit a raw nerve with teachers at Manoel de Paiva School who had already heard from the PT-MSE that curriculum must be made more relevant to students' lives and who had seen with their own eyes (through the Study of the Reality) that what they understood to be students' realities are very different from the actuality. These teachers were aware that changes can be made to make the curriculum more engaging and interesting, but they have not yet found a way that all can pursue comfortably. To have the parents echo these demands was experienced as an insult.

Teachers, on the other hand, while not responding to parents' issues, brought up another tension related to parents' preparation and support of their children. They wanted to see more vigilance on the part of parents to make sure that students arrived at school on time, completed their homework in a satisfactory manner, and generally respected and participated in school life. Like the teachers' response to parents' demands, these teachers' demands were also frustrating to parents who were, for the most part, working full-time, trying desperately to maintain a standard of living that was quickly becoming almost impossible to sustain. Thus, neither the teachers nor the parents were able to acknowledge the perspective of the other and both failed to understand that they were fundamentally trying to solve the same problem.

Finally, teachers at Manoel de Paiva School felt students posed a major challenge to their ability to implement the Inter Project. Student misbehavior was the most common topic in the staff room, though relative to other schools in this study, students at Manoel de Paiva School were very well-behaved and well-mannered. Fights were very rare, classrooms were usually very quiet, and passing periods were a smooth and calm transition. Nevertheless, teachers felt that students' behavior and attitudes compounded the difficulties of their jobs. Again, they attributed this situation to a mismatch between what the teachers viewed as important and central to schooling and what students wanted out of their time in school. One teacher offered this analysis:

> I don't think they [students] are particularly interested in this idea of academics. They come to school more for the socializing and social aspects that it offers than for the intellectual stimulus. The majority—they come looking for things that do not have to do with learning. I don't know if everyone agrees. Regardless of the fact that you try to use materials that are colorful, bright and different, they aren't able to focus on the task because the content of the task, the objective, is not at all what they want. So there is a great loss that we experience as teachers and an inversion in some moments. It's a shock between our values as educators—because we have this ideal that is cognizant of their family income, their lives, etc.—it's not our ideal but the ideal based on these different social factors for the students that we saw in our ER. Even being conscious of these things and adjusting our expectations, we haven't succeeded in reaching the majority of our students.

This teacher posed a more objective and analytical view of the student that takes into consideration both their potential perspectives on the situation as well as the teachers' experiences and feelings. Other teachers were far less charitable. Many times teachers commented on students with such harsh words as "He's lifeless but someone forgot to bury him," or "I wish I could put him in a meat grinder head first," or "She'll never amount to anything." With the exception of three or four teachers, most of the staff at Manoel de Paiva School openly displayed disdain and dislike for their students. Certainly these attitudes compounded any negativity or disinterest that students may have brought with them to the school.

Summary

Conflict and controversy characterized every element of Project implementation at Manoel de Paiva School. The conflict surfaced internally, in the highly contentious relationships between different groups of teachers, and externally, in the tense and often adversarial relationship between teachers and parents. Basic Project tenets created conflicts on an individual and professional level for many teachers, who struggled to integrate their own professional beliefs and values with those proposed by the Project. Key Project procedures, such as the Study of the Reality, also created tension for some teachers, who found themselves unable, even in the face of very clear data, to accept the reality of students' lives.

But the most basic conflict at Manoel de Paiva School seems really to have been one related to social class. There was tension between the PT-MSE's leftist political agenda aimed at creating a public school in the service of the working class and the overwhelmingly middle class status, conservative ideological position and traditional pedagogical approach of the teachers at the school. Teachers struggled with their nostalgia for the glory days of the school, when middle class parents supported classroom instruction by monitoring homework and teaching their children the value of education, and the stark realities of the Brazilian economic crisis, which had, in reality, transformed school clientele into children of working class and poor families. In the face of these conflicts and tensions, full implementation of the Inter Project would have required a level of "pedagogic militancy" that these veteran teachers, on the whole, no longer possessed and were not ideologically nor professionally willing to develop. As a result, their efforts with the Project stalled and only reached fruition in a handful of cases.

Conclusions

Together, these four case studies of schools implementing the Inter Project and the teachers' voices that are heard within the narratives of the experience highlight the difficulties, failures and accomplishments of this extraordinary educational reform effort. Changes perceived by teachers and pedagogic coordinators as a result of the Inter Project experience are summarized in Table 6.2.

Participating schools were given challenging and ambitious goals. They were asked to dramatically transform teacher practice and reorient and curriculum content and development. They were expected to redefine along democratic lines the relationship between students and teachers, teachers and teachers, and the school and the local community within a societal context steeped in authoritarianism and the traditions of hierarchy. They were forced to confront their own complicity in the reproduction of the harsh injustices in Brazilian society, and to use this realization to reorient their work and commitments. Finally, they were invited to participate in a truly liberating, though simultaneously risky and frightening, educational experience and experiment.

TABLE 6.2   Changes Brought About by the Inter Project: From the Perspective of Teachers and Pedagogic Coordinators

Before	*After*
Teachers isolated in the classroom •little contact with other teachers •lack of integration among different disciplines	Teachers work collectively •exchange of ideas •integration of content across different disciplines
Reliance on textbook as main source of curriculum planning and materials	Search for new and diverse sources for curriculum content and materials
Predetermined curriculum •content unrelated to student reality	Curriculum based on lived experience of student
Students passive learners •work individually •academic activity restricte to copying, rote memorization, and regurgitation of curriculum content •knowledge passed from teacher to student	Students active learners •work in collaborative groups •encouraged to be more creative •encouraged to discuss, debate, dialogue •teacher and students work collectively toward the construction of knowledge
Hierarchical/authoritarian relation between school and Secretariat •strict supervisory role of SME •top-down process of policy formulation and implementation	Democratization of relations between school and Secretariat •communication lines open between school and SME •greater autonomy of school in program development

The preceding case studies illustrate the ways in which the Inter Project related to different school cultures and individual personalities and life experiences. We shared in the struggle at Sussumu School to build capacity and pursue the Inter Project independent of constant NAE assistance. We observed the contentious but productive ways in which teachers at Habib School articulated their individual understanding and commitment to the Project, while also trying to find consensus and common ground. At Pracinhas School, the advantages of prior experience, a small staff, and a stable community allowed elements of the Project to flourish and even enhance the original intentions of the PT-MSE, particularly with regard to parent solidarity. And in stark contrast, the example of Manoel de Paiva School demonstrates the theoretical, ideological and practical obstacles that made Project implementation often unattainable.

Amidst this wide range of experiences, it readily becomes evident when listening to the voices of the teachers involved in the Project that one of the most significant accomplishments of the PT administration, (and a common theme whether the Project was well implemented or not), was its support and promotion of collective work by teachers and students. Certainly a hallmark of the PT–MSE is the consistent fact that teachers entered into dialogue with one another about the fundamental issues of educating children from the popular classes. Teachers could no longer avoid responding to the Freirean queries of: What are we teaching? Why and for whom are we educating?

Though this dialogue should be hailed as an important accomplishment, it is also clear that the PT-MSE's efforts, given myriad obstacles including a very brief three year tenure, marked only the initiation of a transformative process to create popular public schools. Though many important questions were raised and acknowledged, many answers still remained elusive. Among these was the teachers' persistent struggle to fully comprehend the Inter Project and translate the ideas of the Project into their daily practice. As an example, in the case study of Sussumu, the juxtaposition of the two curricular plans that were generated at a particular school site at the onset of the Inter Project (when Sussumu School was a pilot site receiving intensive intervention by the NAE Inter team) and one year after the PT administration (with a group of teachers struggling to construct an interdisciplinary curriculum on their own) serves to illustrate the gap between the theory and practice of the Inter Project. The case studies further point out that obstacles to Project implementation were related to the structural and organizational elements of the municipal school system, in addition to the factors that could be attributed to the characterization of the PT administration and the nature of the Project itself. These points are further elaborated in our following and final Chapter VII.

Notes

1. Delizoicov and Zanetic, "A proposta de interdisciplinaridade e o seu impacto no ensino municipal de 1° grau," in Nídia Nacib Pontuschka (org.), *Ousadia no Diálogo: Interdisciplinaridade na escola pública* (São Paulo: Loyola, 1993), p. 10.

2. Ibid., p. 11.

3. John Lofland and Lyn H. Lofland, *Analyzing Social Settings: A Guide to Qualitative Observation and Analysis* (Belmont, CA: Wadsworth Publishing Company, 1984); James P. Spradley, *The Ethnographic Interviewing* (Fort Worth: Holt, Rinehart and Winston, Inc., 1979).

4. SME-SP, *Diretrizes e Prioridades para 1992: Ano 4. Series 1*—Construindo a Educação Pública Popular (January, 1992), pp. 22-23.

5. In effect, the impeachment of Fernando Collor de Mello signified a historical event of primary importance on both a national and international level: Collor was the first president of a republic in Latin America, to be removed from office without the incursion of military force. For Brazil, it meant a strengthening of the precarious democratic institutions that have been in a process of legitimation since the demise of the military dictatorship in 1980. Logically then, the theme of "impeachment" and the related issues of "democracy," "justice"; and "citizenship" became generative themes at many schools participating in the Inter Project.

For example, a teacher [at a school resistant to the PT reform in NAE-4] had his sixth grade History students working in cooperative groups to produce a collective text based on the analysis and interpretation of a poster series, *Patria Amada Esquartejada* (Beloved Dismembered Country), published by the PT Secretariat of Culture: This series depicted social injustices through out Brazilian history and the students were to relate the graphic documentation of historical legacy of grievances of the Brazilian people to the impeachment of then President Collor.

6. Teachers at the intermediate grades specialized in single subjects and often taught for less than a full five-period shift, or they taught at several schools. As a result, many intermediate grade teachers were not present in a single school during the full course of a shift and therefore, were unavailable for meetings that might have logically been scheduled for either before or after a shift.

7. Paulo Freire, *Educação na Cidade* (1991). Op. Cit.

8. Shor, Ira. *Empowering Education: Critical Teaching for Social Change* (Chicago: Chicago University Press, 1992), p. 114.

9. The JTI (*Jornada de Tempo Integral*)—a PT legislative victory in the regulation of the municipal schools—granted teachers the right to ten hours of supplemental pay for class preparation, regardless of participation in the Inter Project, whereas initially only those in the Project received such a stipend.

10. Paulo Freire, *Politics and Education* (Los Angeles: UCLA Latin American Center, in press; São Paulo: Editora Cortez, 1995).

11. Guimar Namo de Mello served as Municipal Secretary of Education for São Paulo from 1983 to 1985 under mayor Mário Covas of the PMDB (Brazilian

Democratic Movement Party). A proponent of the so-called "conteúdista" position, Mello's administration advanced curriculum reforms that sought to enhance
the technical competence of teachers in the muncipal school system in order to
more effectively teach its working class students a well-organized and executed
curriculum founded on the fundamentals of systematized knowledge. See Guiomar
Namo de Mello, *Democracia Social e Educação: teses para discussão* (São Paulo: Cortez;
Autores Associados, 1990).

12. In the Brazilian system, teachers receive tenure for a particular position at a
particular school. They may opt to transfer to another school, but their tenure does
not automatically move with them, though they always have preference at their
school of tenure.

13. Rolnik, Raquel, Lucio Kowarik, and Nadia Somelch, São Paulo: Crise e
Mudança (São Paulo: Secretaria Municipal de Planejamento, 1990).

14. Because of the unique meeting schedule at this school, site visits were conducted on consecutive days for two weeks and then every Monday for a six-month
period.

VII

Conclusion

In this book we have sought to illuminate the interplay among knowledge, popular education, curriculum, teachers and the politics of educational policy in São Paulo. At the same time, we explore the relationship between the state, in this case a socialist party at the helm of a municipal government, and the social movements that the PT-MSE sought to both support and foster. And finally, we examined closely the school realties and teachers' consciousness that evolved out of the Inter Project curriculum reform experience. While explicitly avoiding grand conclusions and claims, our analysis of this complex process of educational change addresses ongoing debates in several areas of scholarship and offers some valuable lessons about what are some of the more relevant problems and possibilities for instituting a Freirean educational proposal in schools. In addition we have made an effort to discuss, however briefly, the nature of the popular state's relation to social movements in the realm of nonformal education, specifically, literacy training for youths and adults.

In our introduction, we posed five questions related to the work of the PT-MSE under Freire's leadership. To briefly recap, we presented the following queries: (1) What kind of knowledge was being produced in São Paulo public schools as a result of the administration's reform efforts? And, was this knowledge production process leading to the creation of critical and active citizens? (2) In what ways did the reform change the professional working conditions and lives of those teachers involved? Did teachers' opinions about their profession, their colleagues and their students change? Moreover, were teachers' working relationships with various school actors—e.g., colleagues, students, and families—transformed? (3) To what extent were various decision-making processes and bodies (e.g., the School Councils) able to democratize school processes and administration? (4) In what ways did teaching and learning change? In what ways did these changes constitute improvements in teaching and learning? And, finally, (5) did the PT-MSE reforms elevate the public's conception of education, and was the idea of a Popular Public School ultimately considered legitimate?

Because our data and analysis focused heavily on the experience of teachers as primary implementors of this radical reform, the previous chapters have focused most extensively on understanding teachers' perspectives, the innovations (however limited) in the teaching and learning process in classrooms, and the overall transformation in teacher culture and practice. In tangential ways, we have also touched on issues related to the ultimate outcomes of this reform (e.g., the creation of critical and active citizens) and the changes in public perception and support of public schooling.

We have divided this final chapter into three sections. The first highlights important concrete conditions that the Freire administration leaves as an on-going legacy to the working class and poor students that frequent São Paulo public schools and the dedicated educators that teach them. In the second section, we analyze in detail the ways in which public schooling, public school teachers, curriculum content and the student experience has been transformed. In doing so, we offer important lessons to be learned with regard to the complexities, the ambiguities and the challenges of creating and implementing a Freirean proposal for public schools. And, the third section revisits an on-going exploration of the relationships between the state and social movements, surfacing several principal questions that remain for future research.

Changes in Concrete Teaching and Learning Conditions

Let us overview some of the direct statistical evidence of positive changes and legislative gains that resulted from Freire's administration of the Secretariat of Education, namely in the areas of student retention and teacher working conditions.

Statistical data show a consistent rise in the student retention rate, which increased from 79.46 percent in 1989 to 81.3 percent in 1990 and to 87.7 percent in 1991 for grades one through eight (the *primeiro grau*, the primary and middle level). These represent the decade's best rates, as the previous high was 77.81 percent in 1985. Educational enrollment kept up with population growth, and the PT government solved the enrollment deficit inherited from the previous municipal administration of conservative populist politician Janio Quadros (1986-88). By the end of the Quadros government, enrollment in the *primeiro grau* had declined to 421,526 students compared with 423,360 toward the end of Mario Covas' administration (1983-85).[1] Under Freire, 50,801 new students were enrolled by 1992, increasing the total to 710,348 students. This 12 percent increase was roughly comparable to the growth of the cohort of seven- to 14-year-olds, which grew 12.5 percent. To reach this goal, Freire's administration increased the capacity of schools by instituting four school shifts of four hours each in 77 percent of the municipal schools.[2] Toward the end of his tenure in 1991, Freire concluded that retention figures demonstrated that "with relation to 1988 this means a conquest [gain] of 15,420 students that would have been failed and would have been candidates to drop out, which in practice means the expulsion of students from schools."[3]

The PT administration worked tirelessly to improve the concrete conditions of teaching, thereby linking improvements in teachers' working conditions and salaries—and by implication in their satisfaction and well-being—to improvements in education. A year after the PT administration took office, nominal salaries had increased by 2,605 percent, well above the inflation rate of 1,173 percent. Government reports state that the salary of a teacher increased by 112.5 percent in real terms during 1989. In 1992, full-time teachers who taught night school (after 7 p.m.) received a 30 percent pay increase above their base salaries.[4]

Table 3.1 shows that the Freire administration invested in areas traditionally neglected, particularly poor urban areas. Rather than push merely for generalized salary increases, the PT, characteristically, created a new salary schedule that kept its commitment to poor students and communities at the forefront. Thus, teachers working in the city's "less desirable" locations (e.g., shantytowns, the inner city) received extra compensation, in some cases up to 50 percent above their base salaries. Likewise, in an effort to increase the number of full-time teachers to the level considered necessary to increase educational quality, the new salary scale gives full-time teachers higher earnings than part-time teachers. (This includes full-time teachers teaching during night shifts, though their increases were somewhat less than those working during day-time shifts.)

Thus, during the PT municipal administration, the working conditions of teachers substantially improved with the approval of the *Estatuto do Magisterio Municipal* and increases in real salaries. Teachers in the municipal system now earn substantially more than their counterparts in the state system, and teachers working at night also have seen their pay increased. In addition, teachers working at more desirable central locations receive comparatively lower salaries than teachers working in less desirable intermediary or peripheral areas. These differential salary scales represent an explicit attempt to attract the best-qualified teachers to the city's poorest areas. By international standards, however, teacher salaries are meager, as the best-paid part-time teachers (category EM-I2-E, 20 contact hours a week) earn $364.75 a month.

Curriculum and Teachers: Transformation and Resistance

As we have consistently argued throughout the book, teachers were the central focus of the PT-MSE reforms, not only in terms of the administration's concrete efforts to improve their working conditions and promote professionalization through the organization of formation groups and legislative advances such as the JTI, but more importantly they constituted a key component of its main policy effort in the schools: teachers were fully charged with interpreting the Secretariat's theoretical principles and devising their own curriculum with the Inter Project. In addition to this universal challenge to link theory with practice, schools in the Inter Project revealed a range of methods for deconstructing and reconstructing the Project in their own vision.

Divergent interpretations of a Project's meaning or purpose, methods or goals, is certainly not particular to this experience in educational reform; but in this case, the design of the Project itself, built on the principles of dialogic reflection and participatory action, made it specially conducive to the development of a variety of interpretations of the Inter Project's objectives, the methods applied and the content matter proposed. In effect, the Secretariat did not present teachers with a discretely packaged project, precisely formulated to carry out its political agenda of radically transforming the city's schools in the service of the working class. Instead, the Project was created in broad brush strokes that outlined general principles for educators to follow in a collective effort to create the so-called Popular Public School.

With the Inter Project, Freire's administration faced the enormous challenge of implementing an educational reform based on the philosophical principles of education as liberating praxis that had mostly evolved in nonformal educational settings by politically militant leaders of grass-roots social movements in the 1960s and 1970s. It is not surprising then that in the 1990s, in an institutional setting of the proportions of the São Paulo municipal school system, the radical elements of Freire's proposal to educate for conscientization would necessarily meet with ideological resistance and methodological problems. Some of the most relevant issues and problems that arose during the Project's implementation are summarized below.

Factors most frequently cited by teachers and secretariat personnel as obstructing the Project's development include:

- large size of the municipal school system.
- uneven distribution of tenured and incoming teachers, with new and inexperienced teachers entering but quickly transferring schools at the periphery with the poorest clientele and more experienced and veteran teachers anxious to maintain their established methods at the more centrally located schools.
- lack of administrative experience of NAE and CONAE personnel.
- ambiguity in Project design and resulting differentiation and inconsistencies in Project interpretation among the different NAEs and schools.
- short time period (four years) for the development and implementation of reform.
- democratic character of administration that led to conflict between the push for school autonomy and the need for NAE and Secretariat coordination and supervision of the Project.
- limited professional preparation of teachers with relation to theoretical complexity of the project.
- resistance to project on basis of political opposition to Worker Party's ideological platform and policy objectives.

We discuss each of these points in depth as follows.

To begin with, the distinctly political focus of the PT's educational reform did not presuppose a partisan alliance on the part of the teachers in the schools as the reforms' detractors might argue. Secretariat staff insisted that a leftist ideological position was not a requirement of the Project but that it did require a certain "idealism, voluntarism, desire and need" for the kind of professional challenges the Inter Project created for teachers.

In the words of one CONAE staff member:

> To work in this proposal you don't necessarily have to be from the left, but you do have to have a series of values; for example, if you have the conception that 'Some of the students I work with can learn, others cannot, it is their problem or a problem that stems from the family,' then you won't do a good job in the Project. So the person need not be explicitly on the left but needs to have certain conceptions of education, knowledge, of students and society, and of life in general, that will allow him to be open to the growth [that the Project implies]. Because in reality all of us here in this administration also are not so certain. We have been constructing [the Project] as we go along, and a person needs to be open to that kind of

professional growth [. . .] the teacher who—and we have many in the
system—acts merely as what we call a public functionary, comes to class,
teaches for four hours, leaves and then blames the student and family and
takes no responsibility for what he/she does will have difficulty working
and growing along with this Project.

Taking into account these and other factors, Secretary Cortella estimated
that among the teachers actually working within the Project only 40 percent fully embraced its methods while another 40 percent were in the process of being convinced and 20 percent, many due to their political opposition to the PT, were very unlikely of ever being convinced of its validity.[5]

Even at the Secretariat level, few were card carrying members of the
party, and although the majority were necessarily supporters of the PT's
educational programs, many sympathized with other parties. Nevertheless, one would be hard pressed to find a Malufista [someone supportive
of Paulo Maluf, the right wing candidate for mayor in 1992] at the level of
the central or regional administrations; however, such individuals, were
not as rare at the school site level. Accordingly, the criteria for hiring subject area specialist to join the coordinating team did not include party membership but had more to do with level of expertise and ability to commit to
the intensive work that the coordination of the Project would entail. The
director for the Division of Primary and Secondary Education heading the
CONAE team pointed out the difficulty they had in getting a qualified
group together citing the fact that many were aware of the hard work it
would involve and turned down the opportunity to take on a leadership
role in the Project on that basis alone.

Hence, beyond resistance to the Project on mere political grounds, several factors which worked against the Project's development were consistently cited by teachers and secretariat personnel. A principal issue was
the large size of the municipal school system coupled with the ambitious
proportions of the Project. Marta Pernambuco characterized the fact that
the Project was implemented on such a large scale (nearly two thirds of the
schools in the municipal system) as "unprecedented in the history of education in Brazil and certainly in the municipality of São Paulo."[6] This broad
implementation had both its positive and negative consequences.

To begin with, if the intention was to create a movement for curriculum reform at the school site level, the PT administrators did not expect to
be met so immediately with the clamoring from teachers for the improvement of working conditions and for greater access to material and technical resources. In effect, the Project's rapid replication throughout the municipal school system, beyond the initial pilot sites—although aimed at
fulfilling the administration's goal of creating a curriculum reform move-

ment in the schools—logically led to a break down in the Secretariat's ability to assist those schools that later opted into the Project. Personnel at the Secretariat level found themselves overwhelmed with the demands being made on them by the steadily increasing number of schools in the Project.

This pointed to another persistent problem which was on one hand, a general lack of administrative experience of NAE and CONAE personnel, and on the other hand, limited professional preparation of teachers to grasp and put into practice a theoretically complex project. Hence teachers, unable to completely pursue the Project without NAE support, consistently voiced their frustration at not receiving the technical support they needed from NAE personnel, already overburdened with wide-ranging responsibilities. In addition, the workload factor also negatively affected teachers' reaction to the Project, considering the limited monetary compensation they received (even with the extra 10 JTI hours) for the intensive work it required.

For their part, the NAE staff complained that many teachers wanted the curriculum handed to them in a ready to teach fashion, which went against the Project's very principles. But for many teachers unaccustomed to taking on such a creative role along side their colleagues, the absence of a curricular package presented an unattractive challenge and therefore resulted in their frustration and disenchantment with the Project. A NAE Inter Team member expressed his own frustration with this situation:

> We [at the NAE] were unable to cover all the bases, you know what they wanted from the advising team, you can ask any one of the advisors, they wanted us to give them the classes ready, prepared for them, "Look you are going to go to your class and do this, this and that." As an advisor you would go crazy. How can you help 40 teachers [asking you for lessons]? Its impossible. As an advisor you don't know the reality of the students, of the neighborhood, of the community of the school. As an advisor it was impossible that you be familiar with all of that but that is what we were being asked [to do].

According to Secretariat personnel, the issue also alluded to a persistent conflict between the democratic principles they endeavored to promote and the need for a more coordinated supervision of the Project (i.e., school autonomy versus accountability and supervision). This conflict was the subject of much debate at the Secretariat level. Project leaders at the NAE and Secretariat level were very insistent about the fact that the Project was never imposed upon the teachers or the schools. The idea was that the school curriculum not be a predetermined package forced on schools from above, as is traditionally the case, but that it be a continually evolving and collectively constructed product generated from within the schools. Yet many teachers, who opted to join more on the basis of peer pressure than pedagogic or political conviction, ultimately resented the casting of the curriculum reform in the light of a political-pedagogical movement within the schools as sheer PT demagoguery.

Another factor that was consistently cited as contributing to teacher resistance to the Project was the uneven distribution of tenured and incoming teachers in the municipal system. CONAE personnel explained that in the more attractive centrally located schools [such as Manoel de Paiva School] where staff turnover is low there was greater resistance to the Project. Teachers in those schools were often more set in their ways and less willing to adopt the sweeping changes the Project entailed: "Why should I change what I've been doing for twenty years if its worked for me up until now," such teachers might chide. Whereas at schools in the periphery, where there is greater teacher turnover, the presence of a high percentage of teachers who have recently entered the profession made them more open to the changes brought on by the Project.

In addition, the ambiguity inherent in the PT proposal contributed to the enormous differentiation and inconsistencies in the Inter Project interpretation among the different NAEs and schools [as the four case studies in chapter VI illustrate]. The Interdisciplinary Project, more than a concrete curriculum proposal, represents above all, an attempt to radically rethink the whole approach to curriculum planning in the schools. This new approach does not adhere to a single curriculum model, but rather promotes the proliferation of ideas that respond to local concerns and are shaped by the creativity of the educators involved. At a CONAE (the Project's coordinating team at the Secretariat level) meeting in 1991, a discussion around the ambiguities that plagued the Project ensued. One member made this emphatic plea to establish a basic structure to the Project that could be more effectively communicated to the teachers:

> We need to stop and reflect on some of the serious problems of conceptualization of the Project. It is not enough to say, "It is resistance on the part of the teacher," it isn't because he was not trained for this kind of work, and neither were we. We have recognize that our technical support is loose. We don't have a generalized approach to the coordination of the Project as a whole and each subject area is not developing in the same direction. The Inter Team at the NAE is being questioned at various points and moments. [. . .] I feel we're in need of something more precise. We are still somewhat loosely defined in this sense and the schools that now are entering the project begin to demand more clarity. In the beginning we could say that they're resisting and don't want to join, but now this is no

longer the case. We need to discuss these problems and somehow bring closure.

This openness in the Project brought forth a series of practical problems for teachers; for example, difficulty in the sequencing of concepts and cognitive abilities being taught. This signified a major obstacle to the continuity of the Inter Project development. Once a set of activities are organized around a Generative Theme, teachers and even NAE team members were stumped as to how to construct a curriculum that maintains continuity and coherence with the different skills of students at a given grade level.

Addressing this issue, Secretary Mario Sérgio Cortella identified as a primary problem of the Project the need to better prepare teachers for this type of pedagogic work: he emphasized that "[the Interdisciplinary Project] demands a broad knowledge base of various elements that connect the production of knowledge . . . it demands a knowledge of the history of science." Secretary Cortella pointed out that the teachers in Brazil are trained in a university where knowledge is compartmentalized making it difficult for them to perceive the lines of communication between the various elements of knowledge. In addition, Secretary Cortella emphasized the persistence of the positivistic ideals on Brazilian pedagogical thinking as contributing to the difficulties teachers had in fully understanding and adopting the Freirean curriculum reform.[7] Accordingly, Torres characterizes a Freirean approach to knowledge as diametrically opposed to the traditional and dominant positivist paradigm. In this regard, Torres has argued elsewhere: "[k]nowledge, for Freire, is a social construction; it constitutes a process of discursive production and not merely an end product consisting of an accumulated cluster of information or facts. Freire's understanding of knowledge as a dialectics of oppositions is fundamentally at odds with traditional-idealist and positivist epistemology."[8]

As a consequence, one of the primary difficulties which arose in the Inter Project's curriculum planning process—pointed out by many of the educators involved in the Project—was the integration of all subject areas around a single generative theme. Teachers and even NAE team members were often stumped as to how to construct a curriculum that maintains continuity and coherence with the different skills of students at a given grade level. The subject areas of History and Geography often became the axis point around which the whole curriculum revolved given the facility with which teachers were able to associate the generative theme—derived from the social reality—to traditional content and skills taught in these areas. Hence at the OC stage of program planing problems came up with regard to the relevance of unifying concepts for all subject areas. Curriculum planning teams found that what might be conceptually important for one subject area was not of profound relevance for another; in other words, what worked for English and Portuguese did not relate to Science, while they were able to unify History, Geography, and Mathematics more easily. One NAE-6 team member pointed out: "If it was difficult for the NAE Inter Team, imagine [how hard it was] for the teachers."

A subject area specialist in Math, working in the CONAE highlights this problem by posing the following questions: "How can I teach math skills without engaging in a classic explanatory format? [. . .] How do you reconcile the most important math content with an interdisciplinary proposal? How to work with "quadratic equations" starting from situations generated in day to day life? Should the teacher always need to start from [real life] situations? If I want to know the general characteristics of a social group I employ the notions of "mean" or "median"—but if probability is not a mathematical topic taught in the fifth grade—what can a teacher do? And factoring? Should I interrupt a discussion within a generative theme in order to present some exercises for practicing skills and techniques in factoring?"[9] Interestingly, these very pragmatic uncertainties expressed by a university specialist at the core of the Inter Project's planning team reflects very accurately the concerns and doubts voiced by teachers at the schools.

Apparently, it was not clear for all teachers that the role of the generative theme was not to restrict the content matter in all subject areas to a single topic but rather to establish the interrelationship of the disciplines around a particular problem facing the community, in this way serving as a point of departure from the immediate reality of the community to the analysis and comprehension of more distant situations at the macro level of society. In this regard, many teachers possessed the erroneous perception that the generative theme was equal to reducing classroom content to talking about misery (i.e., the conditions of impoverishment of the community). In effect, some teachers argued that the generative theme was inappropriate for designing curriculum for small children in the initial cycle (first, second, and third grades).

Such superficial understanding of the Project also created other similar obstacles. Teachers in some schools viewed any attempt to introduce into the classroom a discussion of popular culture or contemporary issues as "doing the Inter-Project." Rudimentary conceptions of the curriculum process under the Inter Project continually cropped up in conversations with teachers and observations of classrooms. Piecemeal approaches to "doing Inter" might consist of writing down questions on the board as opposed to merely dictating factual statements to students or could include using the lyrics of a popular song as the content for a Portuguese class. In this way, "doing Inter" did not necessarily require working from a generative theme based curriculum. Within such a reductionist conception of the Project, it became synonymous with the inclusion in the curriculum of any elements distinct from what would most likely be considered traditional curriculum content. Hence an "any thing goes" approach to content selection was adopted, leading to the disillusionment of many NAE Inter Team members with the path taken in the development of the Project in particular classrooms at the many of the schools where it was supposedly adopted.

In summary, a central problem encountered by Secretariat personnel coordinating the Project stemmed from the difficulty in reconciling teachers' established preconceptions of what constitutes essential content matter to be transmitted to students and the Project's insistence on linking all the subject areas represented in the curriculum to a generative theme of significance to the students. As a result of this persistent conflict between theory and practice, teachers in the Project often left theory behind falling into the above cited practice of presenting standard exercises to cover skills they felt were not being addressed in the interdisciplinary curriculum via the generative theme. Ironically, it was precisely such reductionist interpretations and piecemeal applications of the Inter Project's principles of curriculum construction that represented a primary obstacle to the Project's evolution in a positive [from the perspective of the PT administration] direction. Also, such inconsistencies in the Project's implementation by school staff worked to further fuel the frustration of those who held tenaciously to the conviction that the steady transmission of traditional content matter constituted the "proper" most effect approach to educating the children of São Paulo, in contrast to what they perceived as the "watered down" curriculum that the Inter Project produced. In response to this persistent conflict between teachers' perceptions/interpretations and the Project's intentions, Secretary Mario Sérgio Cortella offered the following words:

> Knowledge in the school serves a double purpose: the role of knowledge is not to make that people understand reality but to give them the power to change reality based on what they understand of it. That is why Interdisciplinariness is not an end in of itself, but an instrument. People should not adopt an interdisciplinary approach because that is what the school exists for, the school does not exist to be interdisciplinary, the school exists to form students with a solid scientific knowledge base and a strong sense of critical citizenship, which are the main objectives of a progressive education.[10]

At the same time, for many teachers the Inter Project signified a transformation of their own professional identity in that they began to

see themselves and their students as active participants in the construction of knowledge not mere transmitters and recipients. In the words of a
CONAE area specialist, "We know of some teachers that underwent a radical change in terms of their attitude towards their students. They always
transmitted knowledge in a structured manner, suddenly they experienced
a dismantling of that structure and perceived that this authoritarian method
of simply transmitting subject matter had nothing to do with educating,
[they came to realize] that it was necessary to hear the student, that the
student also brought knowledge [into the classroom]." Marta Pernambuco,
a central intellectual force and key actor in the reform, also points to the
creation of greater opportunities for dialogue among teachers as the pivotal component in the Secretariat's curriculum reform project:

> We were very clear of the fact that we didn't have a defined project, but
> that we were inaugurating a process. Nothing was resolved for anyone,
> we had defined the broad guidelines, but much was to be constructed
> along the way. For that process to continue, for the movement to happen,
> the most important thing was to create the mechanisms that made it pos-
> sible for the project to happen, hence the *horário coletivo* of teachers; meet-
> ings organized by grade level, by area; the school working as a whole was
> more critical than the content in and of itself. Once those foundations were
> established you could begin to build the rest little by little . . . That was
> guaranteed through the process of expansion that made possible the mo-
> bilization of schools and the continuation of the [reform] process.[11]

According to Secretary Mario Sérgio Cortella, Paulo Freire played a
central role in the creation of the democratic impetus necessary to enlist
the voluntary participation of teachers in the Inter Project. At the onset of
his administration Freire held a conference in which he spoke to 34,000
teachers, and during the time he was Secretary he continually circulated
through out the municipal schools making site visits, speaking in person
with administrators and teachers. Freire's gestures of reaching out directly
to teachers is emblematic of the administration's overall project to transform the relations of power in the organization of the municipal school
system. Secretary Cortella insists on the PT administration's imperative to
move beyond mere rhetoric of democratization of schools: "We have to
demonstrate with gestures, not only with words, but with concrete acts
that promote a democratic quality [of life] and recovery of citizenship . . .
before [the voices of the teachers] were never heard, this administration
has worked for a democratization of communication."[12]

Once those lines of communication were open the next phase was to
address the specific pedagogical aspects of the project. In the first phase of

the Project they were primarily concerned with establishing the mechanisms for its implementation and the democratization of interactions among actors in the municipal schools, and less with the specific formation of teachers with regard to the theory behind the Project and the practice of that theory. The second phase intended to focus in the direction of providing more structured technical intervention at the same time that materials and practices generated at the schools were collected, reviewed and disseminated when appropriate.

In our research we listened directly to the voices from actors at both ends of the spectrum of policy planning and implementation. The overwhelming majority of teachers we spoke with asserted that the one outstanding feature of the PT administration was that for the first time in their professional lives they were afforded the opportunity to have a voice. Their testimony in the case studies underscores the importance of such an opportunity. Efforts along these lines are further exemplified in the two Congresses on Municipal Education held by the MSE in 1991 and 1992. At these two events—the first of their kind in the history of the municipal school system—thousands of the city's educators came together to discuss the direction of the reforms they were carrying out and to share their experiences with the Inter Project, School Councils, Formation Groups and other programs spearheaded under the PT administration.

The State, Educational Policy and Social Movements

We have assumed here that the state becomes an arena for struggle and competition between political-economic forces and educational projects. More investigation is needed, however, about the relationships among municipal educational reform, the role of social movements, and the conflicts and contradictions of Brazilian policy formation. Tensions exist that may limit the participatory character of new educational policies, highlighting the contradictions of such policies in situations of social transition.[13] The PT's fragmented ideological nature is one possible source of conflict, as it comprises up to 15 factions, including five principal ones. Ideologies as different as Liberation Theology (embodied in Christian Base Communities) and Trotskyism are also represented within the party. These differences will be reflected in educational policies, especially in disagreements within the Brazilian Left pitting those who argue for the proposal of a Popular Public Schooling against those who argue for more conventional public schooling as cultural transmission.[14]

A number of political questions also remain. What political and pedagogical differences separate proposals advocated by the PT from those with a conventional social-democratic perspective? What are the possibilities and limits of democratic socialism (and systems built on popular participation) in dependent-development societies such as Brazil, particularly in the context of a rapidly changing world system and with the profusion of neoliberal governments in Latin America?[15]

A second issue is the relationship between democracy as a process and democracy as a method. An argument could be made for the need to enforce procedural democracy in Brazil by creating checks and balances while eliminating clientelist and patrimonialist practices and corruption in the public sector. The dilemma is how to achieve procedural democracy while also pursuing substantive economic and political reforms that will enhance the prospects for economic democracy.[16]

Furthermore, has the proclaimed articulation between public policies and social movements been achieved? This leads to other questions such as, What kind of state and democracy is being constructed, and What kind of education will eventually emerge from popular public education? Through its efforts to both create a Movement for the Reorientation of the Curriculum in schools and to further the impact of existing social movements addressing the problem of illiteracy the PT-MSE initiated an intensive, dynamic, and sometimes conflictual dialogue among educators, learners, and communities throughout the city around these very questions.

Angela Miles has argued that social movements provide congenial ground for a new education, which she describes as teaching and learning that "encourages the spirit of equality and the realization of full human potential in an anti-elitist communal process; provides the students with the skills, resources and intellectual tools to understand and confront the structures and practices which perpetuate inequality; integrates vocational training, personal enlightenment/empowerment, and social action; challenges the separation between the world of knowledge production and daily life; refuses the artificial divisions of subject matter by discipline in an interdisciplinary approach to real world problems; and breaks down the monopoly of knowledge by recognizing the learners as knowledge creators."[17] Any agenda for social transformation should ask whether educational reform in São Paulo, on the basis of a partnership between the state and social movements, has improved public schooling in terms of opportunity and quality. At the same time, we should inquire whether a serious attempt has been made to overcome school and social discrimination based on gender, class, and race.[18] Equally important, is a new educational policy based on a partnership between social movements and the state that is politically feasible, technically competent, and ethically sound?

Very often reforms that are technically competent and politically feasible conflict with ethical principles upholding beliefs in universal social justice and fairness in political and economic democracies. At other times, politically feasible reform projects based on ethics of democratic compassion lack technical expertise, rendering failure inevitable. Finally, situations can also arise in which technically competent and ethically sound democratic projects may not be politically feasible given certain historical conditions.

In his theoretical writings Freire has always advised his readers to remain aware of these tensions, not only as a safeguard for democratic practice but also because such an outlook is necessary for building cooperative and participatory democratic alliances. As a policy maker, Freire certainly has recognized that politics, technical competence, and ethics are deeply interwoven in any attempt at educational reform.[19] For more than three decades he has tirelessly argued that education is not neutral and that the political nature of education is independent of the educator's and the policymaker's subjectivities.

Not surprisingly, then, the orientation of Freire's administration, as we have tried to argue and exemplify, was towards passionately and slowly building a social movement responsive to the educational needs of popular communities rather than coldly and efficiently developing coordinated curriculum packages to be identically replicated in the city's 691 schools. A related impetus for this multifaceted movement was a consciousness on the part of the PT educators in the Secretariat that they may only have four years to carry out their efforts to impact the educational reality of the city's children and the pedagogical minds of the of teachers working in its schools. Movements belie traditional methods of assessment and evaluation. But , in an evaluative and reflective moment, Ana Maria Saúl (director of the DOT) made the following observation regarding the surge in the level of expectations on the part of teachers during the PT administration that resulted from their political mobilization strategy: "this was a very good thing, we didn't expect this, we knew they needed more resources, we were providing the necessary conditions, and [while] we had imagined [that our mobilization efforts] would serve as mechanisms for the organization [of teachers] to pressure future administrations, it [actually] began to happen during this administration. The schools themselves began to make demands of the administration."[20] This was precisely what the PT intended from the notion of creating a movement with the long term effect of mobilizing teachers to continually fight to establish lasting mechanisms of change in the municipal school system.

Still, despite the limited time the PT had to advance its political-pedagogic agenda and the myriad obstacles faced, the Inter Project undoubtedly represents a landmark educational reform. Its roots in the rich tradition of a Freirean based liberatory educational experiences that span the globe and the context of the reform in a large urban school system, make the São Paulo curriculum reform movement one of enormous significance and far reaching consequences. As Cortella, Freire and Erundina proclaimed in 1992: "This experience lived by us—educators, parents, students and functionaries of the government—has demonstrated a fundamental fact to the country: that a Public Education of Quality is possible!"[21] They continued:

> We would like to recall with you the history of those four years, a necessary process in this country so marked by the negation of history, where some put aside the facts of their process as a form of domination, they disseminate their ideas through techniques of political marketing and make millions believe in ideas that attend to the needs of a few. We have the conviction that it will not be by means of empty slogans, presented in a magical and paternalistic fashion, that we will transform the harsh reality of our people. The process of transformation of the conditions of life and citizenship in São Paulo and in the rest of the country requires political will, seriousness and a project that includes as one of its guiding principles the power of interference and decision making on the part of the population. To share the power to think, elaborate and decide requires systematic socialization of information and the ability to coexist and experience the tensions and contradictions inherent in democracy. This only does not occur when authoritarianism reigns and kills the richness and the difficulties of any process that has participation as a [fundamental] presupposition.[22]

In this regard, through its promotion of the Interdisciplinary Project throughout the municipal schools of São Paulo, the party laid the foundation for a new politics of education in Brazil: a politics that seeks to develop the theoretical basis and practical experience of an emancipatory educational paradigm and a new collective approach to curriculum building that speaks to the socio-economic, cultural and political reality of students and their community. Upon that foundation, the São Paulo municipal schools—and municipalities throughout the country—can begin to build their particular conceptualization of the Popular Public School, to investigate the reality of the school and create learning situations of greater relevance for students and opportunities for greater professional development of teachers. In effect, two years after the end of PT administration in São Paulo, schools revisited in 1994 continued to employ elements of a collective curriculum planning process introduced during the Inter Project reform, and even four years later in 1996, a school located in the former NAE-6 region reportedly "tirou o tema gerador."[23] Moreover, other PT municipalities large and small—from Porto Alegre to Angra dos Reis—continue in the footsteps of the São Paulo experience recreating their own versions of Popular Public Schooling and further building the model of an interdisciplinary curriculum via the Generative theme.[24]

It is fitting, however to offer Freire's own evaluation of the experience:

When I was Municipal Secretary of Education for São Paulo I was obviously committed to developing an administration that, in coherence with our political dream and our utopia, would seriously consider, as it would be, the question of popular participation in school issues and we had, my colleagues and I, to start from the very beginning. That is to say we started by making an administrative reform so that the Secretariat could work in a different way. With administrative structures that only made authoritarian power viable, it was impossible to develop a democratic administration that was in favor of school autonomy and recognized that being public the school also belonged to the popular classes. From the Secretary to the immediate directors, and from these directors to the sector chiefs, orders were extended to the schools. In the schools, the administration, taking all of the orders together, would silence the doorkeepers, cooks, teachers, and the students. Of course, there are always exceptions, without which the work of change would be even more difficult.

Given the challenges facing our unfolding Brazilian democracy and the authoritarian tradition of our society, schools had to be given the highest priority. It was necessary, on the contrary, to democratize power to recognize the right of the voice of students and teachers, to diminish the personal power of the directors, and to create new instances of power with the School Councils, which were deliberative and not merely consultative and through which, from the beginning, parents gained an authentic role in determining the destiny of their children's schools. In addition, we hoped to create a very local community that, having the school as something of their own, would make themselves equally present in the policy-making of that school. It was necessary, then to democratize the Secretariat and to decentralize decisions. It was necessary to inaugurate a governing structure that limited the power of the Secretariat. It was necessary to reorient the policy for staff training and development by overcoming the traditional holiday courses that insisted on a discourse about theory, thinking that afterwards the teachers would put directly into practice that theory which was discussed though the practice of discussing practice. Such courses were not developed through an efficacious form of living a dialectic unity between theory and practice. What I would like to make clear is that there was a greater level of democratic participation among students, teachers, parents, and the local community. And this school, being public, intended to transform itself into a popular space, and therefore demanded light structures, ready for change, decentralized, able to facilitate governmental action rapidly and efficiently. What we inherited instead were heavy structures, with centralized power, where solutions required immediate responses but instead crept from sector to sector, waiting for one thing from one end to another from another, which were identified with and served authoritarian, elitist and more than anything, traditional administrations reminiscent of colonial style. Without the transformation of these structures, there was no way to think about community or popular participation. Democracy demands structures that democratize, not structures that inhibit the participatory presence of civil society in the command of *res*-public. It was this that we did. I would have been the Secretariat for whatever little power I had, but for this reason I was able to work effectively and make decisions with others.[25]

For both social movements and the municipal state in Brazil and elsewhere, to develop and sustain an educational policy that was technically competent, ethically sound, and politically feasible represented an immense challenge. This was particularly true for educators, policymakers, and social activists in São Paulo who, following a basic Freirean premise, continue to ask themselves in favor of what and for whom and necessarily against what and whom they were working.

Notes

1. Fernando Rossetti, "Prefeitura de SP em exame: Erundina reduz o déficit educacional," *Folha de São Paulo* (January 3, 1992), p. 1-D. Data are from "Assessoria Técnica de Planejamento/Centro de Informática," Secretaria Municipal de Educação, Evolução de Matricular por Modalidade de Ensino, 1980-1991, unpublished computer printout, June 22, 1991, p. 1.

2. Students attending night schools usually include people who dropped out of the system but have reentered formal schooling through night courses, students who work, older students, and adult learners. They are typically less privileged than their counterparts in day schools.

3. "Uma conquista do trabalho coletivo," *Diario Oficial do Municipio,* São Paulo 36, no. 47 (March 13, 1991), p. 3.

4. In São Paulo's 1991 municipal budget, 10.6 percent was spent on education. Cortella cautiously argued at the time that it was not clear whether increases in teachers' salaries would improve the quality of education; he contended, however, that research clearly shows that meager salaries and poor working conditions have

a negative impact. See Cortella, "Aqui não inaguramos paredes," *Folha Dirigida/ Nacional* (December 24-30, 1991), p. 1.d.

5. Interview with Secretary Cortella (October 1992).

6. Interview with Marta Pernambuco (October 1992).

7. Interview with Secretary Mario Sergio Cortella (October 16, 1992).

8. Carlos A. Torres, *The Politics of Nonformal Education in Latin America* (New York: Praeger, 1990) p. 8.

9. Maria do Carmo D. Mendoça (mimeograph), 1994.

10. Interview, 1992.

11. Interview with Marta Pernambuco, October 1992.

12. Interview with Mario Sergio Cortella (October 1992).

13. For a discussion of the role of education in social transitions, see Carnoy and Samoff, eds., *Education and Social Transition in the Third World* (Princeton, NJ: Princeton University Press, 1990).

14. Moacir Gadotti, *Uma só escola para todos: Caminhos da autonomia escolar* (Petrópolis: Vozes, 1990), pp. 165-183; José Tamarit, "El dilema de la educación popular: Entre la utopía y la resignación," *Revista Argentina de Educación*, 8, no. 13 (1990), pp. 7-45.

15. For a discussion of educational policies under neoliberal governments in Latin America, see Morales-Gómez and Carlos Alberto Torres, eds., *Education, Policy, and Social Change: Experiences from Latin America* (Westport, CT, and London: Praeger, 1992).

16. To this extent, the postmodern notion of the decentralization and fragmentation of power in democratic societies poses many analytical challenges for methodologies of substantive democracy in dependent capitalism.

17. Angela Miles, "Women's Challenge to Adult Education" (Ontario Institute for Studies in Education, Toronto, May 1989, mimeographed), p. 3.

18. For a naturalistic analysis of the role of gender in literacy training in São Paulo, see Nelly Peñaloza Stromquist, "The Intersection of Gender and Social Marginality in Adult Literacy: Becoming Literate in São Paulo" (School of Education, University of Southern California, February 1992, mimeographed).

19. See Paulo Freire and Iván Illich, *Diálogo Paulo Freire e Iván Illich* (Buenos Aires: Editorial Búsqueda-Celadec, 1975).

20. Interview with Ana Maria Saúl (October 1992).

21. *Diário Oficial* (October 15, 1992).

22. Ibid.

23. Translation: "tirou o tema gerador" implies that the school engaged in a thematic investigation of the reality and determined a generative theme for the semester's curriculum. This information was conveyed to us in a phone conversation with a key informant, April, 1996.

24. A key informant of O'Cadiz and Wong's research and a former NAE Inter Team member has been working since 1992 as an advisor to the Secretariat of Edu-

cation of the municipalities of Porto Alegre and Angra dos Reis (both under PT governance) where they are currently implementing curriculum reform based on the São Paulo Inter-Project experience. In 1995, O'Cadiz was able to observe the initiation of this reform process during a visit to the Municipal Secretariat of Education and an elementary school in Angra dos Reis.

25. Paulo Freire, *Politics and Education* (Los Angeles: UCLA Latin American Center, in press).

Index

Lutfi, Eulina P., 134

"Lula" *See* Silva, Luís Inacío da

Luzobrazilian Empire, 7

Mainwaring, Scott, 63

Maluf, Paulo, 24, 238

McCarthy, Thomas, 62, 67

McNeil, Linda M, 67

Mello, Guiomar Namo de, 195, 231-232

Mendonça, Maria do Carmo D., 138

Ministry of Education and Culture (MEC), 8

Miles, Angela, 250, 251

MOBRAL (literacy program for adults by the military government), 158

Moniz de Aragão, Raymundo, 12, 34

Morães Rocha, Maria Selma de, 103

Morais, Regis de, 8, 12-13

Morales-Gómez, Daniel A., 63, 68, 251

Movement for Grassroots Education (*Movimento de Educação & Base*), 46

Movement for Popular Culture (MPC), 21

Movement for the Reorientation of Curriculum *(Movimento da Reorientação Curricular)*, 29, 37, 60, 72, 75, 101, 246

Movement for Youth and Adult Literacy (*Movimento de Alfabetização de Jovens e Adultos*, MOVA), 23, 28, 44-45, 54-61, 67, 189

    literacy training nuclei (*nucleus de alfabetização*), 57-58

    methodology, 58-61

    MOVA Congress, 60

Municipal Secretariat of Education (MSE), 1, 29

Quadros, Jânio, 238

Ramos, Cosete, 36

Regional Council of Representatives of the School Councils (*Conselhos Regionais de Representantes de Conselhos de Escola* CRECEs), 81-83

    Regional Educational Plan, 81, 83

Regional Delegacies for Municipal Education (*Delegacias Regionais de Educação Municipal* DREMs), 77, 103

Reimers, Fernando, 16, 33

Reorientation of Curriculum (MRC), 1, 4

Rogers, Carl, 88, 104

Rosenthal, Gert, 34

Rossetti, Fernando, 250

Santos, Mario R. dos, 61-62

São Paulo, 1, 2, 35, 44, 62-63

    conditions of, 3, 45

    Faculdade de Bellas Artes, 184

    Pontifical Catholic University of, 8, 45, 76, 95, 222

    University of, 8, 76, 95

    See also Case studies of Inter Project/descriptions

Saúl, Ana Maria, 137-138, 247, 251

Schiefelbein, Ernesto, 16, 33

School councils, 53-54, 60, 77, 81-83

    School Plan, 81

Schools,